MICHELIN

Motoring Atlas France

Contents

Inside front cover: key to 1:200 000 map pages

- II — Michelin maps and guides
- III — Introduction
- IV — **Route planning**
- VI — **Paris and suburbs** at a scale of 1:100 000
- VIII — Distances and journey times

- 1 — **Key** to 1:200 000 map symbols
- 2 — **Maps of France** at a scale of 1:200 000

- 182 — **Index** to 1:200 000 maps
  general plans of Bordeaux · Dijon · Lille · Lyon · Marseille
  Nantes · Nice · Rouen · Strasbourg · Toulouse
- 190 — **Paris**

PAUL HAMLYN MICHELIN touring services

MICHELIN maps and guides

MICHELIN, the world's leading manufacturer of radial tyres, is also a well known name in the field of tourist publications; its annual sales of maps and guides exceed 16m in over 70 countries.

Acting on the belief that motoring would have a great future, the Michelin brothers decided to offer the motorist a touring service, an innovative step at the turn of the century: free or inexpensive publications designed to provide information, assistance and encouragement.

At the wheel, touring, on holiday – these three aspects of travel were met by a simple response – a trio of complementary publications to be used together.

The first of these, the Red Guides, which are published annually, present a selection of hotels and restaurants, with a wide range of prices and facilities. It is, however, probably their award of the stars for good cooking that has established their international reputation; as well as the wealth of essential touring information included in them. There are several guides covering Europe, including the Red Guide to France which alone has sold over 20m copies to date. Readers have such faith in their reliability that the Red Guides are foremost among reference books in this field.

The role of the Michelin Green Guides is to provide tourists with an introduction to the regions of France and other foreign countries. The guides describe the sights, the countryside and picturesque routes; they also contain maps, plans and practical information as well as illustrations and photographs which whet one's appetite for travel. There are over 70 titles covering Europe and North America, which are published in French and other European languages and are revised regularly.

This Motoring Atlas of France is composed of the series of detailed maps originally published in 1910; they have benefited from the evolution of technical processes and have kept up to date with changes in the road network and the needs of the modern motorist. Over the years new symbols have been devised to facilitate the 'reading' of the map.

To improve their service to the customer, Michelin call upon the latest techniques in the compilation and production of their maps and guides. Because of their practical approach, their regular revision and their common concepts, these publications will continue to be an indispensable aid to travel.

MICHELIN
maps and guides
complement one another:

use them together!

First published 1987 by
Paul Hamlyn, an imprint of
The Hamlyn Publishing Group Limited
now a Division of The Octopus Publishing Group plc
Michelin House, 81 Fulham Road
London SW3 6RB

All maps and index   Copyright © Michelin et Cie
Propriétaires-Éditeurs 1987, 1988
Creation, graphic arrangement and text pages I-VIII
Copyright © The Hamlyn Publishing
Group Limited 1987, 1988

Second edition 1988

All rights reserved. No part of this publication may be reproduced, stored in a retrieval system or transmitted, in any form or by any means, electronic, mechanical, photocopying, recording or otherwise, without the permission of the Publishers and the copyright owners.

In spite of the care taken in the production of this book, it is possible that a defective copy may have escaped our attention. If this is so, please return it to your bookseller, who will exchange it for you, or contact The Hamlyn Publishing Group Limited at the address above.

The representation in this atlas of a road is no evidence of the existence of a right of way.

ISBN 0 600 55863 0

Printed in Great Britain

Introduction

The first maps

André Michelin published his first guide book in 1900, to provide 'information which will be useful to a motorist travelling in France', and logically this led to the first Michelin road map, in 1907, and then to the first 1:200 000 series which covered the whole of France.

The first edition of this series, published between 1910 and 1913, was the forerunner of the modern series of Michelin sheet maps, still published at the scale decided by André Michelin early in the century. These maps in turn are the basis of this atlas, which, like the first Michelin maps and guides, is a thoroughly practical companion for travellers using the roads of France; it also looks beyond the roads to many of the topographical and man-made features of this varied country.

The roads of France

In European terms France is a large country, and it is still predominantly rural, characterized more by open country and villages or small towns than sprawling urban areas – outside Paris, only the conurbations of Lyon and Marseille have populations of more than a million. It is thus a country where the road network has traditionally been important, and it has become steadily more important through the last three decades.

There are more than 1.5 million kilometres (930 000 miles) of roads. The network includes over 6500 km (over 4000 miles) of motorways, some 800 000 km (almost 500 000 miles) of main roads, and around 700 000 km (around 435 000 miles) of minor roads. The main roads are either 'N' roads, which are regarded as part of the international or national routes network, or 'D' roads which are inter-regional; these are the red and yellow roads on the maps. Other roads are shown in white on the maps.

Many of the trunk roads, most logically those which do not duplicate motorway routes, have been uprated. Often superbly aligned, sometimes still lined with the poplar trees that were once traditional, these can make for enjoyable driving and overall journey speeds very near to the governing legal speed limit. From a driver's point of view the motorways are less interesting, but they do provide straightforward routes between main centres. Most are *autoroutes à péage*, or toll roads. The charge per kilometre varies from motorway to motorway and the toll payments on a long journey can be high. Different rates apply to coaches, goods and utility vehicles, cars towing caravans or trailers, motorcycles, and so on.

Overall, congestion is not a feature of motoring in France, though city rush hours are best avoided. The routes out of Paris or back into the capital can be very congested at weekends or holiday periods, while the almost perpetual congestion on the *périphérique* has become notorious. This ring road does, however, offer quick and easily understood routes from one side of the capital to another, or between suburban districts, and it links the motorways radiating out to the provinces. At peak holiday periods routes through Lyon can be very crowded but are difficult to avoid. Other traffic trouble spots are predictable – for example, parts of the south coast during the summer, or routes to winter sports resorts early in the year.

Using this atlas

The Michelin maps in this atlas provide the best possible guidance for drivers in France, from route pre-planning to on-the-spot selection to avoid a delay. Each spread of two pages in this atlas covers an area of approximately 79 by 114 kilometres (49 by 71 miles), displaying a sizeable area of country. Through routes are obvious and the painstaking work of the cartographers also ensures that the detail of road widths can be seen in advance. Diversions can be devised quickly, perhaps using the yellow or white minor roads.

The yellow roads are often used in signposted alternative routes, with signs frequently directing drivers to good 'D' roads; these can be particularly useful in avoiding built-up areas and often provide good, less congested long-distance routes. This system uses green signs which incorporate the word *Bis* since the routes are known as *Itinéraires Bis* in France.

Many of the 'D' roads are keys to intrinsic delights and the map symbols guide tourists to sites ranging from historic buildings to viewpoints. Many of the places picked out on the maps also merit entries in the renowned Michelin Green Guides, which cover regions of France with detailed descriptions of places of interest and suggestions for tours; the outline maps can be used in conjunction with this atlas. Picturesque roads are distinguished on the maps with green borders.

General rules

- Driving in France is straightforward, with regulations and road signs generally similar to those in most West European countries. The basic rule is drive on the right, overtake on the left.
- Visitors should carry a full driving licence, vehicle registration document and evidence of insurance cover.
- Hazard warning lights or a red warning triangle must be carried, and used in a case of breakdown or accident. A spare set of light bulbs should be carried on a vehicle. Cars and commercial vehicles should have an external mirror on the left-hand side.
- Seat belts must be worn by the driver and front-seat passenger; children under ten may not travel in a front seat unless the car is a two-seater. Motor cyclists and pillion passengers must wear crash helmets.
- Full or dipped headlights must be used in poor visibility and at night and motor cyclists must use dipped headlights at all times, except when full beam is called for. Side lights should be used only as parking lights. Yellow-tinted headlights are preferred but are not compulsory for tourist vehicles.
- Overtaking must not be attempted where a 'no overtaking' sign (a red vehicle and a black vehicle side by side) is displayed, where the manoeuvre would entail crossing an unbroken line on the road, or at the brow of a hill even if the road is not marked.
- Studded tyres may be used between November 15 and March 15, on light vehicles (up to 3500 kg), which are then subject to a 90 kmh/56 mph speed limit.
- Speeding or drink-driving offences are subject to on-the-spot fines, payable in cash, while a drink-driving offence may also result in the vehicle being immobilized on the spot.
- An accident causing injury must be reported to the police or gendarmerie. After an accident causing damage but not injury a Notice of Motoring Accident should be completed and signed by both parties.

Full information on motoring in France is available from French Government Tourist Offices or motoring organizations such as the Automobile Association or the Royal Automobile Club.

Speed limits

Urban areas: 60 kmh/37 mph

Single carriageway roads: 90 kmh/56 mph (**on wet roads:** 80 kmh/50 mph)

Dual carriageway roads: 110 kmh/68 mph (**on wet roads:** 100 kmh/62 mph)

Motorways: 130 kmh/80 mph (**on wet roads:** 110 kmh/68 mph)
A *minimum* speed limit of 80 kmh/50 mph applies to the overtaking lane of motorways in daylight and good weather.

These limits apply to motor cycles over 81cc; light motor cycles (51–80cc) are subject to a 75 kmh/47 mph limit.

Local variations are indicated on speed limit road signs. The *rappel* sign indicates a continuing restriction.

Priority

The system giving priority to traffic entering a road from the right now applies in built-up areas only, and then not in every case; main roads outside built-up areas have priority. Visual confirmation of a 'priority' road is displayed in yellow and black signs; the same sign with a diagonal cancel stripe clearly indicates the end of a 'priority' stretch. Stop signs must be observed as such, with drivers bringing their vehicles to a standstill. In roundabouts with the approach sign illustrated drivers must give way to vehicles already on the roundabout.

More broadly, topography can be read off the maps, with hill shading, for example, fleshing out the bare bones of a named mountain pass or throwing into relief the sweep of one of the superb French river valleys which have provided routes for travellers since prehistoric times.

The maps are also related very directly to the Michelin Red Guide; places, not simply towns but villages and isolated hamlets, that merit entries in the Guide are underlined in red on the maps, while red frames pick out the towns with street plans included in the Guide.

This atlas has been planned as an end in itself, and as part of the Michelin tourist library, where it complements the series of well-established maps and guides. It does not take the place of the yellow sheet maps, which slip conveniently into a pocket or handbag with the local Green Guide, but, in combination, this atlas, the guides and the sheet maps are invaluable to travellers in France.

Route planning

Scale 1:2 600 000   1cm:26km   approx 41 miles:1 inch

- Motorway
- Dual carriageway with motorway characteristics
- Major road
- Secondary through route
- Motorway or road number
- 17 Intermediate distances in kilometres
- ⊙ Regional prefecture
- • Prefecture
- ○ Other principal town

The blue rectangles outline the coverage of each page in the 1:200 000 maps sequence which starts on page 2. The blue numbers are map pages.

Road signs

The background colours of direction signs are appropriate to categories of roads:

- blue – motorways
- green – main roads
- white – local roads

The *Itinéraire Bis* road signs are used to indicate less congested alternative routes.

Yellow signs with black lettering are used for temporary routes, especially diversions (*déviations*).

Traffic information

Centre de Renseignements Autoroutes (9-12h, 14-18h)
Monday-Friday (1) 47 05 90 01   **Minitel** 3614 Code ASFA
Centre National (0-24h) (1) 48 94 33 33   **Minitel** 3615 Code ROUTE
Centres Régionaux d'Information et de Coordination Routière

Bordeaux 56 96 33 33	Marseille 91 78 78 78
Ile de France/ Centre (1) 48 99 33 33	Metz 87 63 33 33
Lille 20 47 33 33	Rennes 99 32 33 33
Lyon 78 54 33 33	

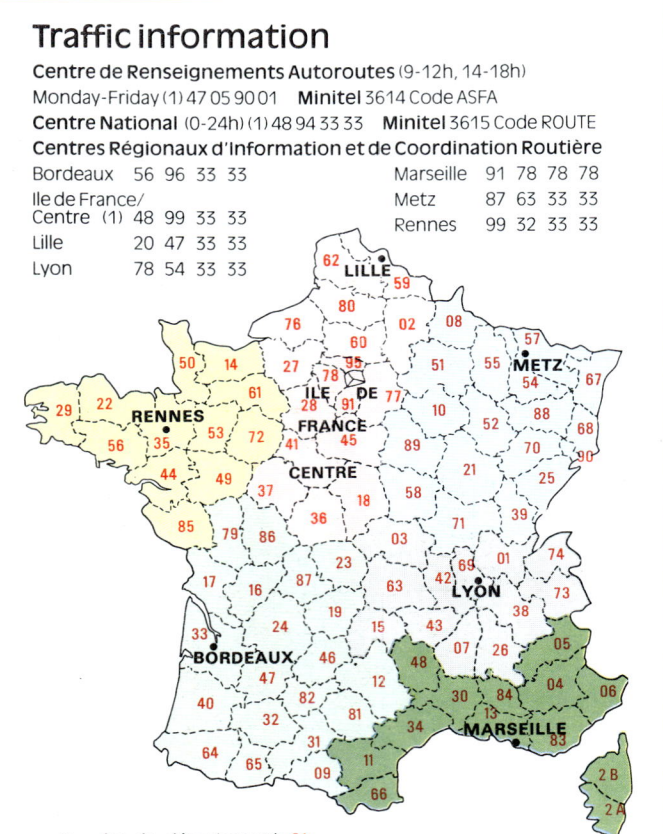

Numéro de *département* 21

Départements

01 Ain	32 Gers	64 Pyrénées-Atlantiques
02 Aisne	33 Gironde	65 Hautes-Pyrénées
03 Allier	34 Hérault	66 Pyrénées-Orientales
04 Alpes-de-Haute-Provence	35 Ille-et-Vilaine	67 Bas-Rhin
05 Hautes Alpes	36 Indre	68 Haut-Rhin
06 Alpes Maritimes	37 Indre-et-Loire	69 Rhône
07 Ardèche	38 Isère	70 Haute-Saône
08 Ardennes	39 Jura	71 Saône-et-Loire
09 Ariège	40 Landes	72 Sarthe
10 Aube	41 Loir-et-Cher	73 Savoie
11 Aude	42 Loire	74 Haute-Savoie
12 Aveyron	43 Haute-Loire	75 Paris
13 Bouches-du-Rhône	44 Loire-Atlantique	76 Seine-Maritime
14 Calvados	45 Loiret	77 Seine-et-Marne
15 Cantal	46 Lot	78 Yvelines
16 Charente	47 Lot-et-Garonne	79 Deux-Sèvres
17 Charente-Maritime	48 Lozère	80 Somme
18 Cher	49 Maine-et-Loire	81 Tarn
19 Corrèze	50 Manche	82 Tarn-et-Garonne
2A Corse-du-Sud	51 Marne	83 Var
2B Haute-Corse	52 Haute-Marne	84 Vaucluse
21 Côte-d'Or	53 Mayenne	85 Vendée
22 Côtes-du-Nord	54 Meurthe-et-Moselle	86 Vienne
23 Creuse	55 Meuse	87 Haute-Vienne
24 Dordogne	56 Morbihan	88 Vosges
25 Doubs	57 Moselle	89 Yonne
26 Drôme	58 Nièvre	90 Territoire-de-Belfort
27 Eure	59 Nord	91 Essonne
28 Eure-et-Loir	60 Oise	92 Hauts-de-Seine
29 Finistère	61 Orne	93 Seine-St-Denis
30 Gard	62 Pas-de-Calais	94 Val-de-Marne
31 Haute-Garonne	63 Puy-de-Dôme	95 Val-d'Oise

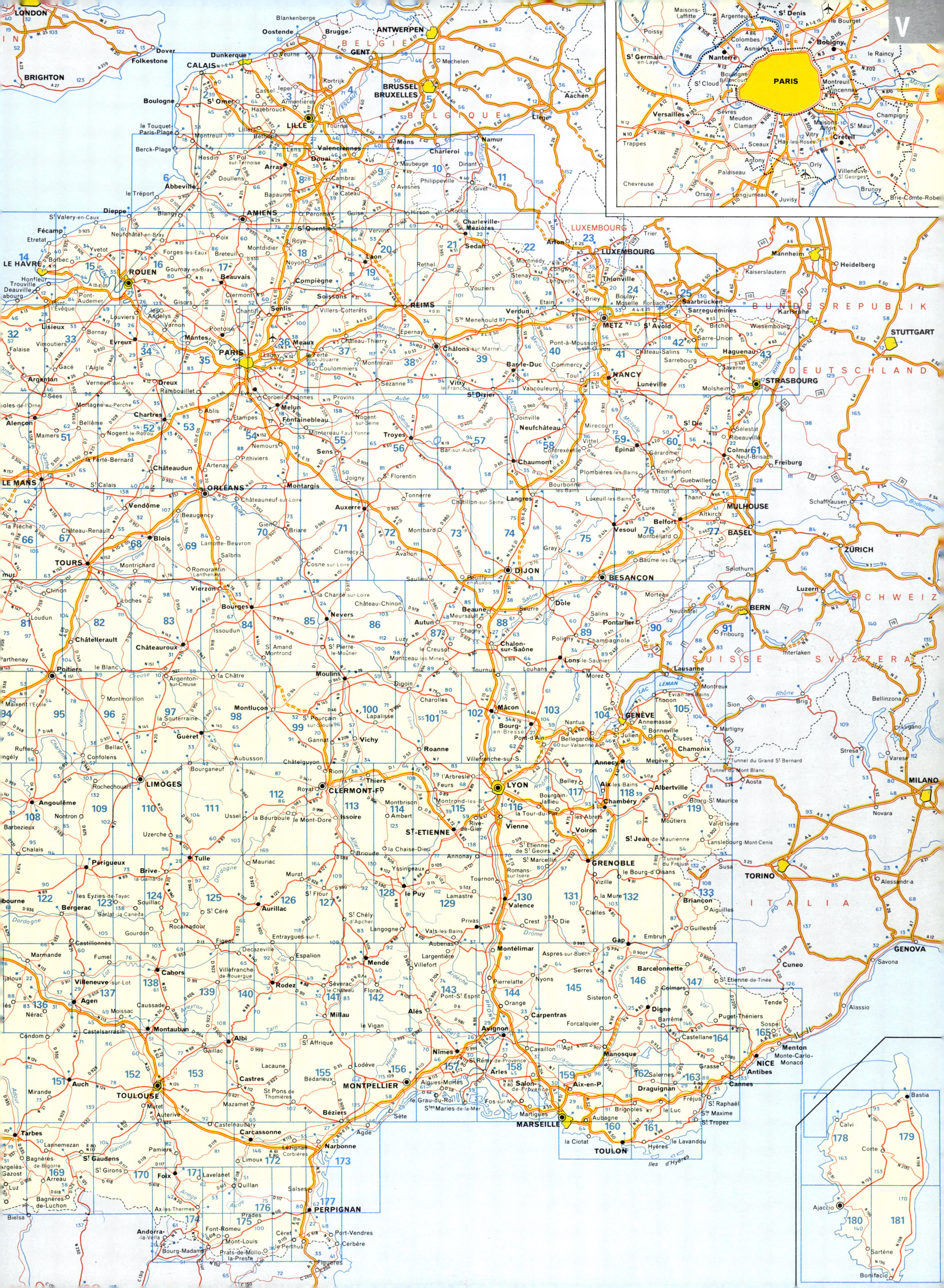

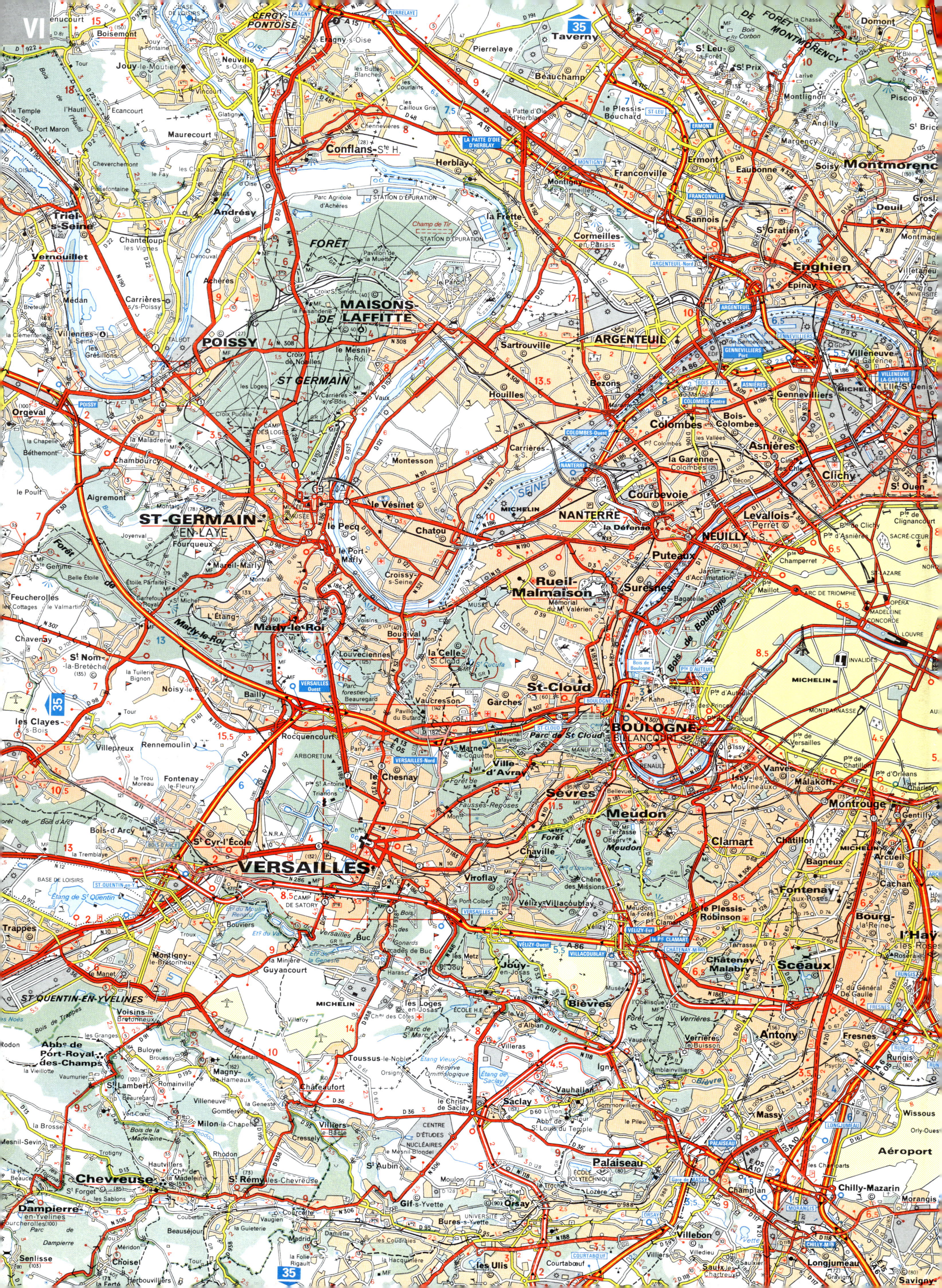

Distances and journey times

Distances between principal towns

Distances are shown in kilometres and are calculated from centres and along the best roads from a motoring point of view, not necessarily following the shortest routes. To obtain a round figure conversion from kilometres to miles multiply the kilometre figure by 5 and divide by 8; for a more precise conversion, multiply by 0.6214.

Journey times between principal towns

The times are shown in hours and minutes and are calculated for an average car taking into account normal driving conditions and excluding any stops.

Verklaring van tekens / Zeichenerklärung / Légende / Key

Autobahnen – Straßen / Wegen / Motorways – Roads / Autoroutes – Routes

Autobahn: getrennte Fahrbahnen	Autosnelweg: met gescheiden rijbanen	Motorway: dual carriageway	Autoroute: à chaussées séparées
Autobahn: nur eine Fahrbahn	Autosnelweg: met één rijbaan	Motorway: single carriageway	Autoroute: à une seule chaussée
zweibahnige Straße, autobahnähnlich	Weg met gescheiden rijbanen van het type autosnelweg	Dual carriageway with motorway characteristics	Double chaussée de type autoroutier (sans carrefour à niveau)
Numerierte Anschlußstellen: uneingeschränkt	Aansluiting met nummer: volledig (in alle richtingen)	Numbered junctions: complete	Échangeur numéroté: complet
Numerierte Anschlußstellen: eingeschränkt	Aansluiting met nummer: gedeeltelijk	Numbered junctions: limited	Échangeurs numérotés: partiels
Hauptverkehrsstraße mit Vorfahrtsberechtigung	Hoofdweg	Major road (having priority)	Route principale (en France classée à grande circulation)
Straße 2. Ordnung	Secundaire verbindingsweg	Secondary road network	Itinéraire régional ou de dégagement
Nebenstraße befestigt	Andere weg: verhard	Other road: surfaced	Route: revêtue
unbefestigt oder in schlechtem Zustand	Andere weg: onverhard of slecht berijdbaar	Unsurfaced or of doubtful quality	Non revêtue ou de mauvaise viabilité
Radweg	Fietspad	Cycle track	Piste cyclable
Wirtschaftsweg, Pfad	Bedrijfsweg of karrespoor; voetpad	Service road or cart track, footpath	Chemin d'exploitation, sentier
Autobahn/Straße, im Bau befindlich	In aanleg: autosnelweg; andere weg	Motorway, road under construction	Autoroute, route en construction
Datum der Verkehrsfreigabe	Vermoedelijke datum van openstelling	Scheduled opening date	Date prévue de mise en service

Straßenbreite / Breedte / Road width / Largeur des routes

Getrennte Fahrbahnen	Gescheiden rijbanen	Dual carriageway	Chaussées séparées
4 Fahrspuren, 3 Fahrspuren	4 rijstroken; 3 rijstroken	Four lanes, three lanes	Quatre voies, trois voies
2 breite Fahrspuren, 2 Fahrspuren	2 brede rijstroken; 2 rijstroken	Two wide lanes, two lanes	Deux voies larges, deux voies
1 Fahrspur, 1 sehr schmale Fahrspur	1 rijstrook; 1 smalle rijstrook	One lane, one narrow lane	Une voie, une voie étroite

Entfernungen (in km) / Afstanden / Distances in kilometres / Distances

Gesamtentfernung	Totale afstanden	Total	Sur autoroute: totalisées
Autobahnen, Mautstrecke, mautfreie Strecke	Autosnelwegen: tolweg; tolvrij	Motorway toll section, free section	Sur section à péage, sur section libre
Teilentfernung	Tussenstanden	Intermediate	Sur autoroute: partielles
Gesamtentfernung	Totale afstanden	Total	Sur route: totalisées
übriges Straßennetz	Andere wegen	On other roads	
Teilentfernung	Tussenstanden	Intermediate	Sur route: partielles

Verkehrshindernisse / Hindernissen / Obstacles / Obstacles

Steigung, Gefälle: 5 – 9%, 9 –13%, 13% u.m. (Steigung in Pfeilrichtung)	Hellingen, afdalingen 5-9%; 9-13%; +13% (pijlen in de richting van de helling)	Gradient: 5-9%, 9-13%, 13%+ (ascent in the direction of the arrow)	Pente: 5-9%, 9-13%, 13% et plus (flèches dans le sens de la montée)
Paß mit Höhenangabe (in m über N.N.)	Bergpas en hoogte boven de zeespiegel	Pass and height in metres above sea level	Col et sa cote d'altitude
Schwierige oder gefährliche Strecke	Moeilijk of gevaarlijk traject	Difficult or dangerous stretch of road	Parcours difficile ou dangereux
Bahnübergänge, schienengleich, Unter- Überführung	Spoorwegovergangen: gelijkvloers, overheen, onderdoor	Level crossing, railway under, over road	Passages: à niveau, supérieur, inférieur
Zulässige Gesamthöhe (angegeben wenn unter 4,50 m)	Vrije hoogte (aangegeven onder 4,50 m)	Headroom (given when less than 4.50 m)	Hauteur limitée (ind. au-dessous de 4,50 m)
Autofähre (Im Roten Michelin-Führer - Telefonnummern der wichtigsten Fährunternehmen).	Auto-veerpont (tel.nr. in Rode Michelingids van Frankrijk)	Car ferry (Michelin Red Guide France gives the phone numbers of main ferries)	Bac passant les autos (le Guide Michelin France donne le numéro de téléphone)
Personenfähre	Pont voor voetgangers en fietsers	Ferry (pedestrians and cycles only)	Bac pour piétons et cycles
Höchstbelastung einer Brücke, einer Fähre (angegeben wenn unter 19 t)	Maximumdraagvermogen van een brug, van een veerpont (aangegeven onder 19t)	Load limit of a bridge, of a car ferry (given when less than 19 tonnes)	Limite de charge d'un pont, d'un bac (indiquée au-dessous de 19 t)
Zugbrücke oder Drehbrücke	Ophaalbrug, beweegbare brug of draaibrug	Drawbridge or swing bridge	Pont mobile
Beschränkung des zulässigen Gesamtgewichts	Maximumdraagvermogen van een hoofd- of secundaire weg	Load limit of a major or secondary road	Limite de charge d'une route
Einbahnstraße	Weg met eenrichtingsverkeer	One-way road	Route à sens unique
Schmale Straße: Überholen schwierig oder unmöglich, Nebenstraße mit Gewichtsbeschränkung	Smalle weg (passeren moeilijk of onmogelijk), kleine weg met beperkt draagvermogen	Narrow road: passing difficult or impossible, local road with load limit	Une voie étroite: croisement difficile, impossible; route communale à charge limitée
Straße mit eingeschränkter Befahrbarkeit	Beperkt toegankelijke weg	Road subject to restrictions	Route réglementée
Gesperrte Straße	Verboden weg	Prohibited road	Route interdite

Unterkünfte / Plaatsen en verblijf / Accommodation / Hébergement

Gekennzeichnete Orte sind in den Michelin-Führern aufgeführt	Het onderstaande verwijst naar diverse Michelingidsen	The information below corresponds with places selected in the Michelin Guides	Indications limitées aux ressources sélectionnées dans les Guides Michelin
Rote Umgrenzung: Stadtpläne im Roten Michelin-Führer	Rood-omlijnde plaats: stadsplattegrond in de Rode Michelingids van Frankrijk	Red frame: town plans in the Michelin Red Guide France	Schémas encadrés: plans traités dans les Guides "Hôtels et Restaurants"
Rot unterstrichen: Im Roten Michelin-Führer aufgeführter Ort	Rood onderstreepte plaatsnaam: plaats die vermeld is in de Rode Michelingids van Frankrijk	Red underlining: town or place mentioned in the Michelin Red Guide France	Noms soulignés: localités ou sites figurant dans ces mêmes guides
Im Michelin-Führer "Camping Caravaning France" gelistete Campingplätze	Kampeerterrein dat vermeld is in de Michelingids "Camping Caravaning France"	Camp sites listed in the Michelin Camping Caravanning Guide	Localités ou sites retenus dans le Guide "Camping-Caravaning"
Abgelegenes Hotel oder Restaurant	Afgelegen hotel of restaurant	Secluded hotel or restaurant	Hôtel, restaurant isolé
Campingplatz	Kampeerterrein	Location of camping site	Terrain de camping

Sehenswürdigkeiten / Bezienswaardigheden / Tourist information / Eléments touristiques

Orte in den Grünen Michelin-Reiseführern aufgeführt	De meeste bezienswaardigheden zijn beschreven in de Groene Michelingidsen	Most of these sites are described in the Michelin Green Guides	Les Guides Verts Michelin décrivent la plupart de ces curiosités
Orientierungstafel, Rundblick, Aussichtspunkt	Oriëntatietafel met panorama, uitzichtpunt	Viewing table, panorama, viewpoint	Table d'orientation, panorama, point de vue
Landschaftlich schöne Route, Kirchliches Gebäude	Schilderachtig traject, kerk of kapel	Scenic route, ecclesiastical building	Parcours pittoresque, édifice religieux
Schloß, Burg, Ruine, Megalith, Leuchtturm	Kasteel, ruine, hunebed of dolmen, vuurtoren	Chateau, ruins, megalith, lighthouse	Château, ruines, mégalithe, phare
Windmühle, Höhle, sonstige Sehenswürdigkeit	Windmolen, grot, andere bezienswaardigheid	Windmill, cave, other place of interest	Moulin à vent, grotte, autre curiosité

Sport- und Freizeiteinrichtungen / Sport, Recreatie / Sports and recreation facilities / Sports – Loisirs

Stadion, Golfplatz, Pferderennbahn	Stadion, golfbaan; renbaan	Stadium, golf course, race course	Stade, golf, hippodrome
Reitanlage, Strandbad, Schwimmbad	Manege; zwemgelegenheid; zwembad	Equestrian centre, swimming place, pool	Centre équestre, baignade, piscine
Jachthafen, Segelflugplatz, Freizeitpark	Zeilsport, zweefvliegen; recreatiepark	Sailing, gliding, country park	Voile, vol à voile, parc de loisirs
Seilbahn, Sessellift, Schutzhütte	Kabelspoor of stoeltjeslift; berghut	Cable car, chair lift, mountain hut	Téléphérique, télésiège, refuge de montagne
Fernwanderweg	Lange-afstands-wandelpad	Long distance footpath	Sentier de grande randonnée

Sonstige Symbole / Andere tekens / Other features / Equipements – Environnement

Bahnlinie mit Bahnhof, Straßenbahn	Spoorweg met station; tramweg	Railway, station, tramway	Voie ferrée, station, tramway
Landeplatz im Gebirge, Flugplatz, Flughafen	Landingsbaan in de bergen; vliegveld; luchthaven	Mountain airfield, airfield, airport	Altiport, aérodrome, aéroport
Funk-, Fernsehturm	Telecommunicatietoren of -mast	Telecommunications tower or mast	Tour ou pylône de télécommunications
Notrufsäule	Telefoon voor noodgevallen	Emergency telephone	Borne d'appel d'urgence
Staatsgrenze	Rijksgrens	National boundary	Frontière
Zollstation	Douanekantoor	Customs post	Bureau de douane
Erdöl- oder Erdgasquelle, Steinbruch, Bergwerk	Olie- of gasput, steengroeve, mijn	Oil or gas well, quarry, mine	Pétrole ou gaz naturel, carrière, mine
Materialtransportbahn, Fabrik, Staudamm	Kabelvrachtvervoer; fabriek; stuwdam	Overhead conveyor, factory, dam	Transporteur aérien, usine, barrage
Leuchtturm, Windmühle, Wasserturm	Vuurtoren, windmolen; watertoren	Lighthouse, windmill, water tower	Phare, moulin à vent, château d'eau
Krankenhaus, Kirche oder Kapelle	Verpleeginrichting; kerk of kapel	Hospital or hospice, church or chapel	Hôpital ou hospice, église ou chapelle
Friedhof, Bildstock, Schloß, Burg, Festung, Ruine	Begraafplaats; kruisheuvel; kasteel, fort, ruine	Cemetery, cross, chateau, fort, ruins	Cimetière, calvaire, château, fort, ruines
Denkmal, Höhle, Forsthaus	Monument; grot; boswachtershuis	Statue or building, cave, forester's lodge	Monument, grotte, maison forestière
Wald oder Gehölz, Staatsforst	Bos; domaniaal woud	Forest or wood, state forest	Forêt ou bois, forêt domaniale

Verwaltungssitz / Hoofdplaats van / Seat of local government / Chef-lieu de

Präfektur (Departement)	Departement (Prefectuur)	Prefecture	Département
Unterpräfektur (Bezirk)	Arrondissement (Onderprefectuur)	Sub-prefecture	Arrondissement
Kanton (Kreis)	Canton	Canton	Canton

Maßstab 1:200 000 — 1cm entspricht 2 km
Schaal 1:200 000 — 1cm op de kaart = 2km in het terrein
Scale 1:200 000 — 1cm:2km approx 3 miles:1 inch
Échelle 1/200 000 — 1cm: 2 km

0 1 2 3 4 5km

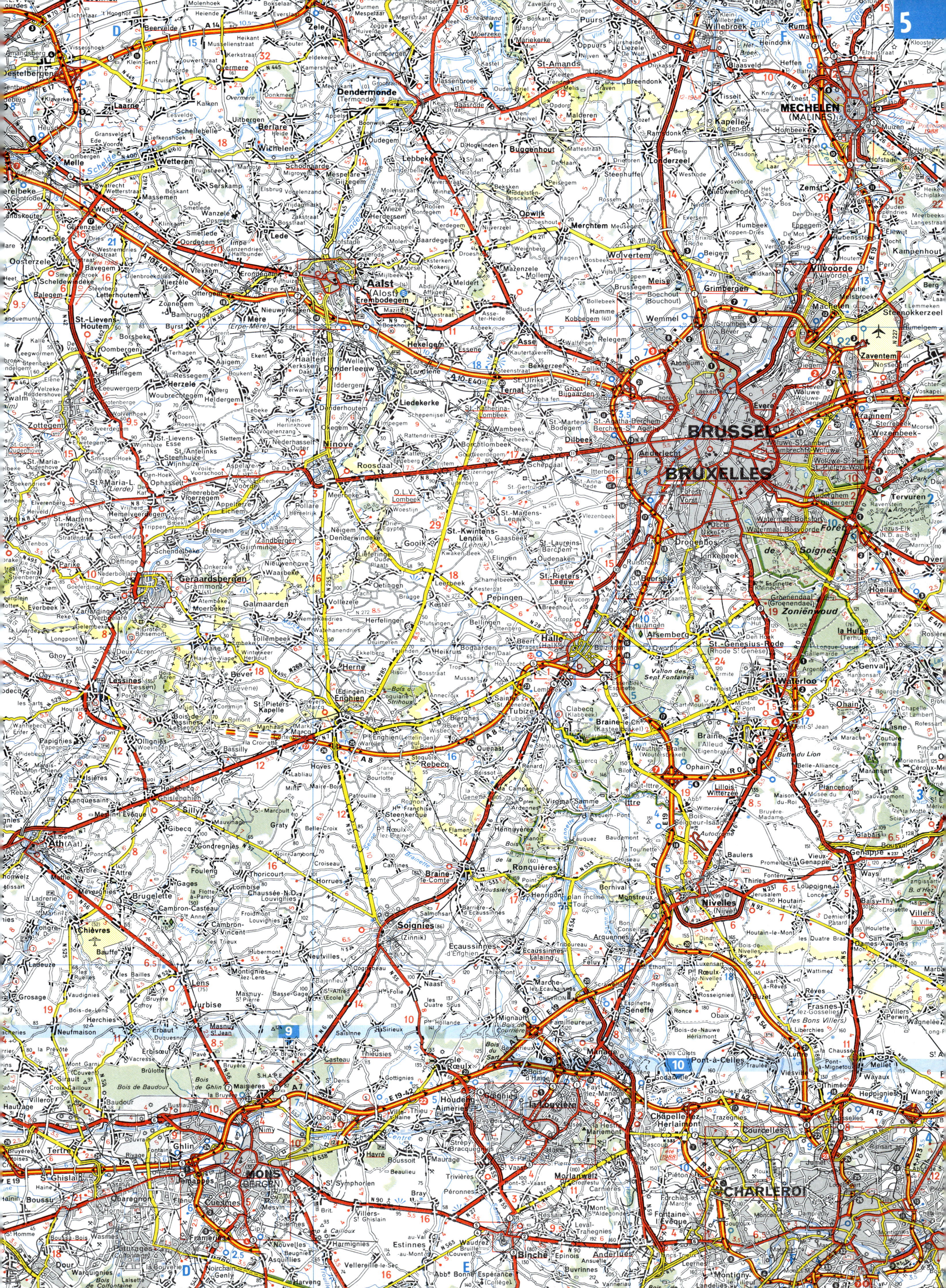

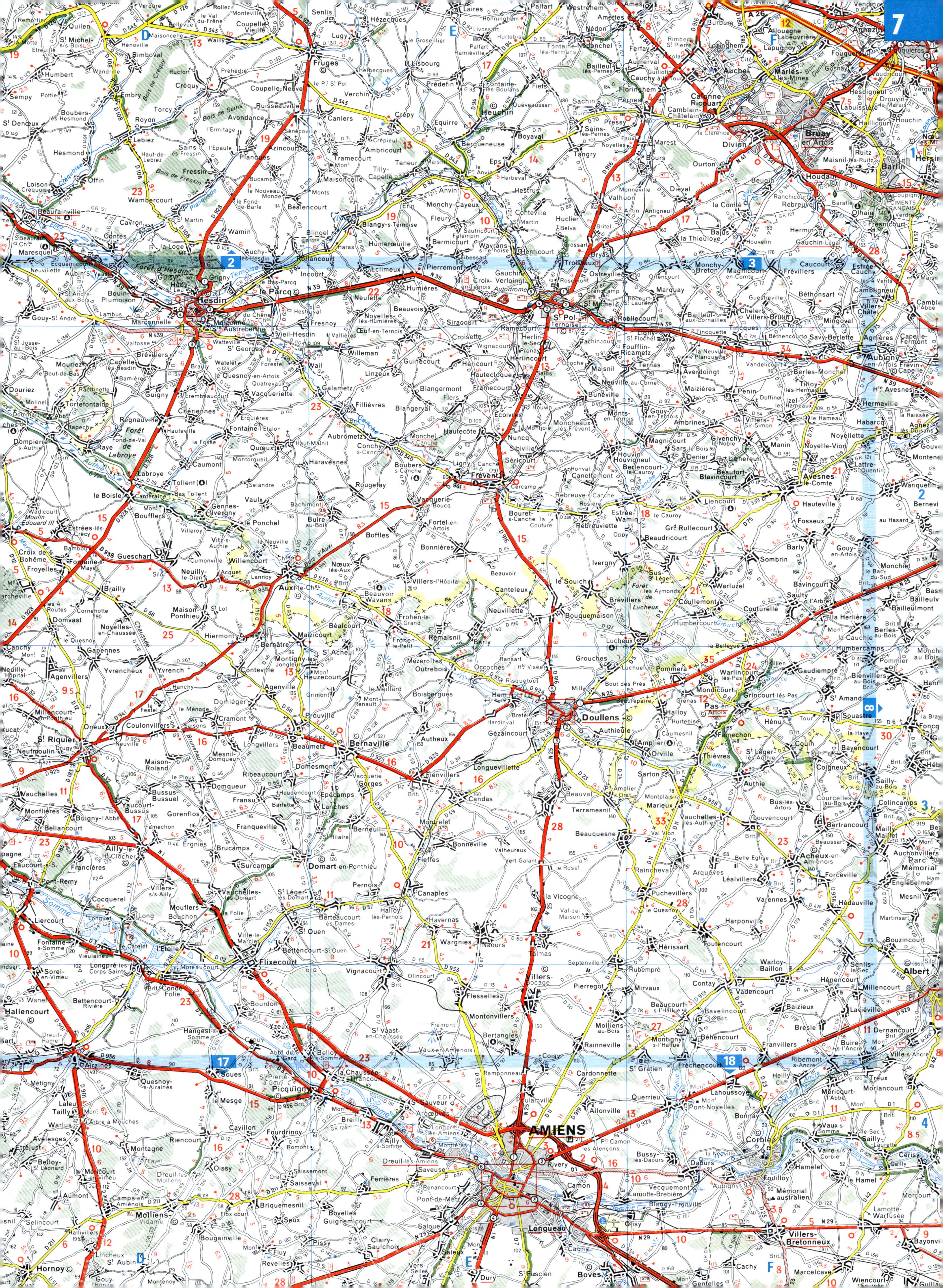

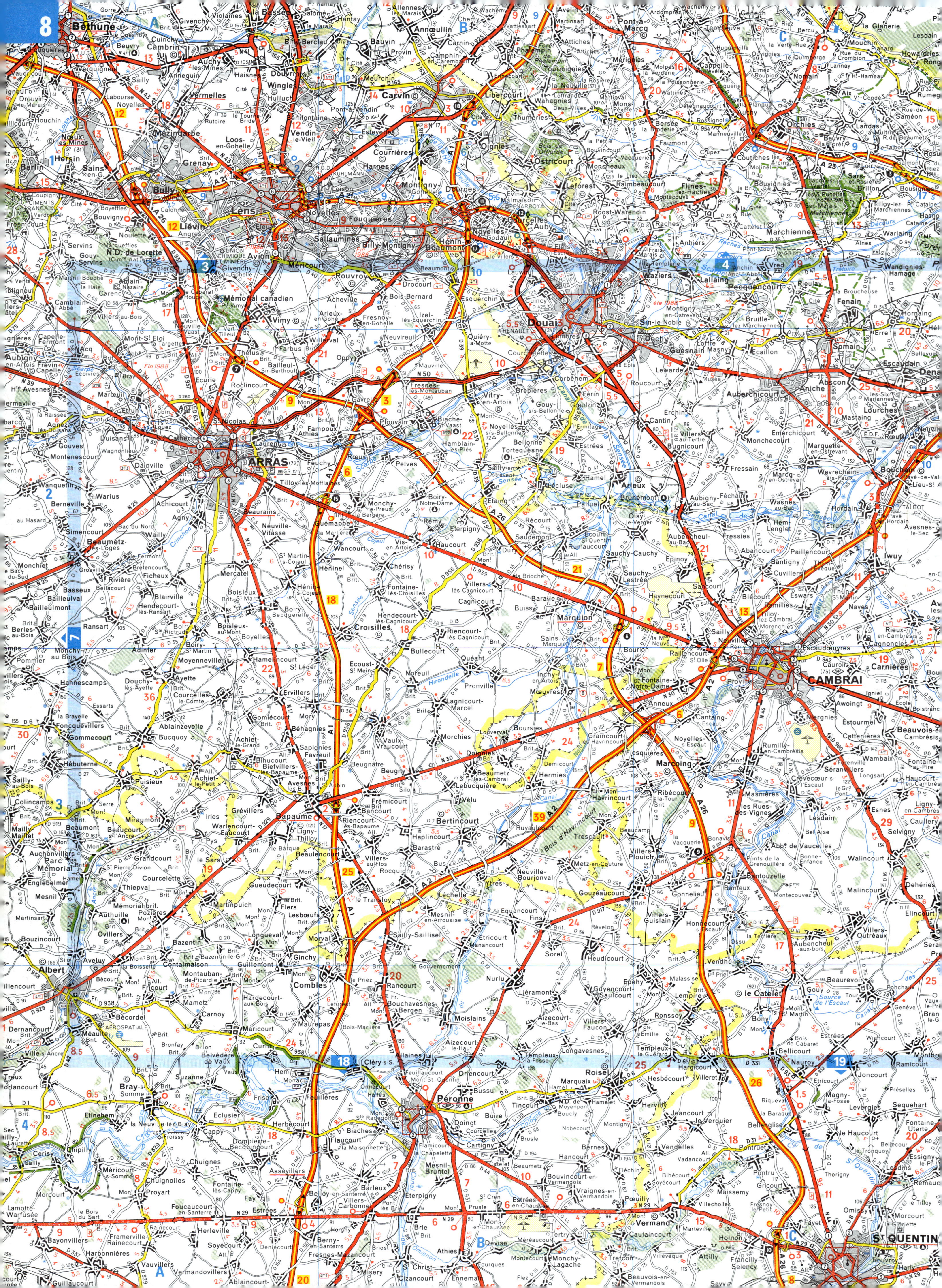

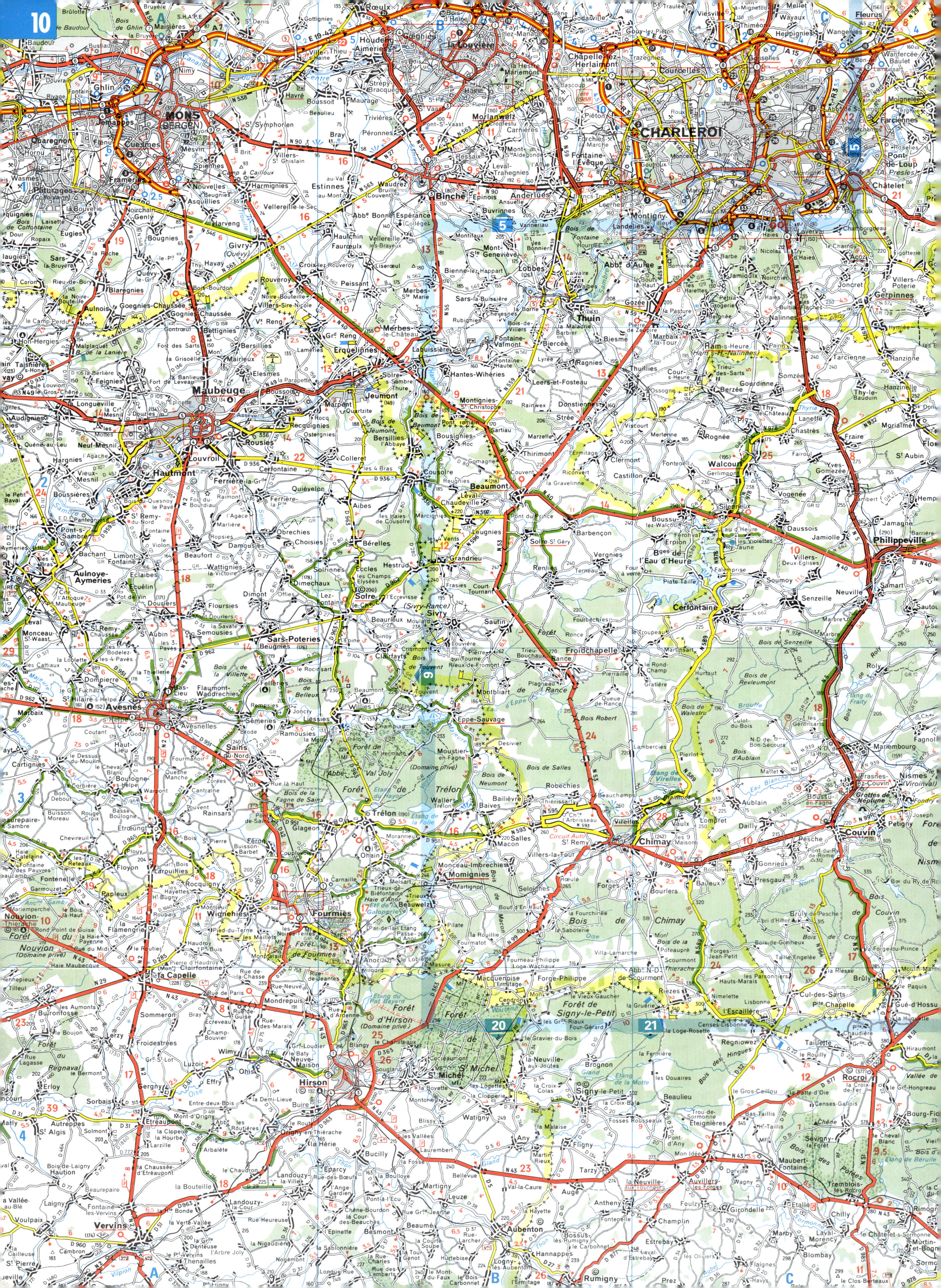

MONS
BERGEN
CHARLEROI
La Louvière
Binche
Maubeuge
Jeumont
Hautmont
Beaumont
Thuin
Avesnes
Aulnoye-Aymeries
Sivry
Froidchapelle
Chimay
Couvin
Philippeville
Walcourt
Trélon
Fourmies
Wignehies
La Capelle
Hirson
Signy-le-Petit
Rocroi
Aubenton
Rumigny
Vervins
Sars-Poteries
Solre-le-Château
Momignies
Fleurus
Montigny-le-Tilleul
Anderlues
Mariembourg
Nismes
Forêt de St-Michel
Forêt d'Hirson
Bois de Chimay
Lobbes
Erquelinnes
Bavay

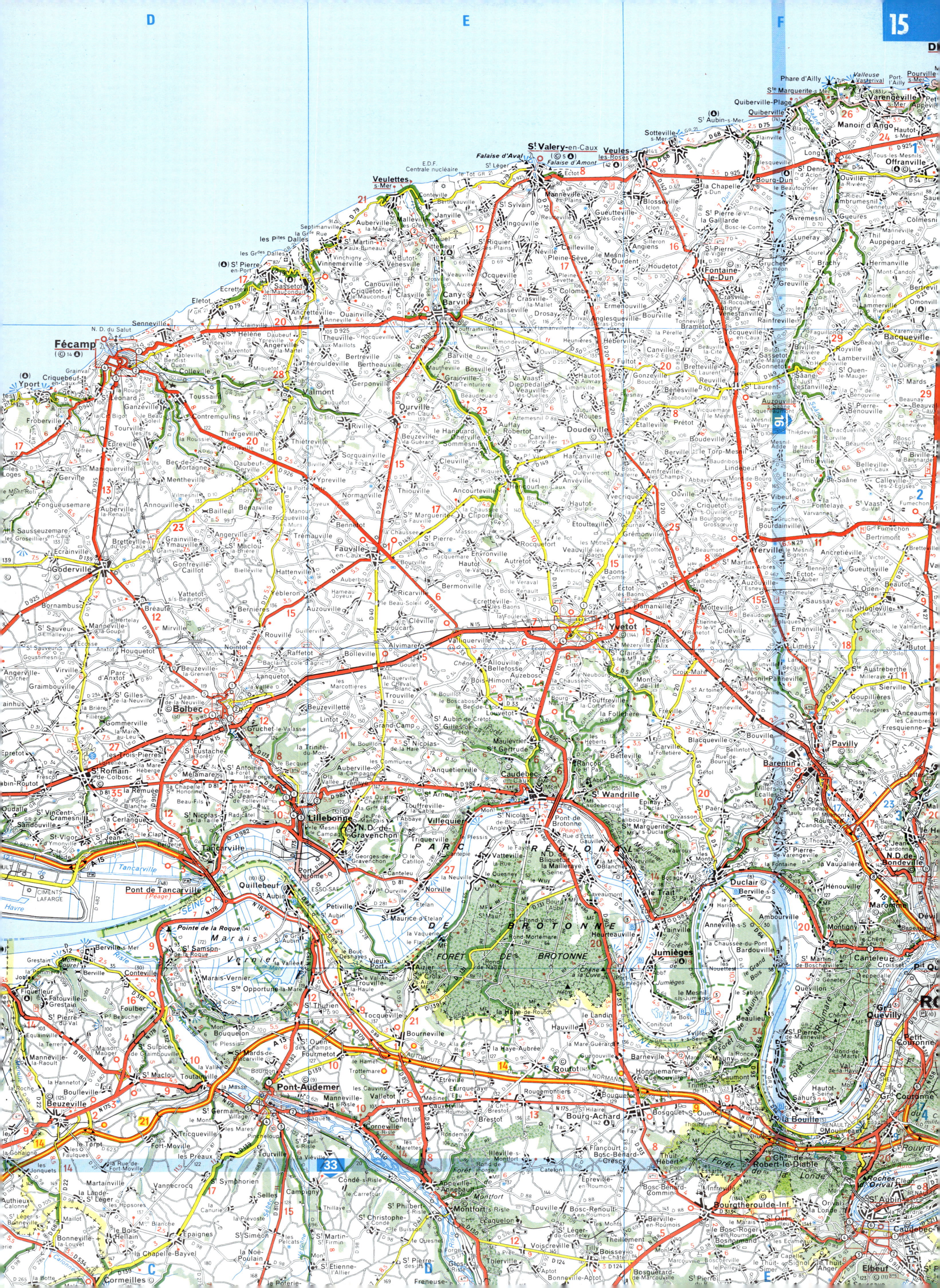

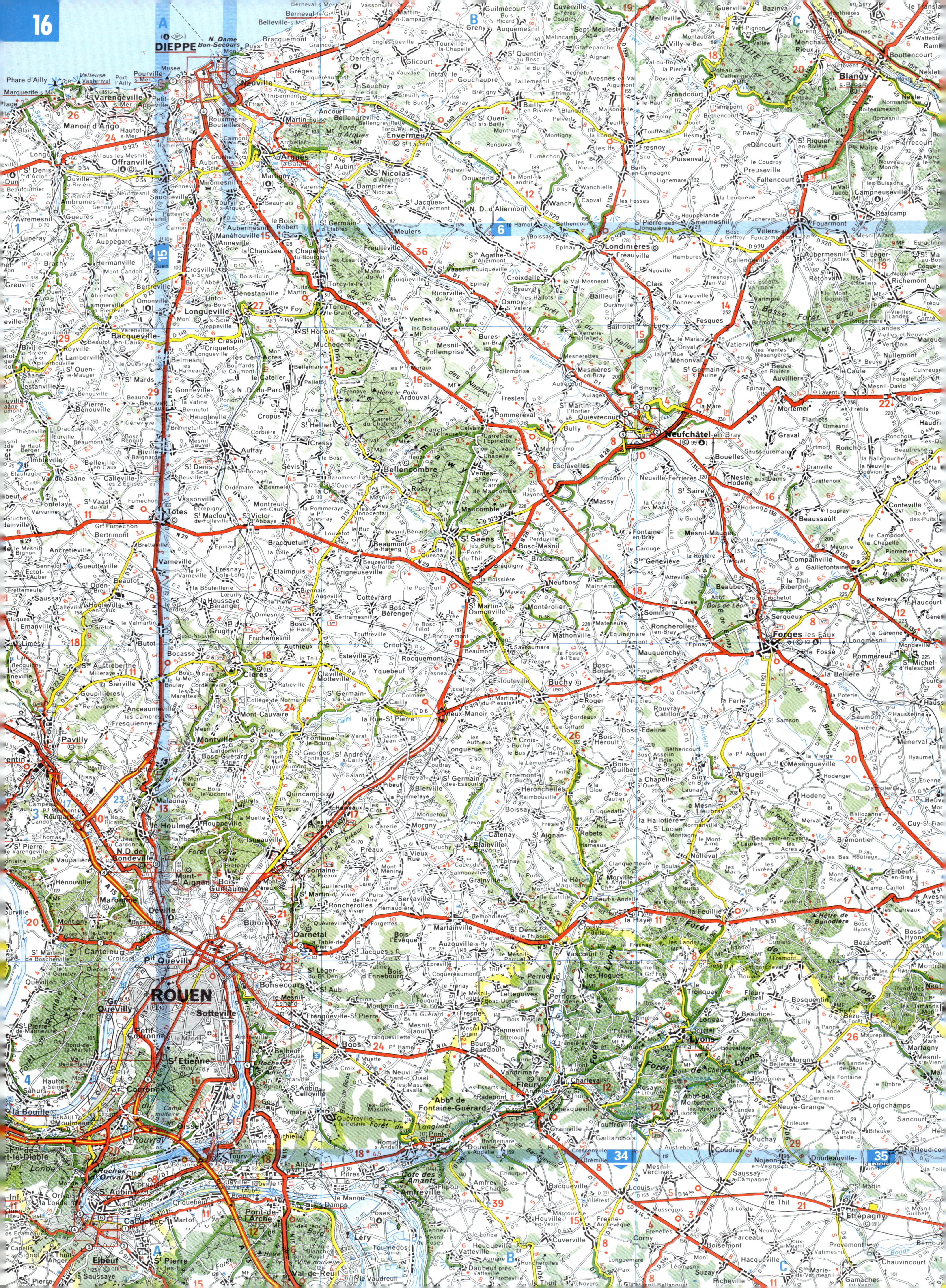

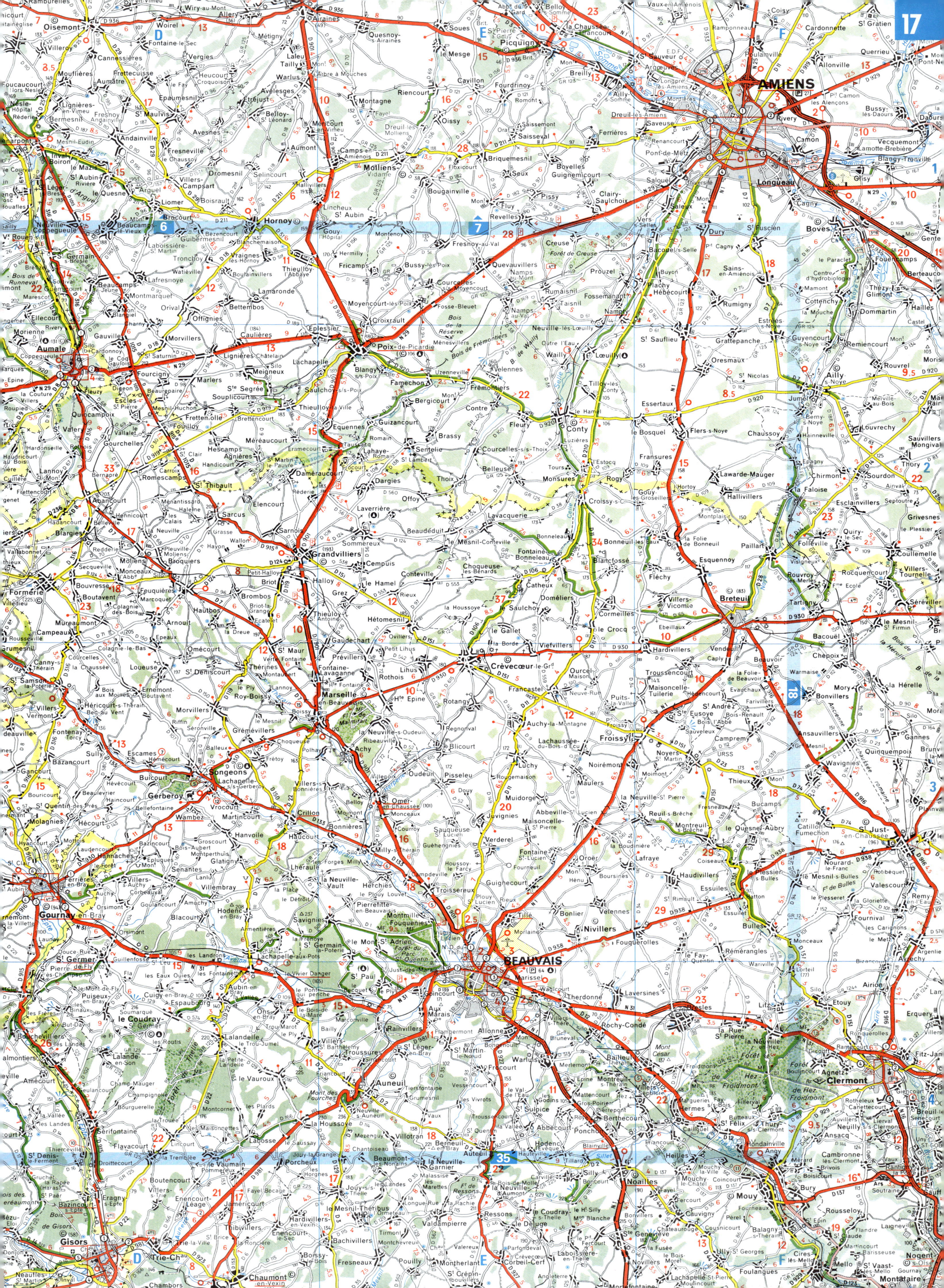

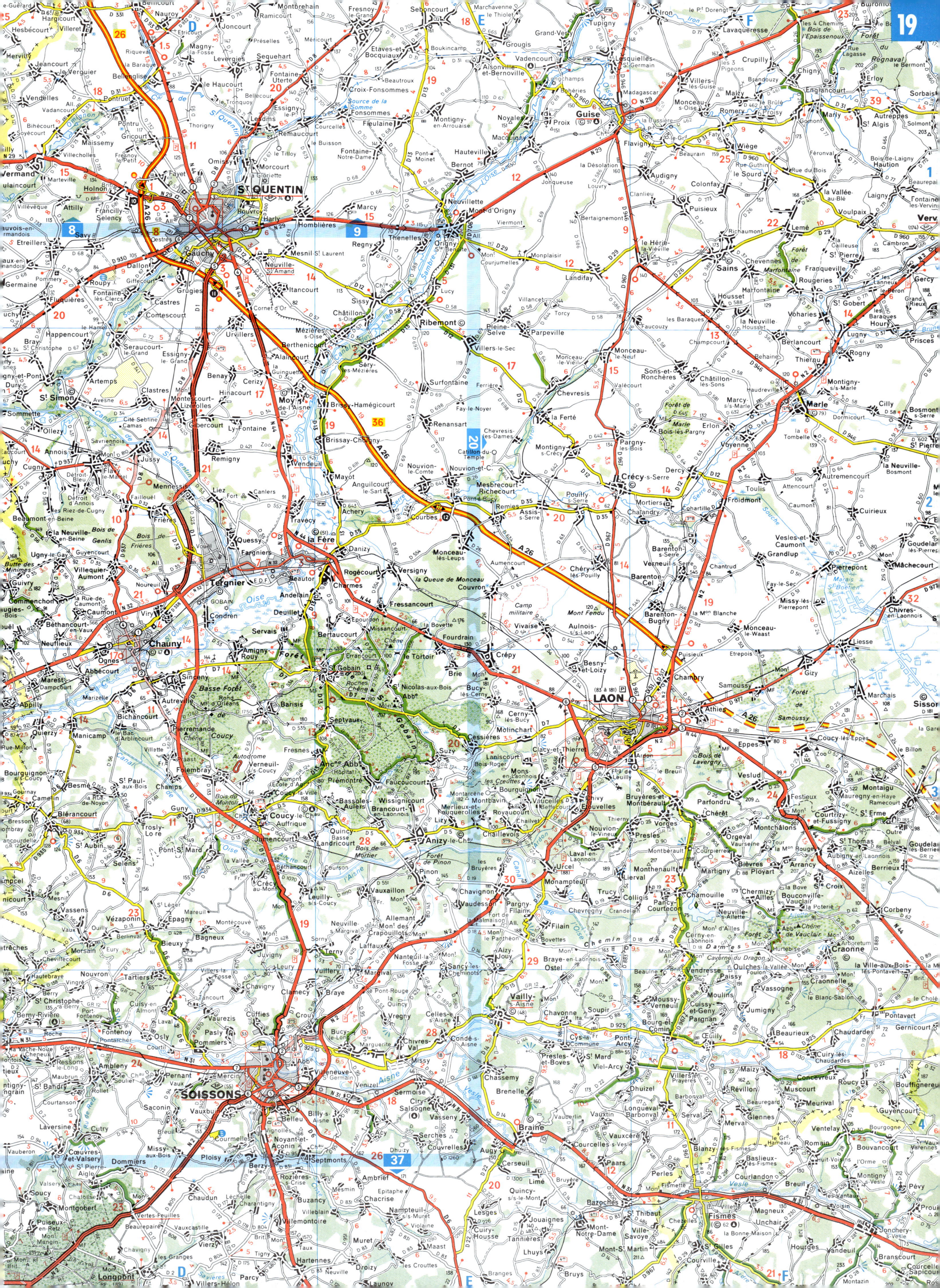

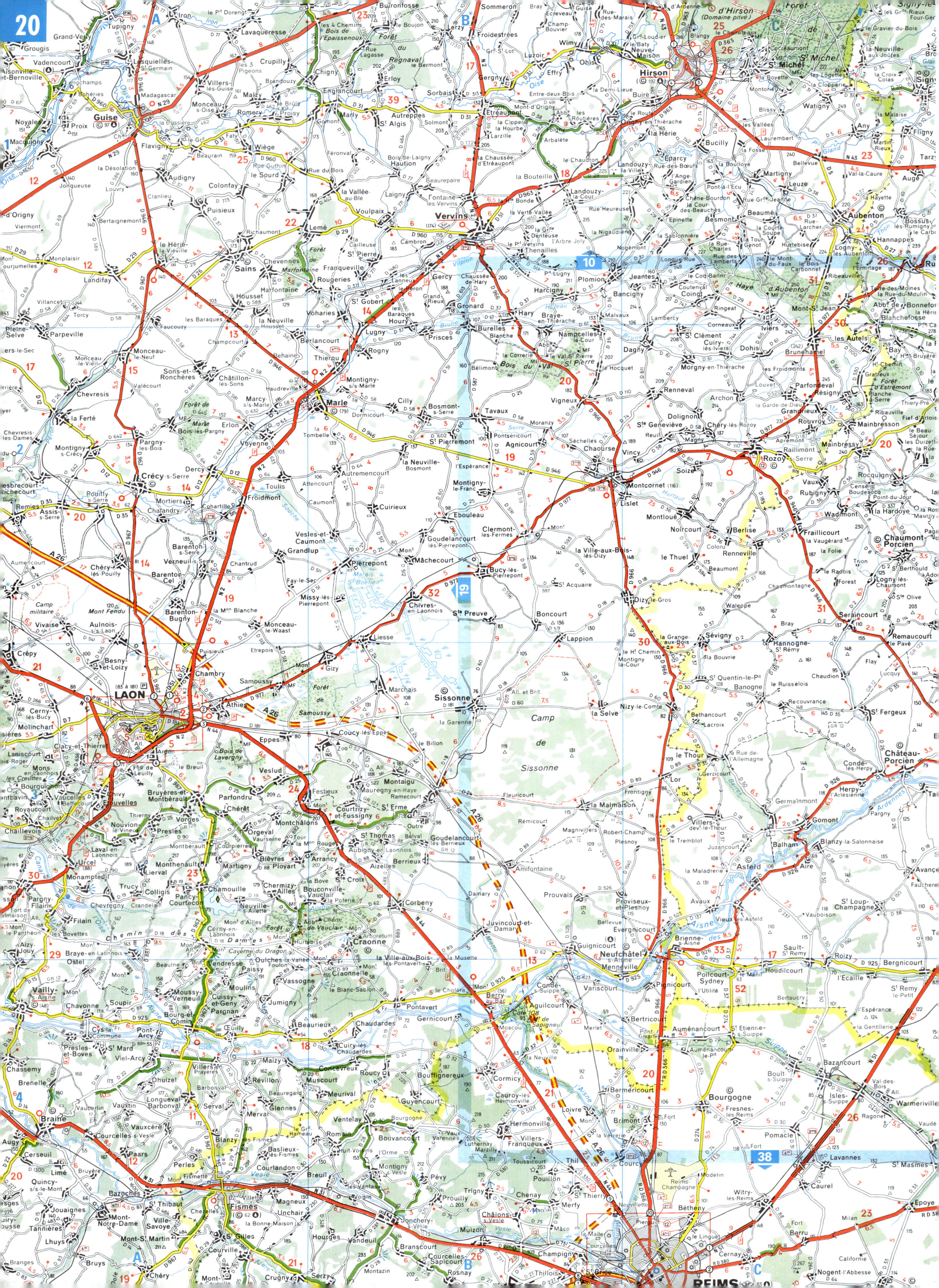

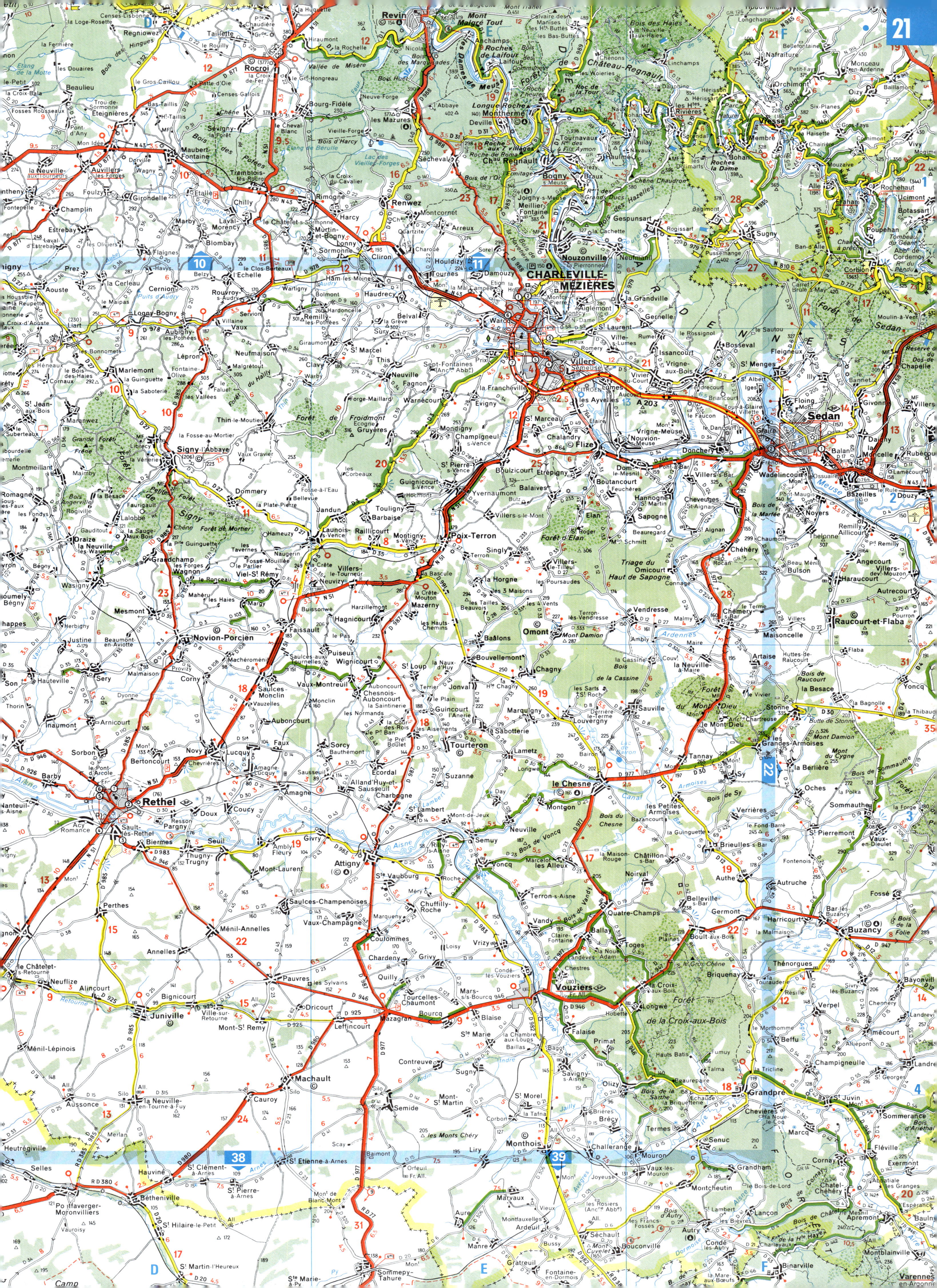

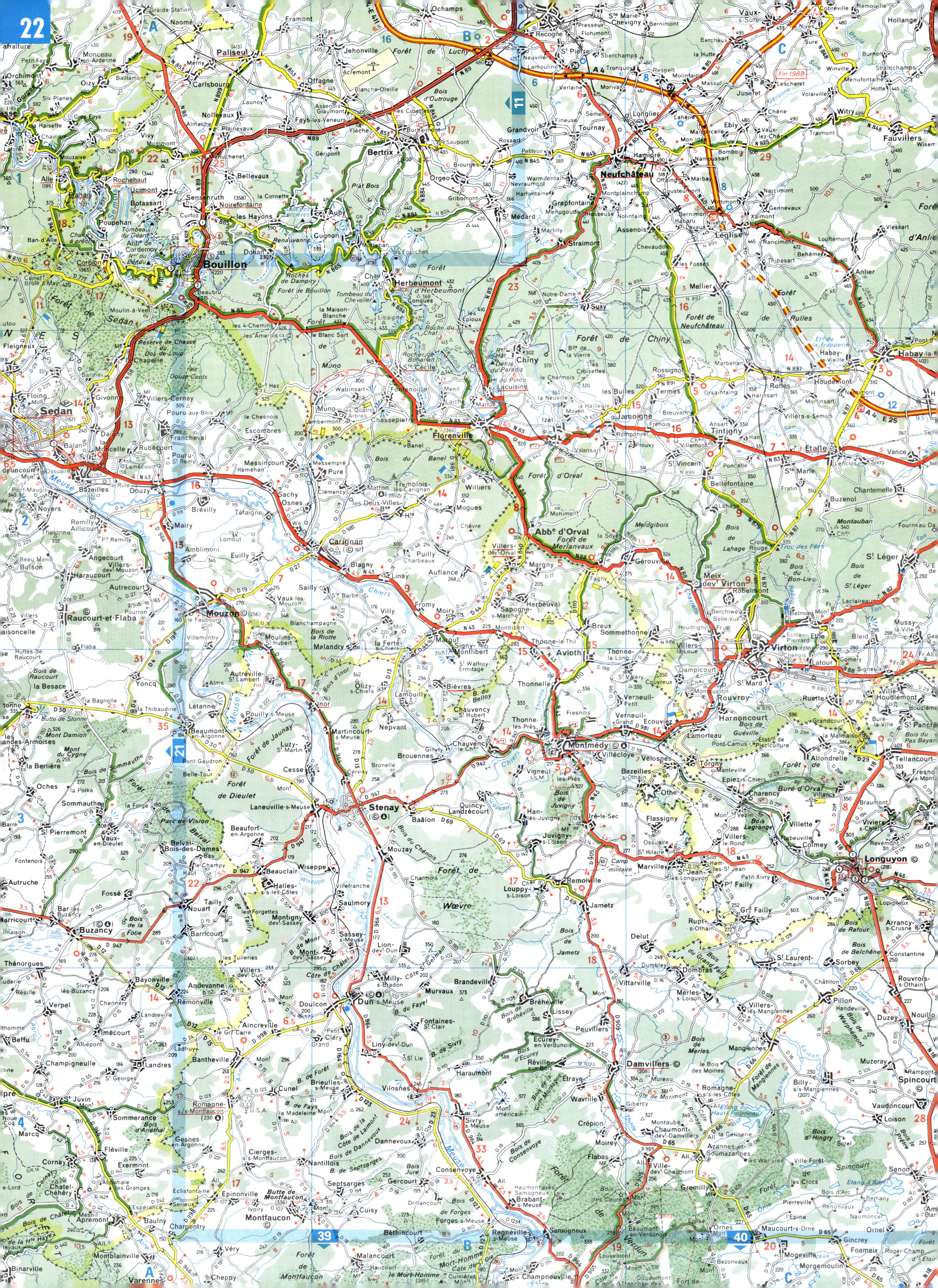

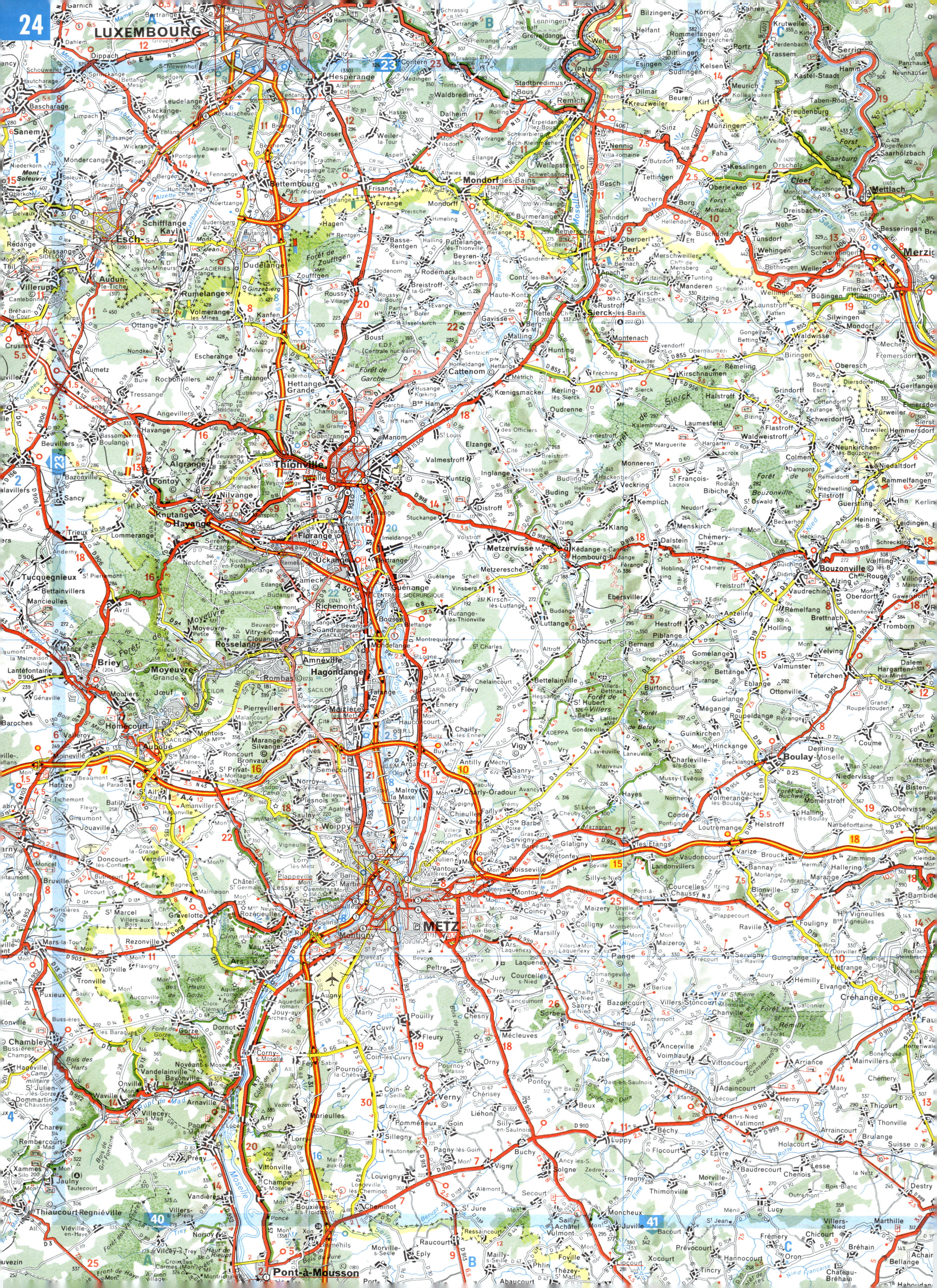

SAARBRÜCKEN
SAARLOUIS
Völklingen
Neunkirchen
St. Ingbert
HOMBURG
St. Wendel
Kusel
Zweibrü
Dillingen
Saarwellingen
Lebach
Tholey
Wadern
Weiskirchen
Schmelz
Ottweiler
Bexbach
Blieskastel
Sulzbach
Quierschied
Heusweiler
Püttlingen
Riegelsberg
Wallerfangen
Wadgassen
Überherrn
Forbach
Stiring-Wendel
Freyming-Merlebach
St. Avold
Creutzwald
Sarreguemines
Puttelange-aux-Lacs
Sarralbe
Sarre-Union
Grostenquin
Rohrbach-lès-Bitche
Kirkel
Mandelbachtal
Gersheim
Kleinblittersdorf

A
B
C
PERROS-GUIREC
Ploumanach
Trégastel
Port-Blanc
Plougrescant
Tréguier
Lézardrieux
Paimpol
Ile de Bréhat
Pointe de l'Arcouest
Phare du Paon
Lannion
La Roche-Derrien
Pontrieux
La Roche-Jagu
Chât. de Tonquédec
Bégard
Plouaret
Belle-Isle-en-Terre
Guingamp
Lanvollon
Plouha
St Quay-Portrieux
Binic
St Brieuc
Châtelaudren
Bourbriac
Callac
Plésidy
Quintin
St Gilles-Pligeaux
St Nicolas-du-Pélem
Corlay
Rostrenen
Gouarec
Mûr-de-Bretagne
Uzel
Plouguenast
Plœuc-s-Lié
Forêt de Lorge
Gorges de Toul Goulic
Gorges du Corong
Forêt de Duault
Bois d'Avaugour
Plaine-Haute
St Gilles-Vieux-Marché
Glomel
Ménez-Bré
Lac de Guerlédan
27
46
47

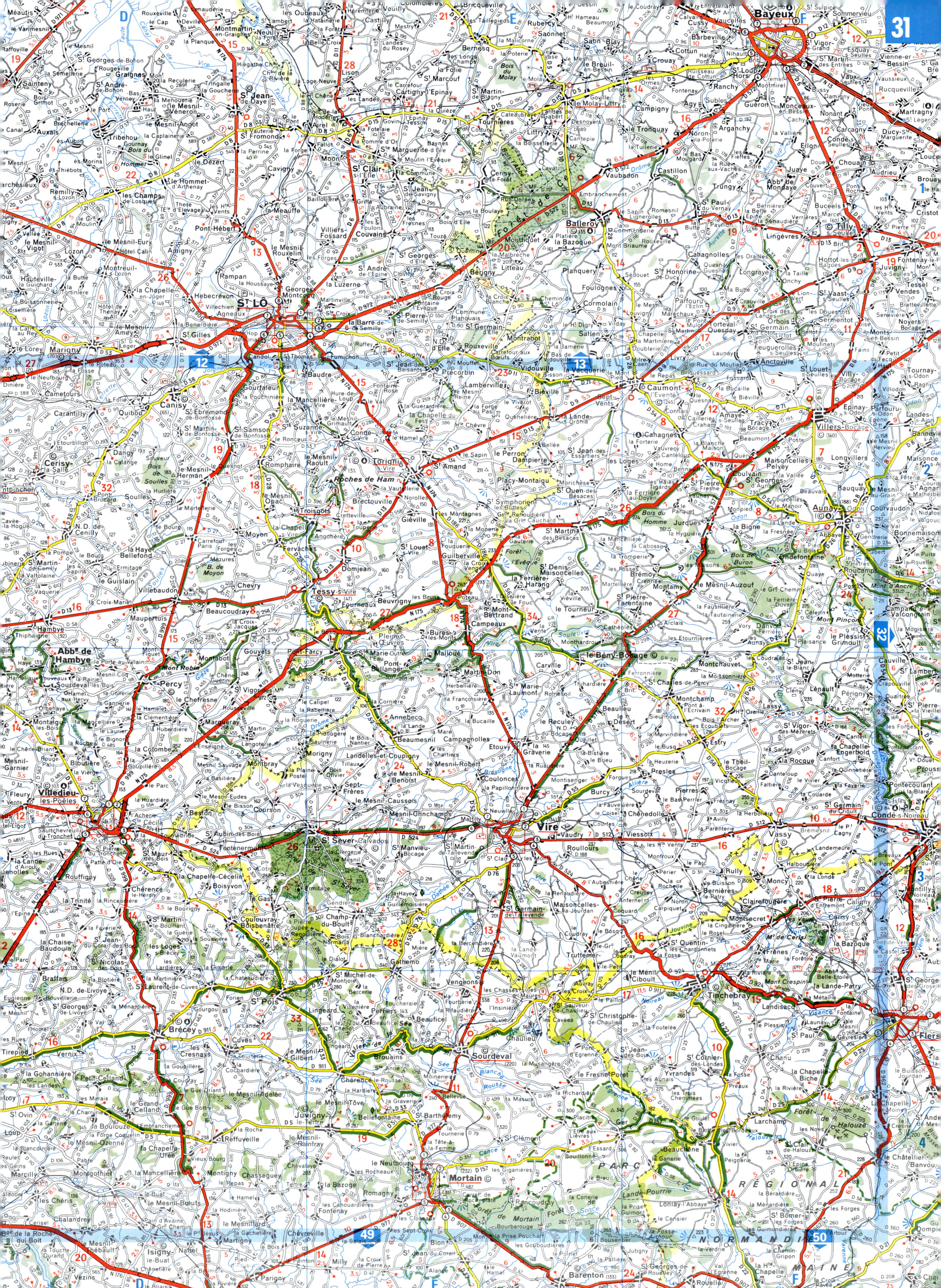

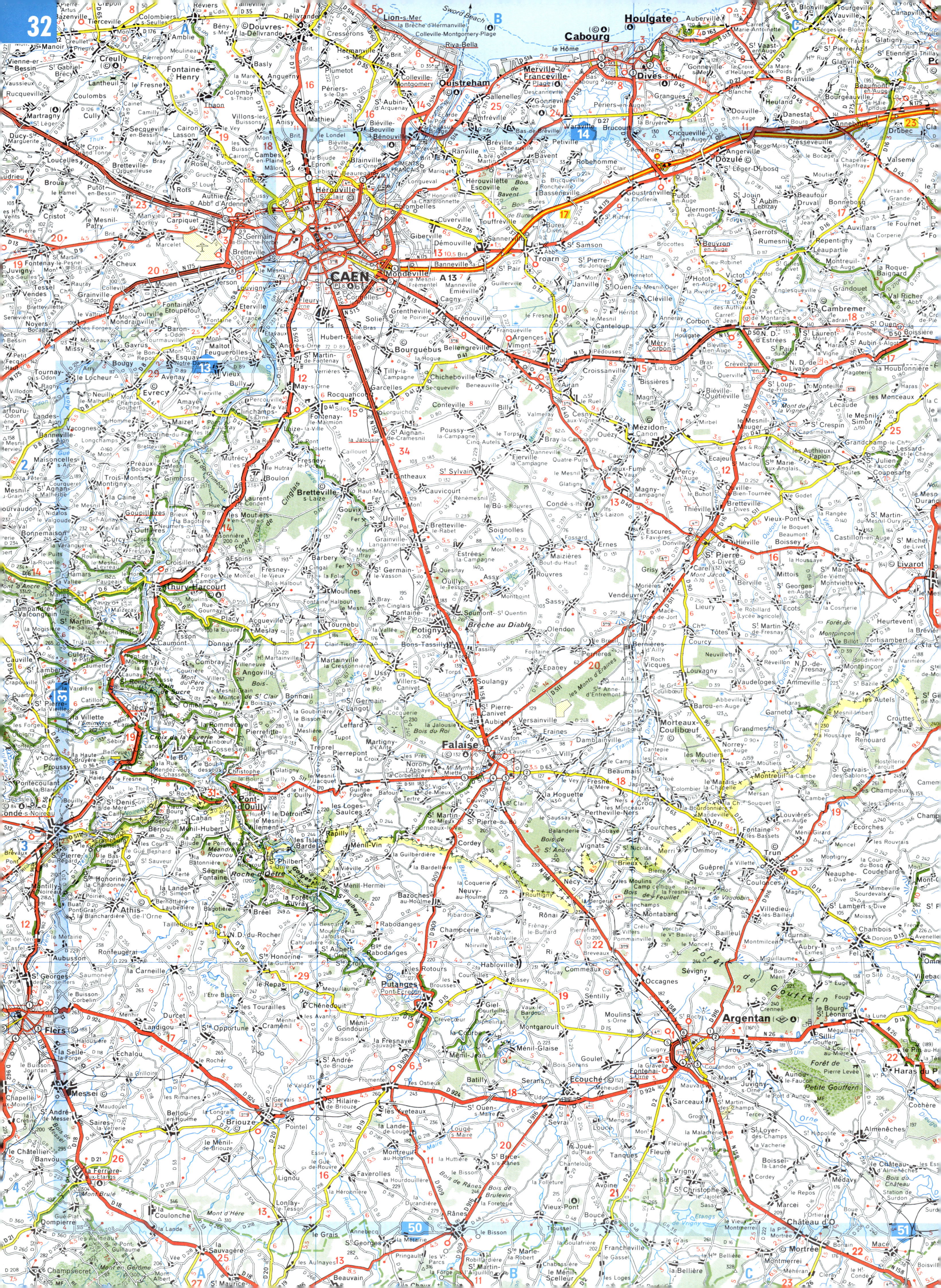

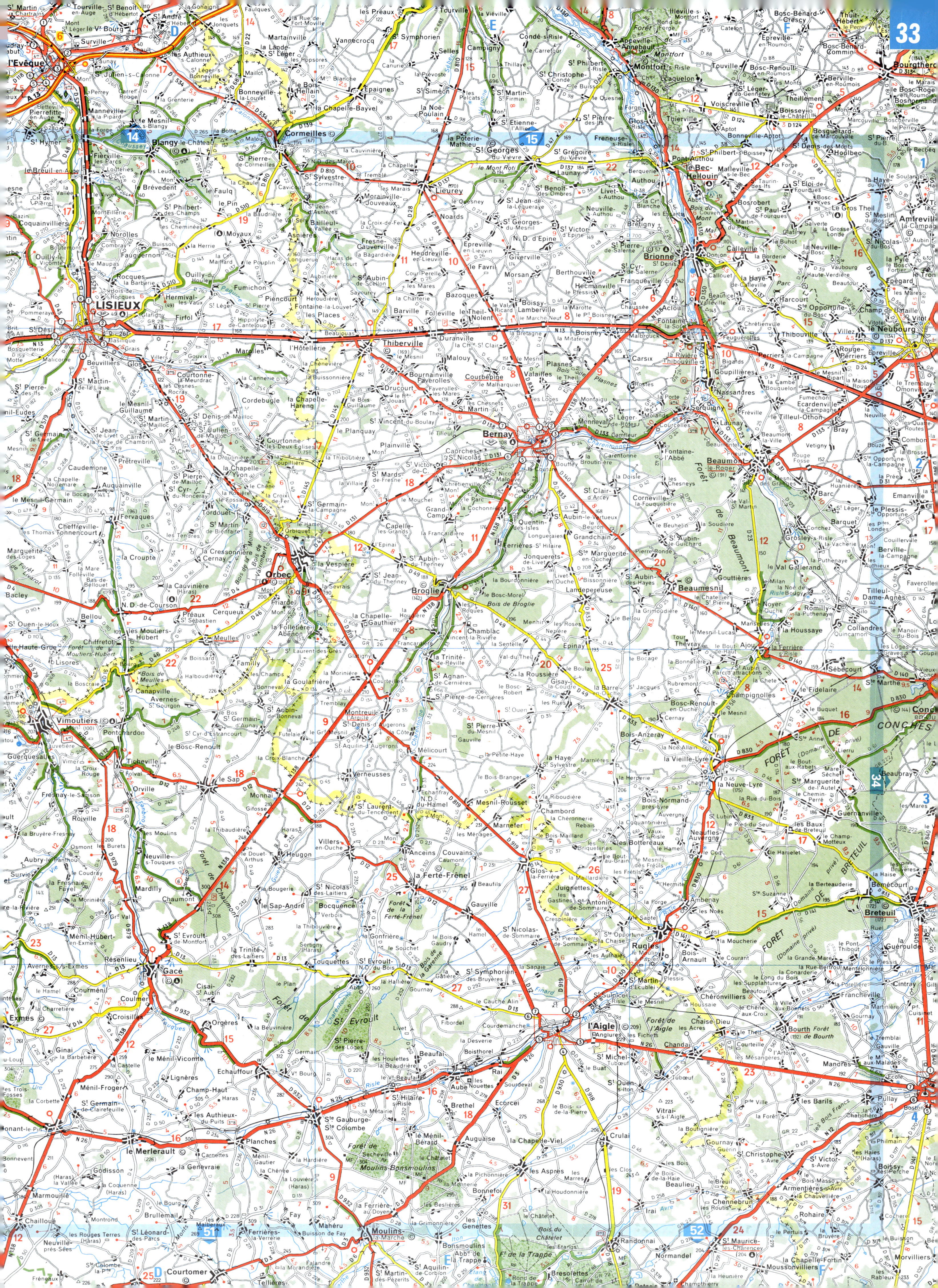

Lisieux
Cormeilles
Blangy-le-Château
Lieurey
Montfort
Pont-Authou
le Bec-Hellouin
Brionne
Bourgtheroulde
le Neubourg
Thiberville
Bernay
Orbec
Broglie
Beaumont-le-Roger
Beaumesnil
Vimoutiers
Gacé
la Ferté-Frênel
Rugles
Breteuil
l'Aigle
Moulins-la-Marche
le Merlerault
Forêt de Conches
Forêt de Breteuil
Forêt de St Evroult

Elbeuf
Pont-de-l'Arche
Val-de-Reuil
Louviers
les Andelys
Gaillon
Vernon
Neubourg
EVREUX
Pacy-s-Eure
Bonnières
Conches-en-Ouche
la Bonneville-s-Iton
Damville
St-André-de-l'Eure
Ivry-la-Bataille
Anet
Nonancourt
Verneuil
Dreux
Brezolles
Houdan
Nogent-le-Roi
SEINE
Forêt des Andelys
Forêt de Bizy
Forêt de Dreux
16
52
33

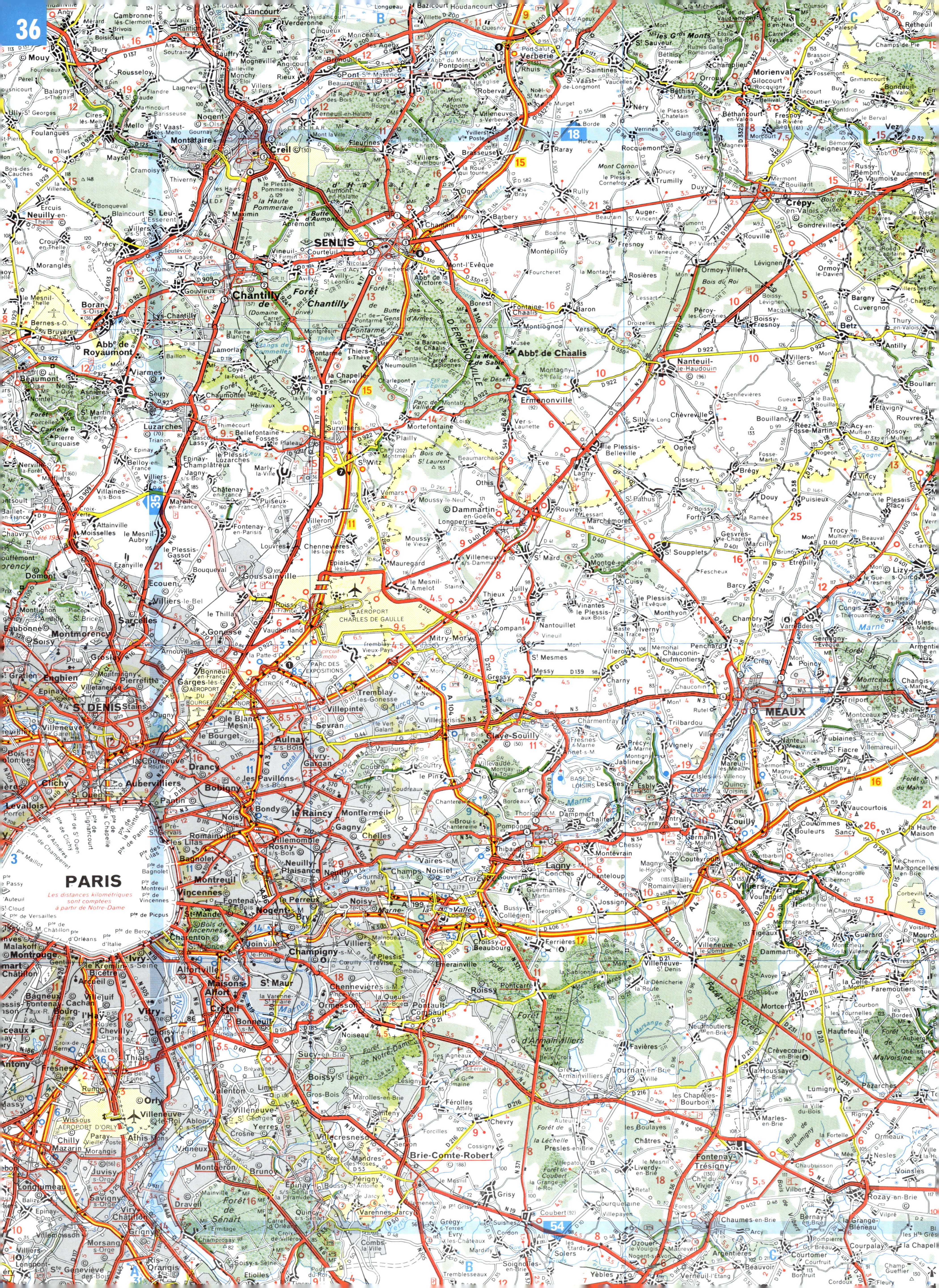
SENLIS
Chantilly
Forêt de Chantilly
Creil
Crépy-en-Valois
Nanteuil-le-Haudouin
Abb. de Chaalis
Ermenonville
Luzarches
Dammartin-en-Goële
AEROPORT CHARLES DE GAULLE
Montmorency
Sarcelles
St DENIS
Aubervilliers
Le Bourget
Villepinte
Claye-Souilly
MEAUX
PARIS
Les distances kilométriques sont comptées à partir de Notre-Dame
Vincennes
Montreuil
Champigny
Noisy-le-Grand
Lagny
Coulommes
St Maur
Créteil
Vitry
Orly
Boissy-St Léger
Brie-Comte-Robert
Tournan-en-Brie
Forêt d'Armainvilliers
Forêt de Sénart
Rozay-en-Brie

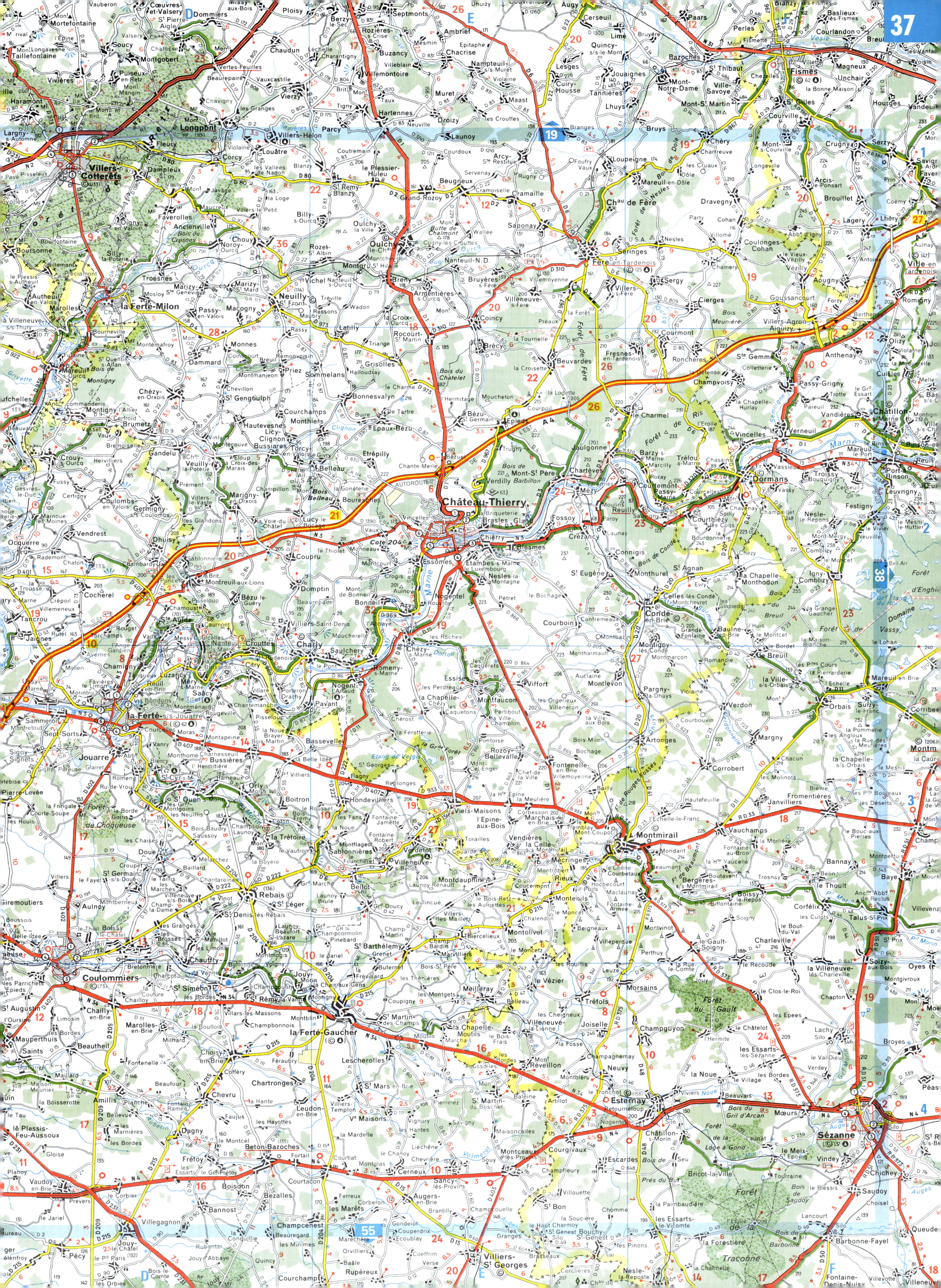

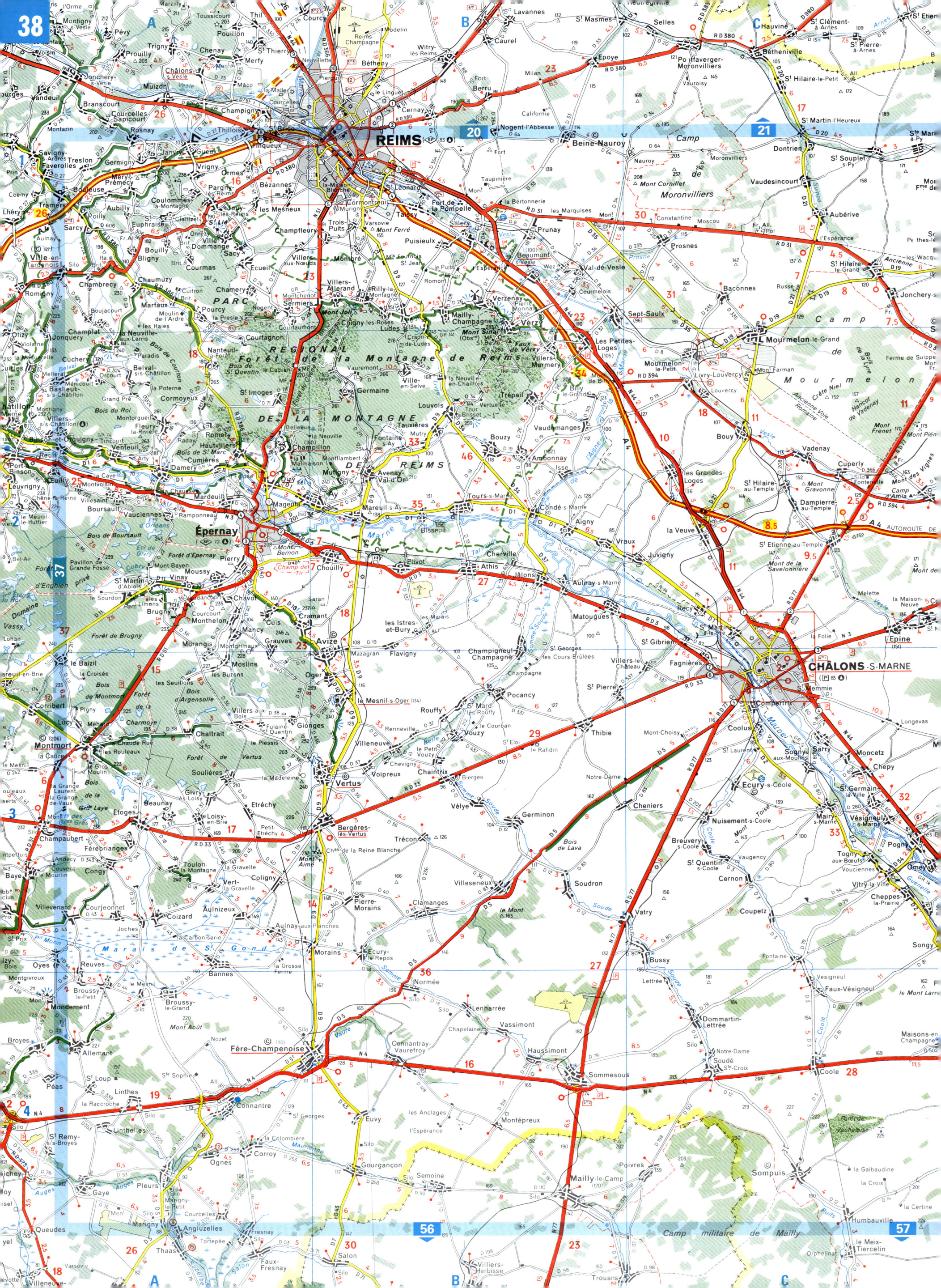

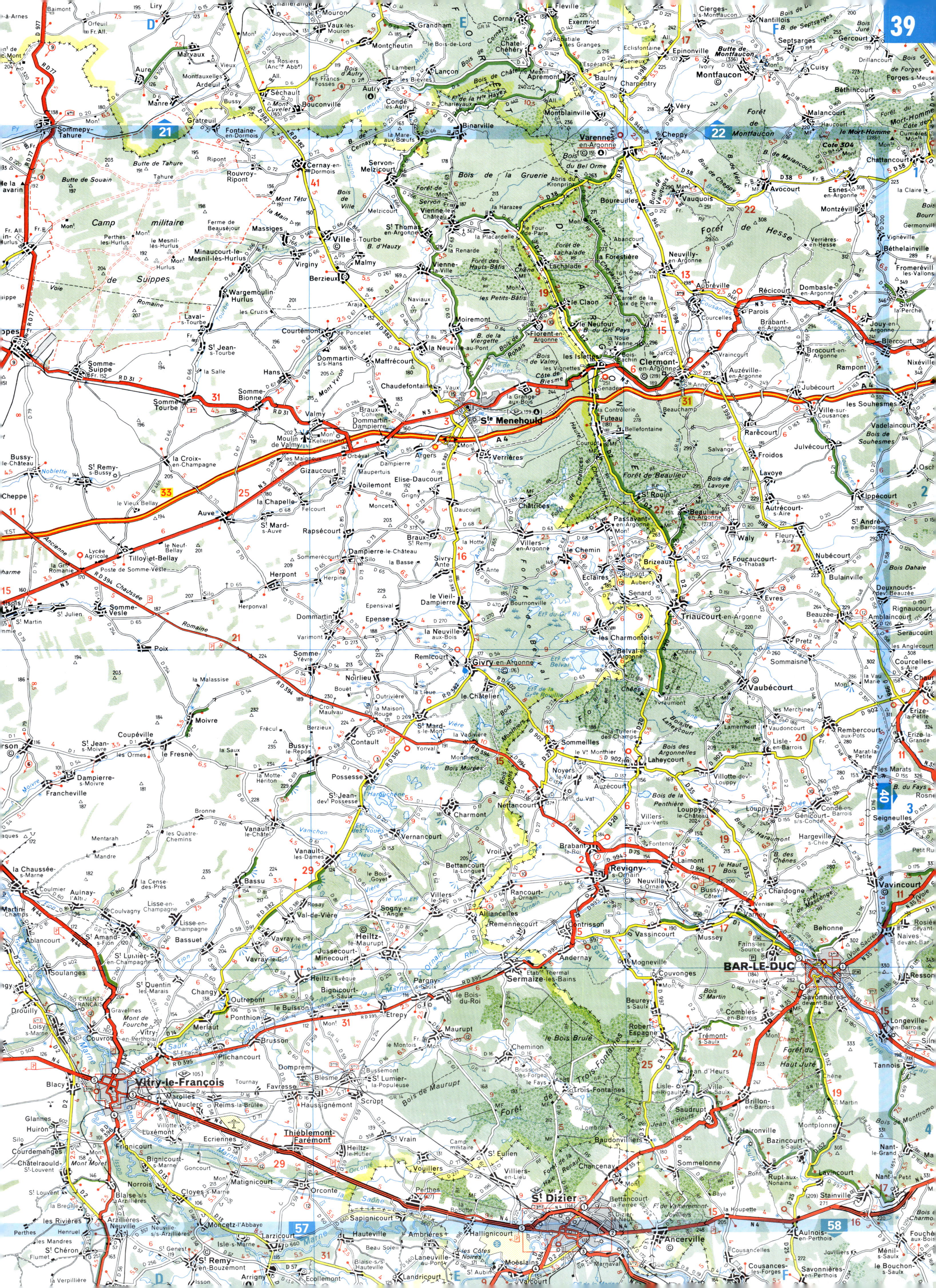

VERDUN
Etain
Conflans-en-Jarnisy
Jarny
Briey
Fresnes-en-Woëvre
Hattonchâtel
Vigneulles-lès-Hattonchâtel
Thiaucourt-Regniéville
St Mihiel
Commercy
Ligny-en-Barrois
TOUL
Vaucouleurs
Void
Pierrefitte-s-Aire
Souilly
Chambley
PARC RÉGIONAL DE LORRAINE
Forêt de Commercy
Forêt de Souilly
Forêt d'Amblonville
Forêt de la Reine
Meuse
Madine

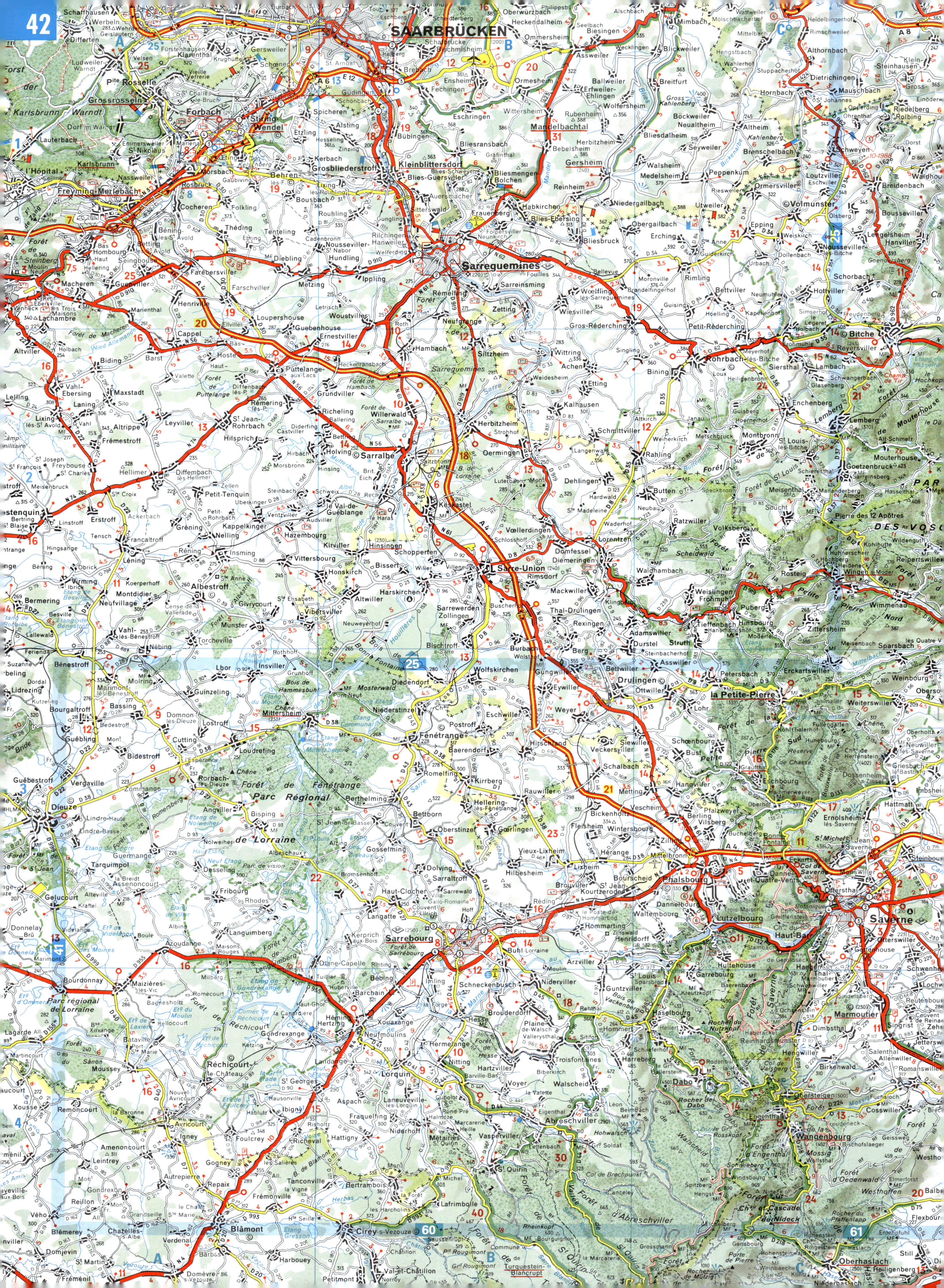

Pirmasens
Landau in der Pfalz
Hinterweidenthal
Hauenstein
Dahn
Lemberg
Klingenmünster
Bad Bergzabern
Kandel
NATURPARK PFÄLZERWALD
Herxheim
Wissembourg
Ch. de Fleckenstein
Lembach
Niederbronn-les-Bains
Reichshoffen
Philippsbourg
Lauterbourg
Seltz
Rastatt
Haguenau
FORÊT DE HAGUENAU
Soufflenheim
Bischwiller
Drusenheim
Brumath
Hochfelden
Bouxwiller
Ingwiller
Wasselonne
Marlenheim
Molsheim
Mutzig
STRASBOURG
Kehl
Achern
Oberkirch
Bühl
Rheinau
Renchen
Appenweier
Hagenau
Sinzheim
Baden-Baden
Gambsheim
La Wantzenau
Schiltigheim
Bischheim
Illkirch-Graffenstaden
Mundolsheim
Lingolsheim
Kappelrodeck
Lichtenau
Stollhofen
Iffezheim
Hügelsheim

Carhaix-Plouguer
Maël-Carhaix
Rostrenen
Plouguernével
Gouarec
Corlay
Mûr-de-Bretagne
Gourin
Le Faouët
Guémené-sur-Scorff
Cléguérec
Pontivy
Plouay
Quimperlé
Hennebont
Lanester
LORIENT
Port-Louis
Larmor-Plage
Ploemeur
Le Pouldu
Baud
Pluvigner
Auray
Ste Anne-d'Auray
Belz
Etel
ILE DE GROIX
Groix
Kernascléden
Bubry
Locminé
Camors
Landévant
Riantec
Pont-Scorff
Guidel
Arzano
Quistinic
Melrand
St Nicolas-des-Eaux
Forêt de Quénécan
Lac de Guerlédan
Forêt de Camors
Forêt de Lanvaux
Roches du Diable
Basse des Bretons
Passe de l'Ouest
Passe du Sud
Roches de Magouërb
Barre d'Etel
Anse du Pouldu

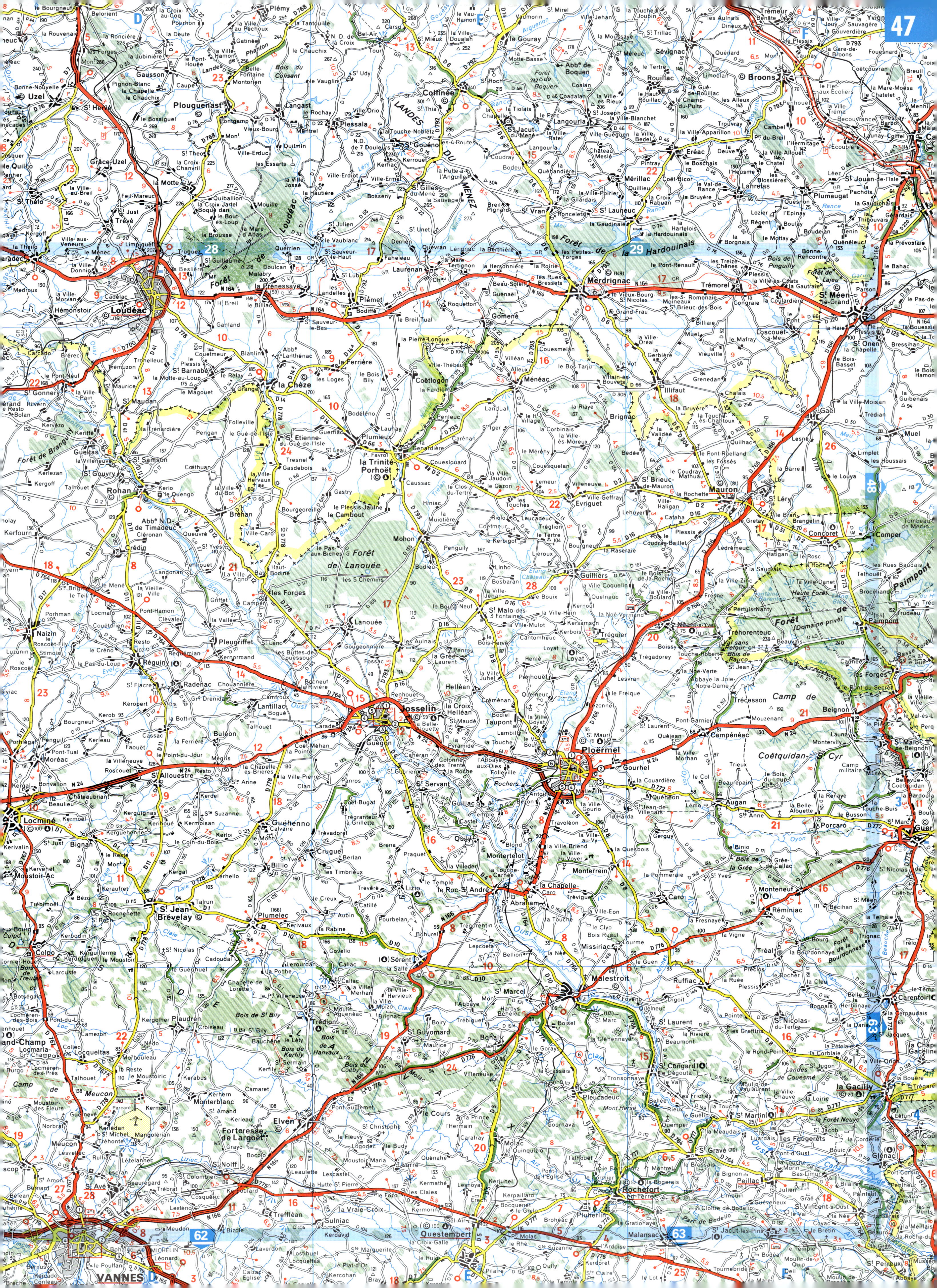

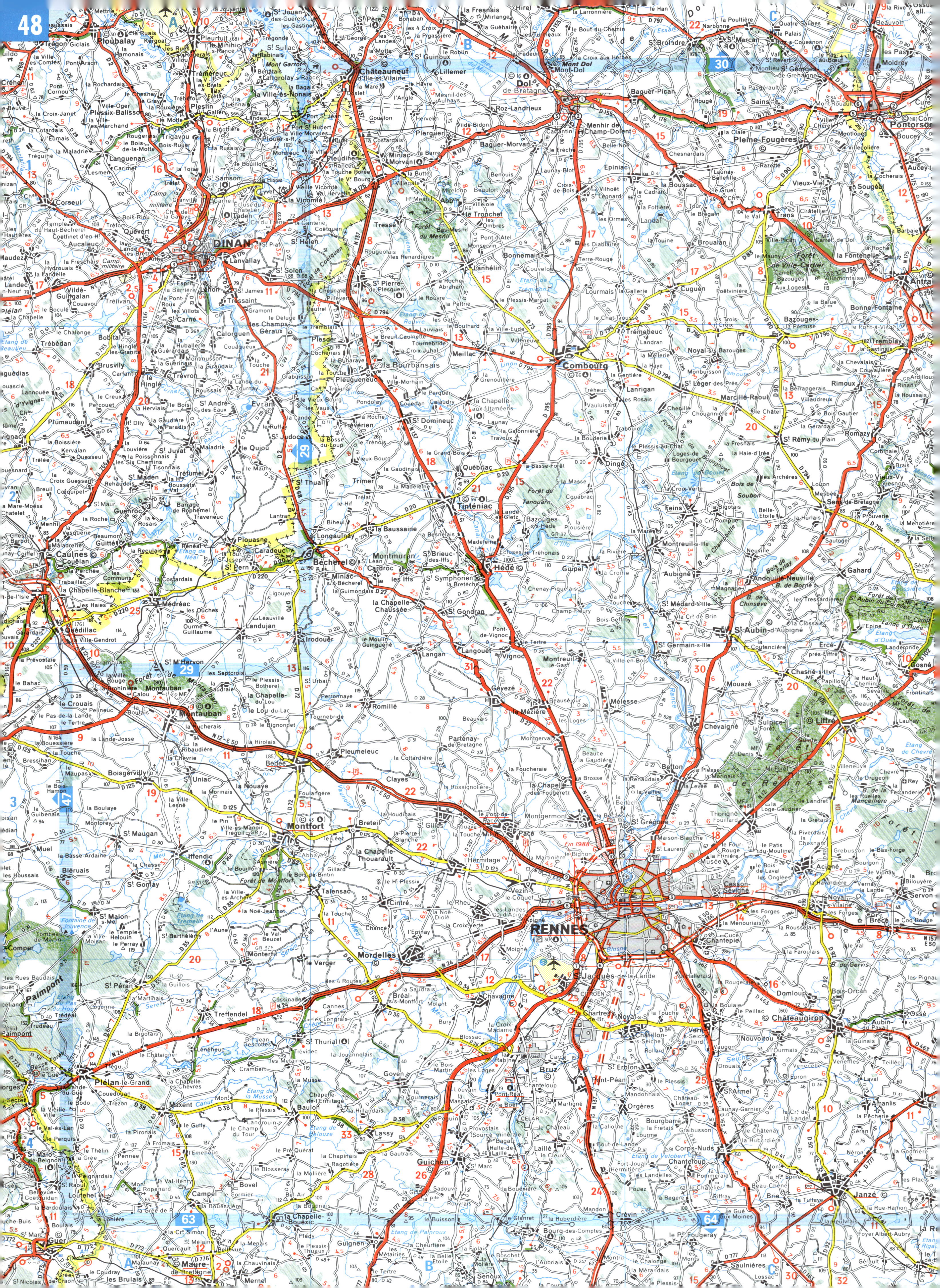

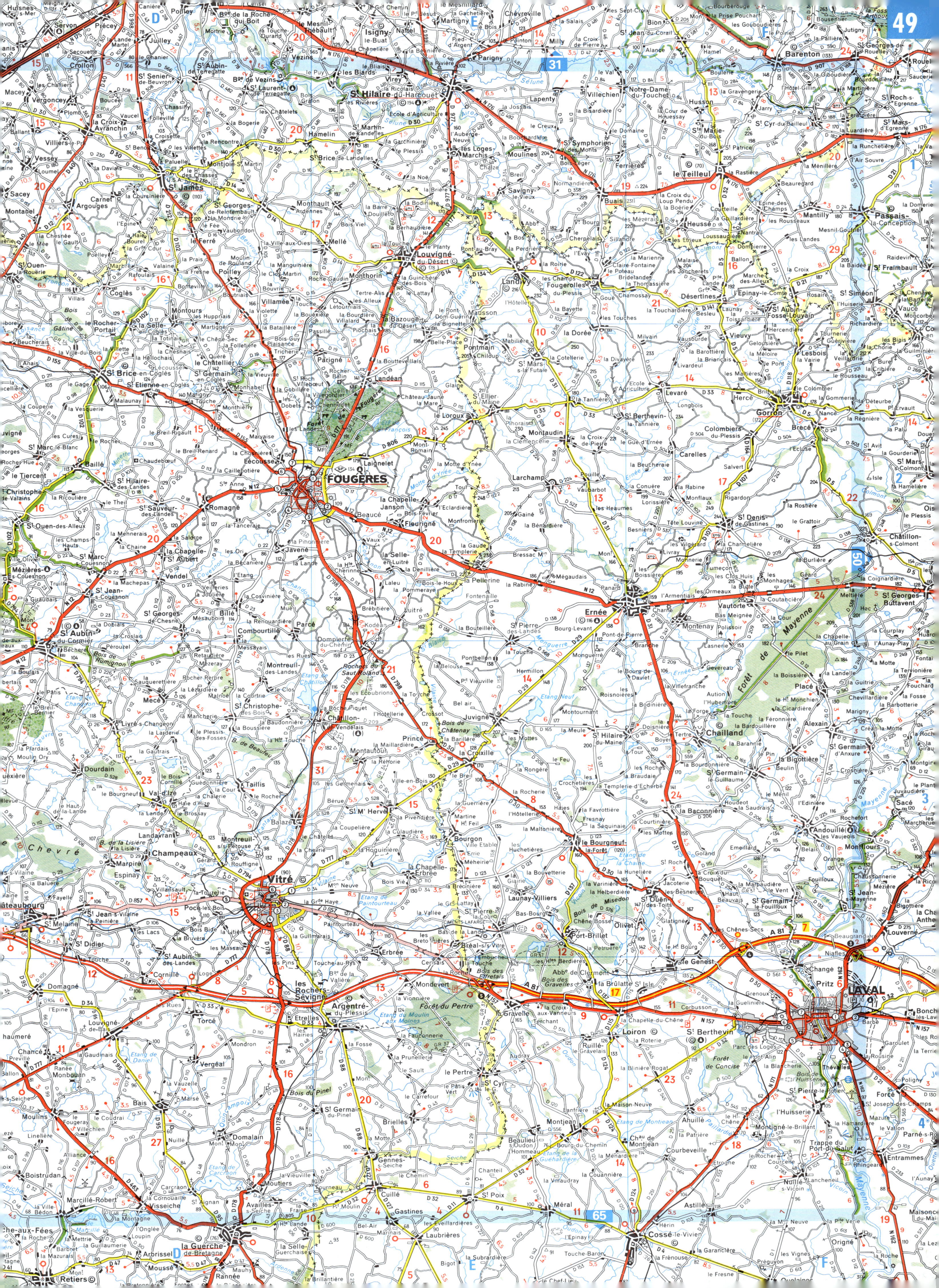
FOUGÈRES
LAVAL
Vitré
Ernée
St Hilaire-du-Harcouët
Louvigné-du-Désert
Landivy
Gorron
Isigny-le-Buat
Barenton
St James
Le Teilleul
Ducey
Pontmain
Fougerolles-du-Plessis
Désertines
Landéan
Laignelet
St Brice-en-Coglès
Romagné
Javené
Beaucé
Fleurigné
Larchamp
Montaudin
Vautorte
Chailland
Andouillé
Changé
Argentré-du-Plessis
Étrelles
la Guerche-de-Bretagne
Cossé-le-Vivien
Loiron
St Berthevin
Montjean
Gennes-sur-Seiche
Cuillé
Méral
Retiers
Châteaubourg
Champeaux
Dourdain
Chatillon-en-Vendelais
Princé
Bourgon
la Croixille
Juvigné
St Pierre-des-Landes
Port-Brillet
Olivet
le Bourgneuf-la-Forêt
St Ouën-des-Toits
le Genest
la Brûlatte
Brécé
Colombiers-du-Plessis
Carelles
Lévaré
Mantilly
Passais
Forêt de Mayenne
Bois de Misedon
Forêt du Pertre
Bois du Pinel
Chevré
Les Rochers-Sévigné
Vergéal
Domalain
Moutiers
Visseiche
Marcillé-Robert
A 81
N 12
N 157
N 176
31
50
65

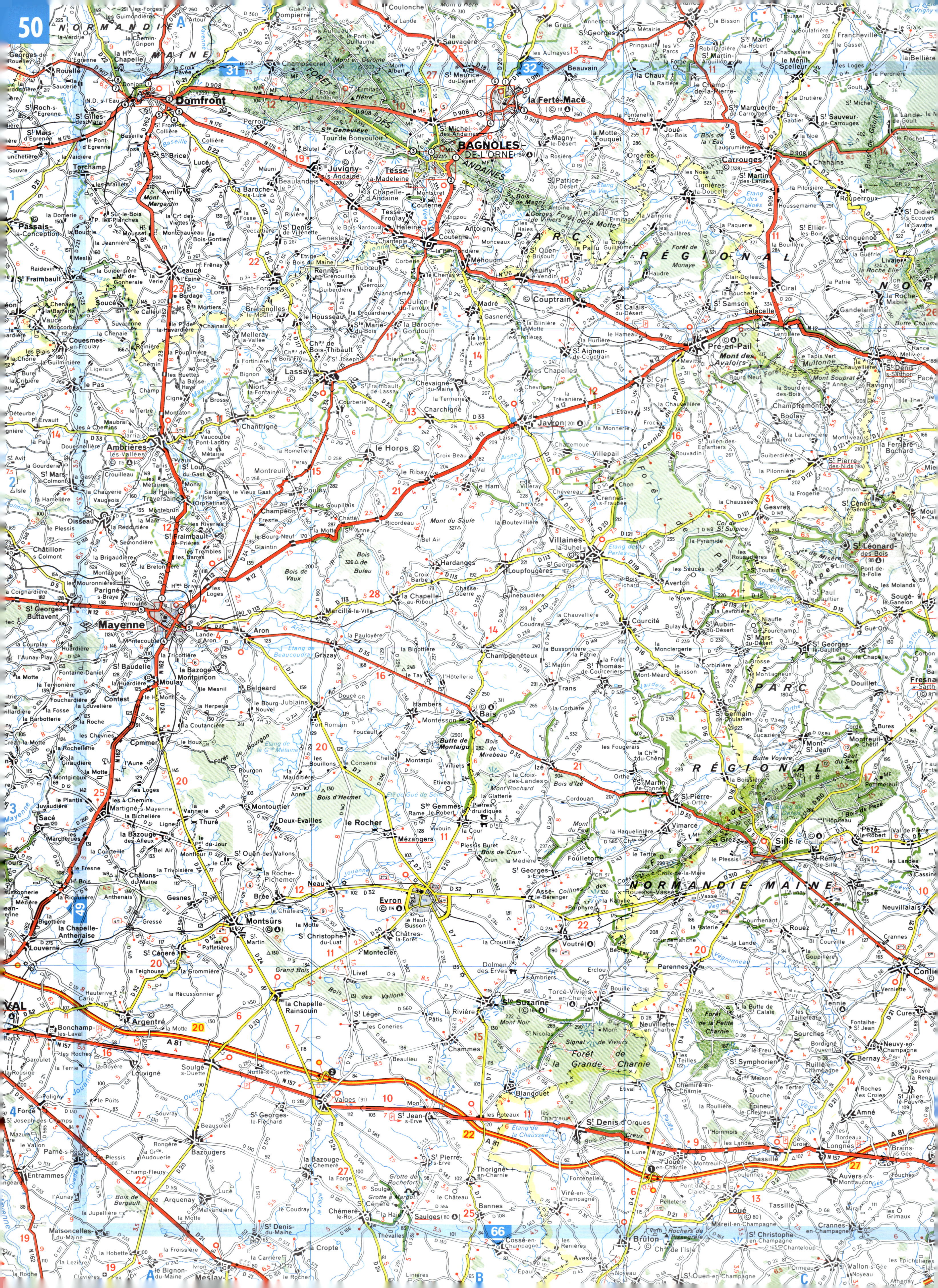

Alençon
Sées
Mortagne-au-Perche
Bellême
Mamers
Le Mans
La Ferté-Bernard
Bonnétable
Beaumont-s-Sarthe
Ballon
Connerré
Montfort-le-Rotrou
Le Mêle-s-Sarthe
Courtomer
Moulins-la-Marche
Fresnay
Forêt d'Écouves
Forêt de Perseigne
Forêt de Bellême
Forêt de Bonnétable
Forêt du Perche
Forêt de Vibraye
Maine

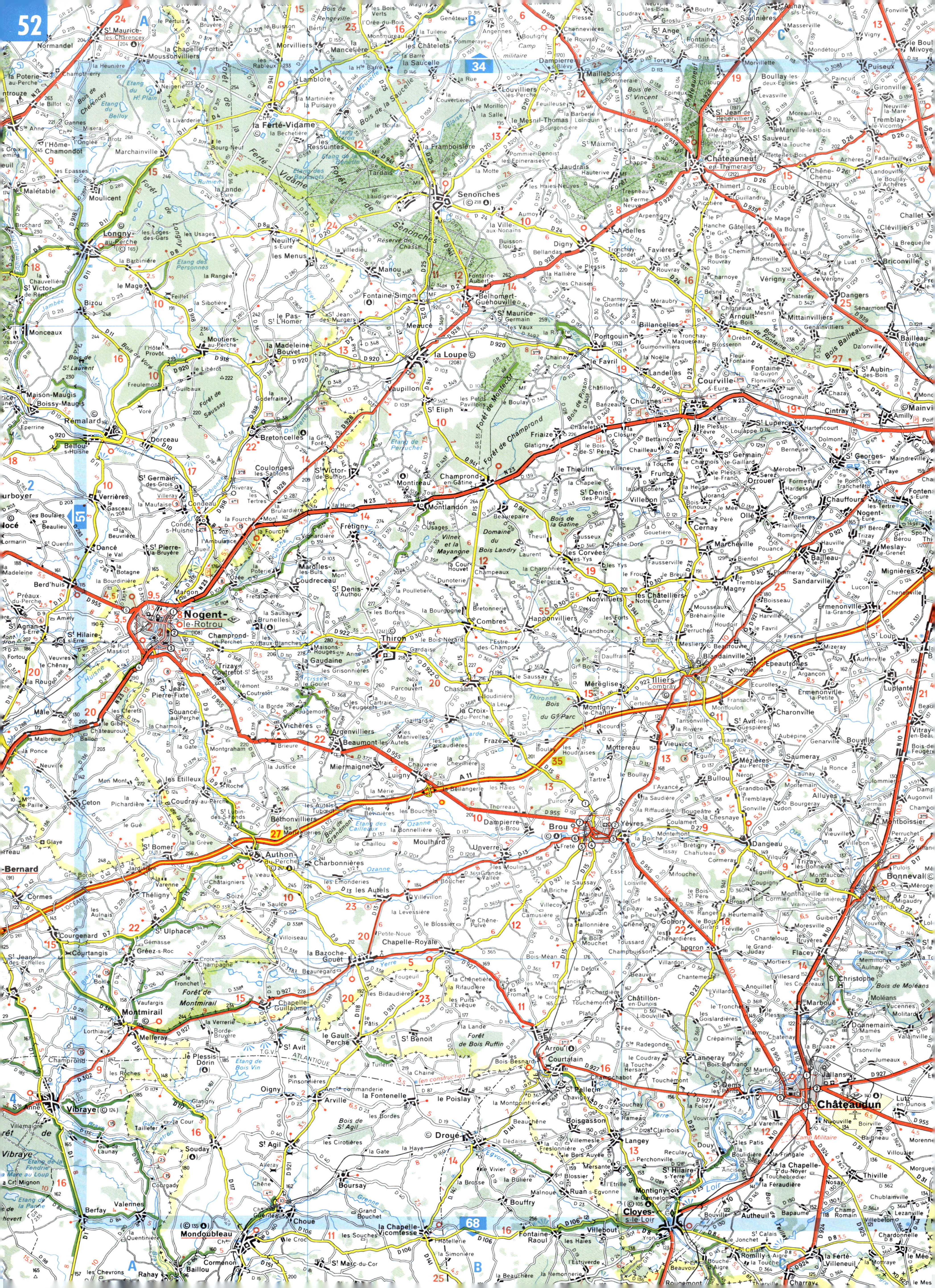

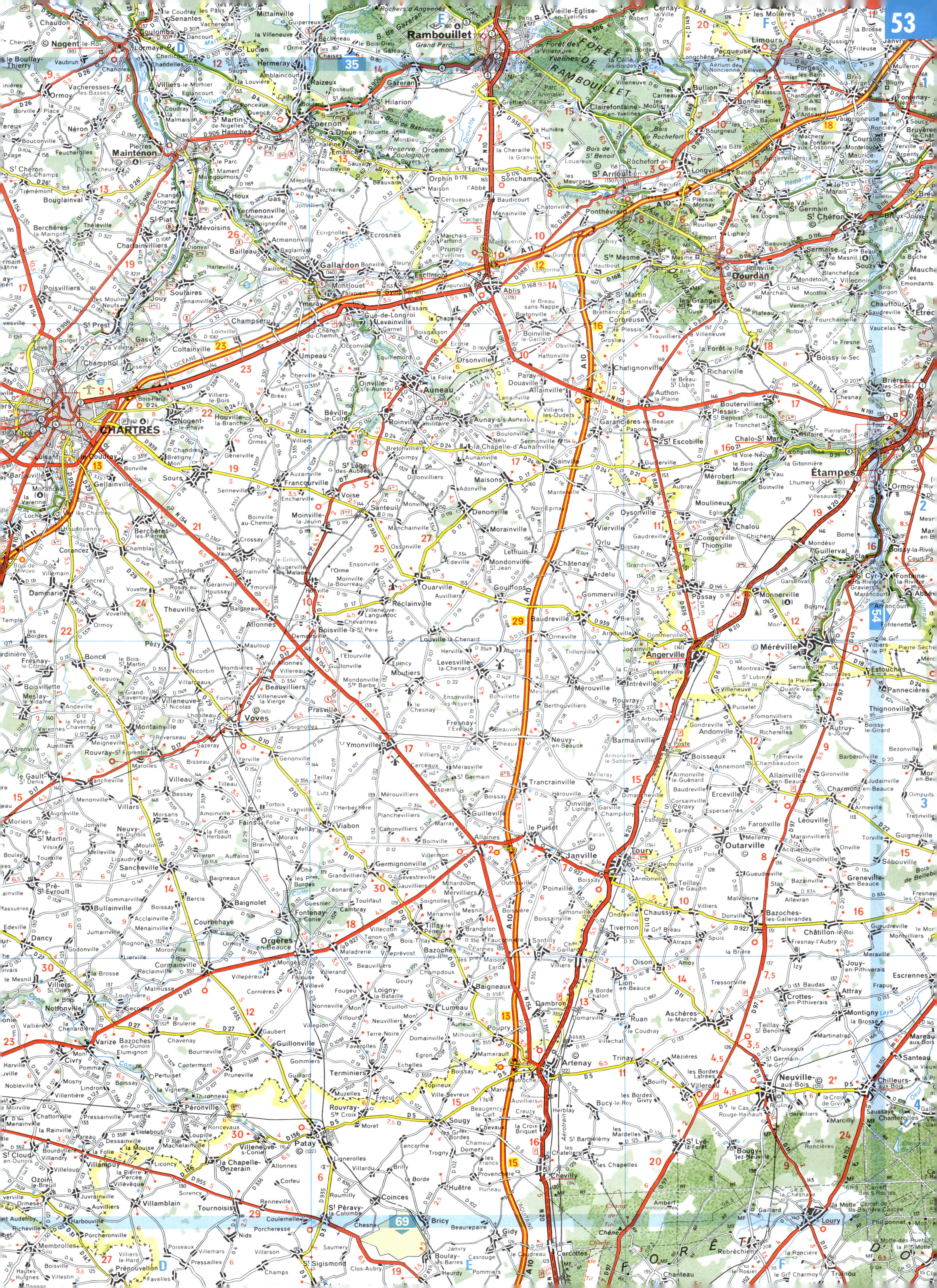

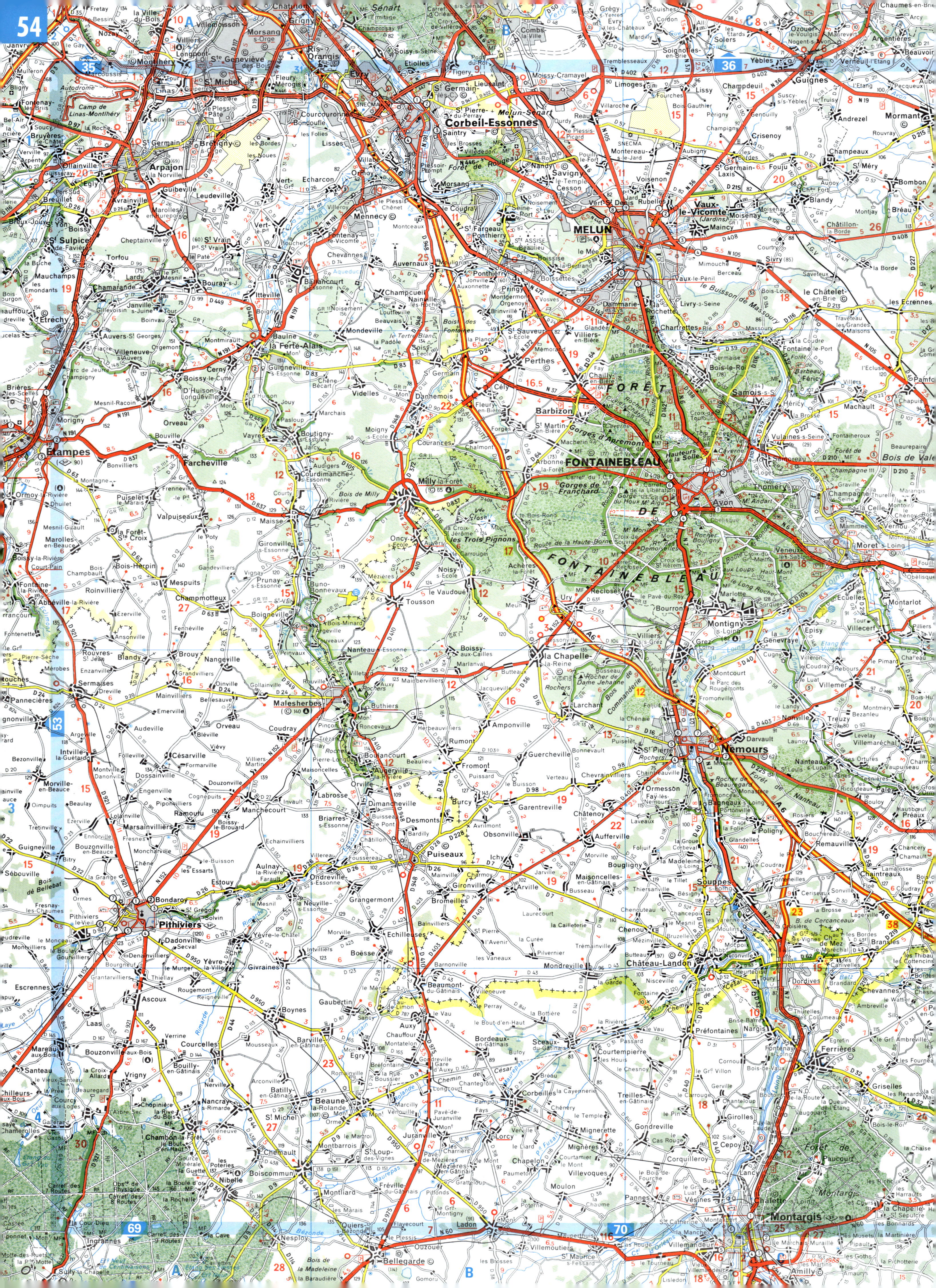

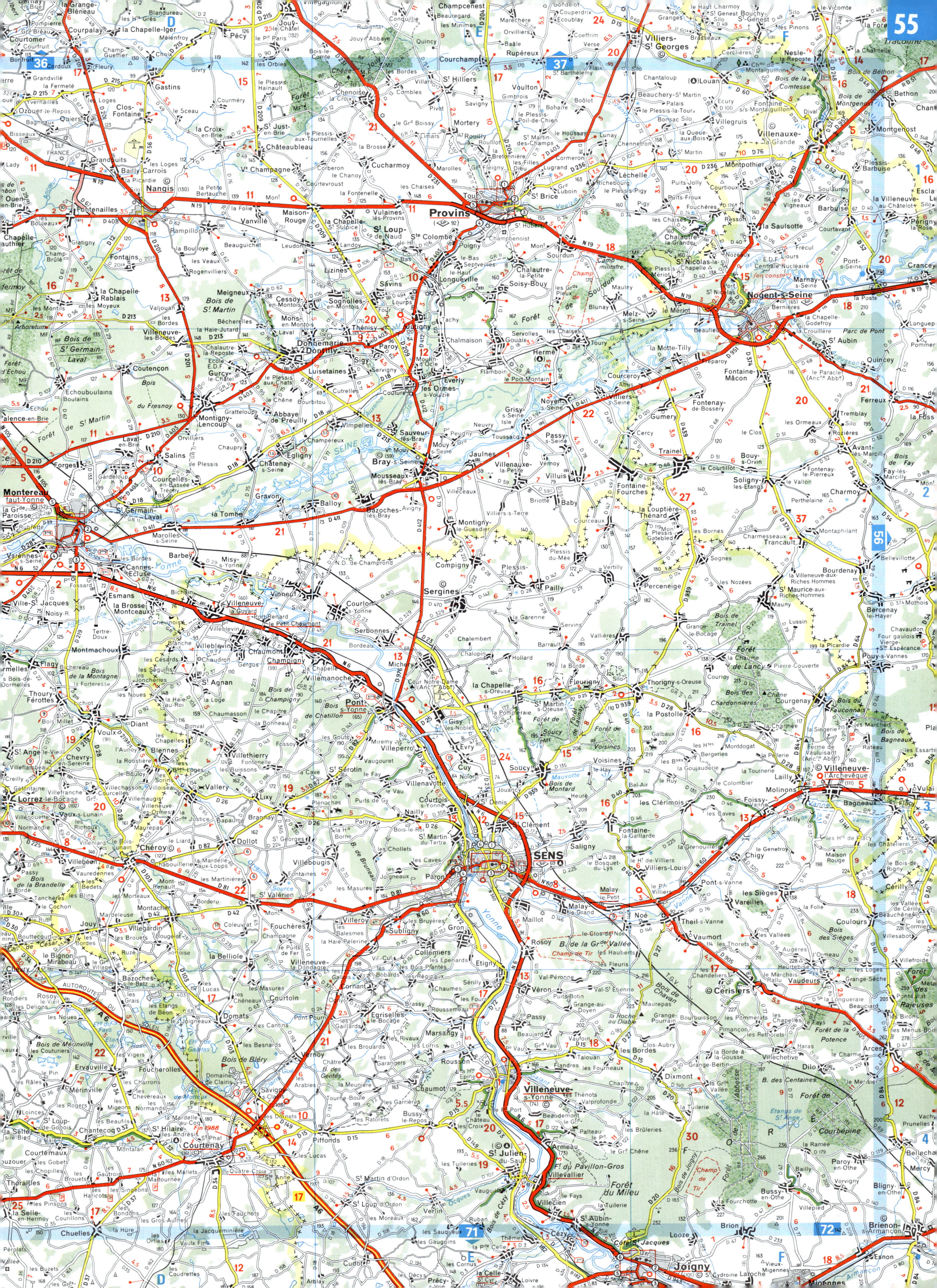

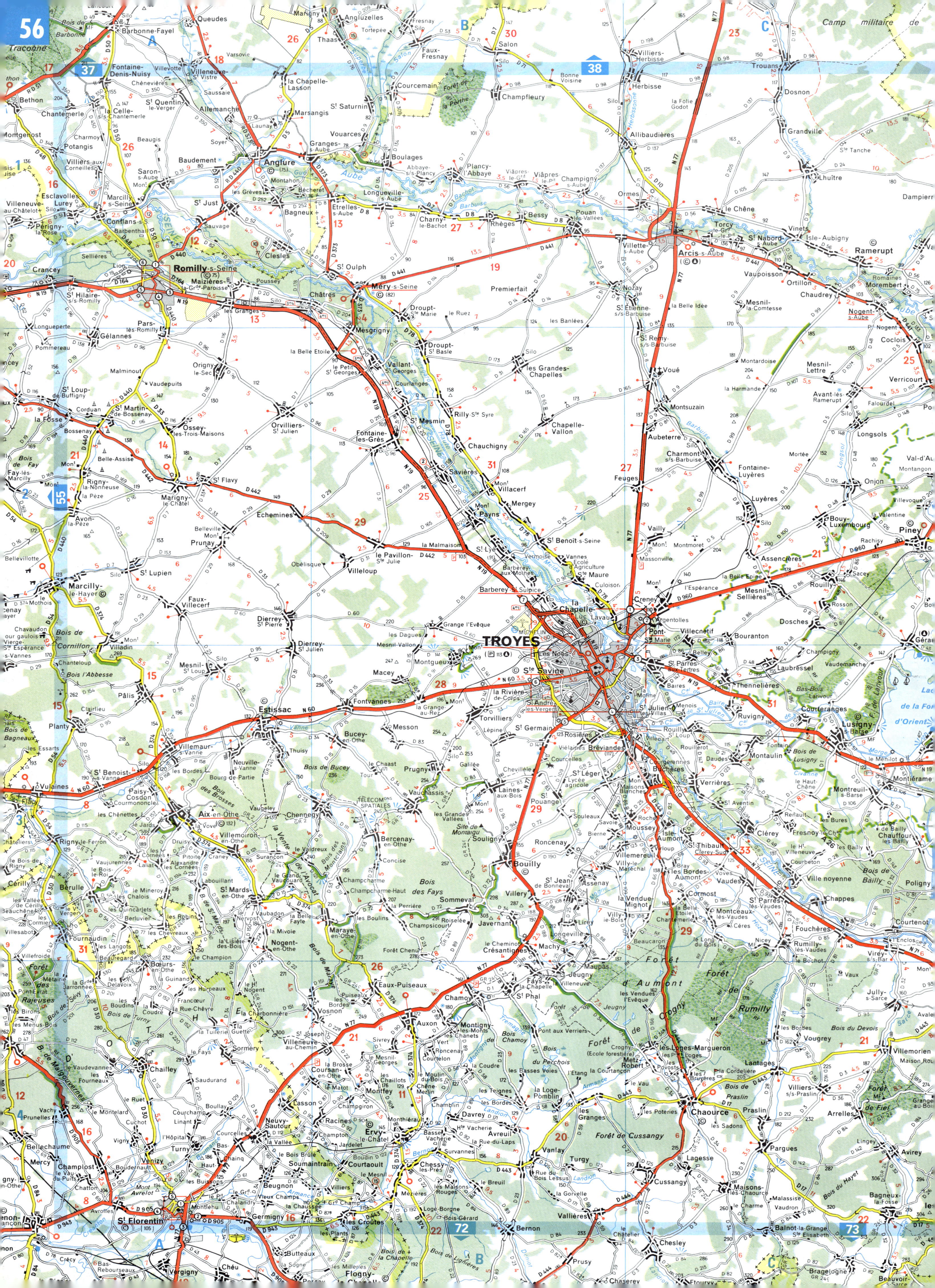

38
39
58
73
74
St Dizier
Ancerville
Humbaville
Larzicourt
Hauteville
Ambrières
Hallignicourt
Moëslains
Valcourt
Eurville
Chamouilly
Roches-s-Marne
Bienville
Narcy
St Remy-en-Bouzemont
Arrigny
Ecollemont
Landricourt
Ste Livière
Eclaron
Humbécourt
Forêt du Val
Lac du Der-Chantecoq
Presqu'île de Larzicourt
Port de Chantecoq
Giffaumont-Champaubert
Presqu'île de Champaubert
Allichamps
Louvemont
Braucourt
Frampas
Wassy
Brousseval
Attancourt
Villiers-aux-Bois
Troisfontaines
Magneux
Sommancourt
Fays
Dommartin-le-Franc
Doulevant-le-Petit
Doulevant-le-Château
Morancourt
Forêt de Mathons
Brachay
Blécourt
Flammerécourt
Montier-en-Der
Droyes
Puellemontier
Planrupt
Ceffonds
Robert-Magny
Laneuville-à-Rémy
Voillecomte
Ville-en-Blaisois
Courcelles-s-Blaise
Sommevoire
Mertrud
Dommartin-le-St Père
Forêt du Der
Chavanges
Joncreuil
Arrembécourt
Margerie
Outines
Châtillon-s-Broué
Bailly-le-Franc
Lentilles
Montmorency-Beaufort
Drosnay
Somsois
Chapelaine
Corbeil
Bréban
Donnement
Jasseines
Brillecourt
Aulnay
Magnicourt
Molins-s-Aube
Lesmont
St Christophe-Dodinicourt
Précy-St Martin
Pel-et-Der
Brienne-le-Château
Brienne-la-Vieille
Blaincourt-s-Aube
Radonvilliers
Dienville
Mathaux
Epagne
Rosnay-l'Hôpital
Lassicourt
Maizières-lès-Brienne
Perthes-lès-Brienne
Juzanvigny
Crespy-le-Neuf
Epothémont
Louze
Longeville-s-la-Laines
Thilleux
Rozières
Sauvage-Magny
Anglus
Soulaines-Dhuys
Forêt de Soulaines
Morvilliers
Bois de Chantecoq
La Chaise
Nully
Trémilly
Blumeray
Thil
Villiers-aux-Chênes
Arnancourt
Cirey-s-Blaise
Bouzancourt
Beurville
Forêt de Blinfey
Ville-s-Terre
Fresnay
Fuligny
Vernonvilliers
Eclance
Lévigny
Bois de Beauregard
Thors
Maisons-lès-Soulaines
Saulcy
Rizaucourt
Champcourt
Daillancourt
Blaise
Marbéville
Curmont
Lamothe-en-Blaisy
Forêt de l'Etoile
Colombey-les-Deux-Eglises
Colombé-le-Sec
Colombé-la-Fosse
Rouvres-les-Vignes
Lignol-le-Château
Engente
Arrentières
Voigny
Bar-s-Aube
Proverville
Fontaine
Baroville
Bayel
Ailleville
Arsonval
Montier-en-l'Isle
Jaucourt
Dolancourt
Bossancourt
Trannes
Jessains
Juvanzé
Unienville
Amance
Vauchonvilliers
Vendeuvre-s-Barse
Magny-Fouchard
Maison-des-Champs
Argançon
Spoy
Fravaux
Forêt d'Orient
Parc Régional de la Forêt d'Orient
Réservoir Aube (en construction)
Brevonnes
Chaumesnil
Rothière
Petit Mesnil
La Giberie
Thieffrain
Puits-et-Nuisement
Montmartin-le-Haut
Meurville
Couvignon
Longpré-le-Sec
Bois de Bossican
Beurey
Magnant
Fralignes
Bligny
Urville
Bergères
Champignol-lez-Mondeville
Arconville
Clairvaux
Longchamp-s-Aujon
Maranville
Rennepont
Juzennecourt
Lachapelle-en-Blaisy
Sexfontaines
Gillancourt
Blaisy
Montheries
Lavilleneuve-au-Roi
Forêt des Dhuits
Forêt de Clairvaux
Eufligneix
Vaudrémont
Autreville-s-la-Renne
Buxières-lès-Villiers
Cirfontaines-en-Azois
Aizanville
Braux-le-Châtel
Valdelancourt
Bricon
Orges
Juvancourt
Laferté-s-Aube
Pont-la-Ville
Essey-les-Ponts
Silvarouvres
Dinteville
Blessonville
Châteauvillain
Forêt de Châteauvillain
Richebourg
Villars-en-Azois
Lanty-s-Aube
Créancey
Montribourg
Coupray
Cour-l'Evêque
Arc-en-Barrois
Latrecey
Gevrolles
Montigny-s-Aube
Riel-les-Eaux
Autricourt
Essoyes
Verpillières-s-Ource
Loches-s-Ource
Landreville
Celles-s-Ource
Merrey-s-Arce
Bar-s-Seine
Polisot
Polisy
Buxeuil
Gyé-s-Seine
Neuville-s-Seine
Courteron
Mussy-s-Seine
Gommeville
Plaines-St Lange
Grancey-s-Ource
Cunfin
Fontette
St Usage
Noë-les-Mallets
Chacenay
Bertignolles
Buxières-s-Arce
Ville-s-Arce
Viviers-s-Artaut
Vitry-le-Croisé
Eguilly-s-Bois
Bourguignons
Villy-en-Trodes
Marolles-lès-Bailly
Vaudrémont
Bois de Beaumont
Forêt de Beaumont
Bois du Charmoi
Forêt de Bois-Rouge
Bois de Lanty
Bois de la Longe
Ormoy-s-Aube
Veuxhaulles

61

LORIENT
Lanester
Hennebont
Port-Louis
Larmor-Plage
Locmiquélic
Riantec
Gâvres
Pte de Gâvres
Kervignac
Merlevenez
Nostang
Landévant
Languidic
Brandérion
Baud
Locminé
Camors
Forêt de Camors
Pluvigner
Landaul
Plumergat
Grand-Champ
Brech
Ste Anne-d'Auray
Auray
Pluneret
Plouharnel
Erdeven
Etel
Belz
Ploemel
Carnac
Carnac-Plage
la Trinité
Crach
Locmariaquer
Baden
Arradon
VANNES
Séné
Sarzeau
Arzon
Port-Navalo
Ile aux Moines
Ile d'Arz
GOLFE DU MORBIHAN
Presqu'île de Rhuys
St Gildas-de-Rhuys
Pointe de St Jacques
PRESQU'ILE DE QUIBERON
St Pierre-Quiberon
Quiberon
Port-Haliguen
Pointe du Conguel
Côte Sauvage
Penthièvre
Ile Thévlec
Plateau des Birvideaux
BAIE DE QUIBERON
Passage de la Teignouse
Chaussée de la Teignouse
la Teignouse
Ile de Houat
Houat
Ile de Hœdic
Hœdic
les Grands Cardinaux
les Petits Cardinaux
Plateau de la Recherche
la Calebasse
BELLE-ILE
Le Palais
Sauzon
Bangor
Locmaria
Pointe des Poulains
Grotte de l'Apothicairerie
Port Donnant
Grand Phare
Aiguilles de Port Coton
Port Goulphar
Pointe de Kerdonis
Pointe du Talus
Côte Sauvage
Pointe de Taillefer
Rade du Palais
Roches de Magouëro
Barre d'Etel
Pte d'Erdeven
Meaban
A
B
C
2
3
4
46
47
45

Malestroit
Questembert
Rochefort-en-Terre
Redon
St Nicolas-de-Redon
la Gacilly
Carentoir
Guer
Maure-de-Bretagne
Elven
Forteresse de Largoët
Theix
Muzillac
Péaule
Allaire
la Roche-Bernard
Missillac
Pontchâteau
St Gildas-des-Bois
Herbignac
Guérande
le Croisic
Pointe du Croisic
Piriac-s-Mer
Pointe du Castelli
la Turballe
Rade du Croisic
Batz-s-Mer
LA BAULE
le Pouliguen
Pornichet
St NAZAIRE
St Brevin-les-Pins
Paimbœuf
Donges
Montoir-de-Bretagne
Trignac
Savenay
Campbon
PARC RÉGIONAL DE BRIÈRE
GRANDE BRIÈRE
Pénestin
Camoël
Arzal
Damgan
Sulniac
Pointe de Penlan
Rade de Penerf
Ile Dumet
Pointe de Chémoulin
Côte Sauvage
Chenal du Sud
Forêt de la Roche Bernard
Landes de Couesme
Vilaine
Loire
Pointe de Kervoyal
Pointe de Merquel
Plage de la Mine d'Or
Plage Valentin
Pointe de Penchâteau
Pointe du Halguen
Corsept
D
E
F
47
48
69
78

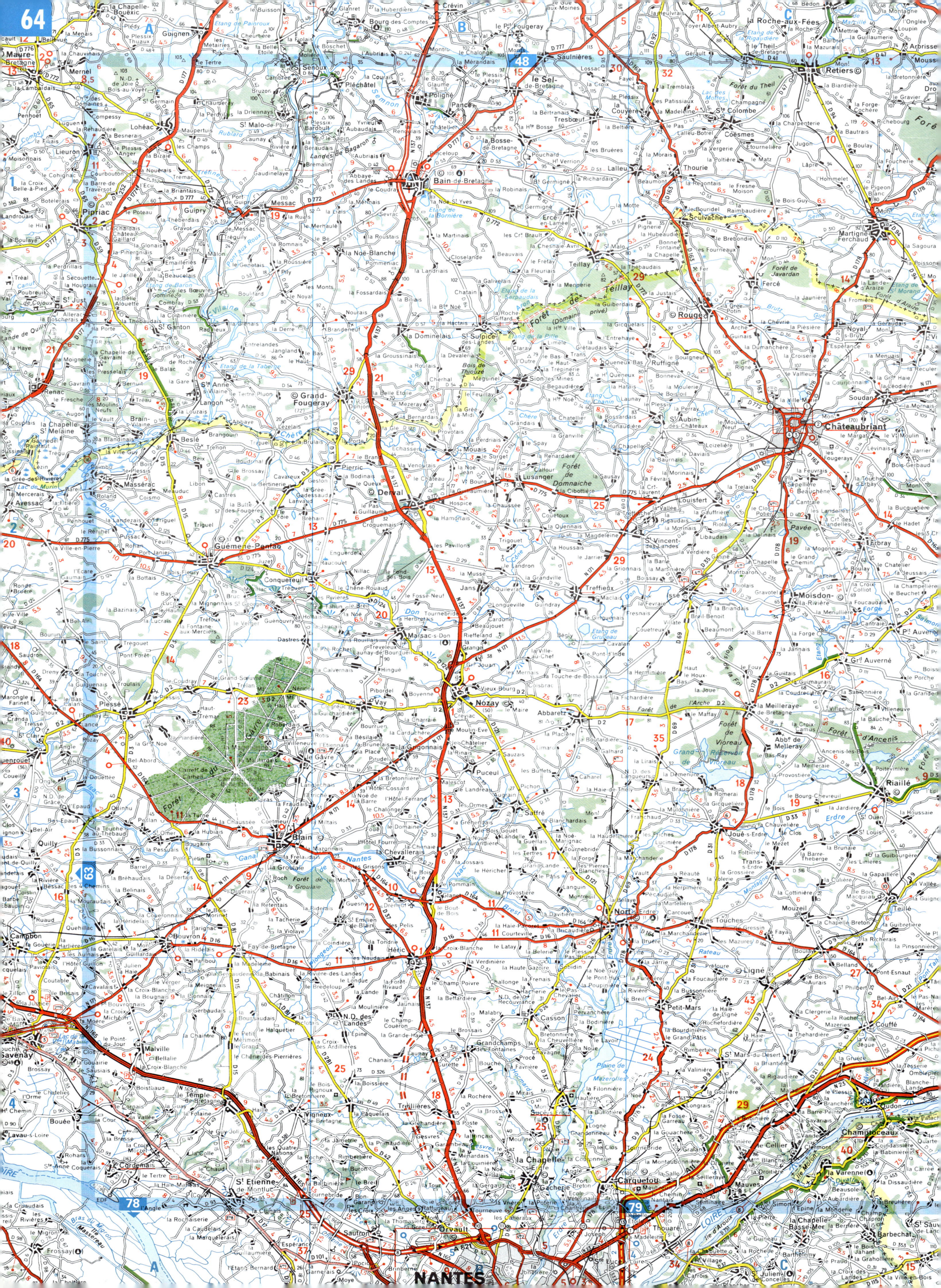

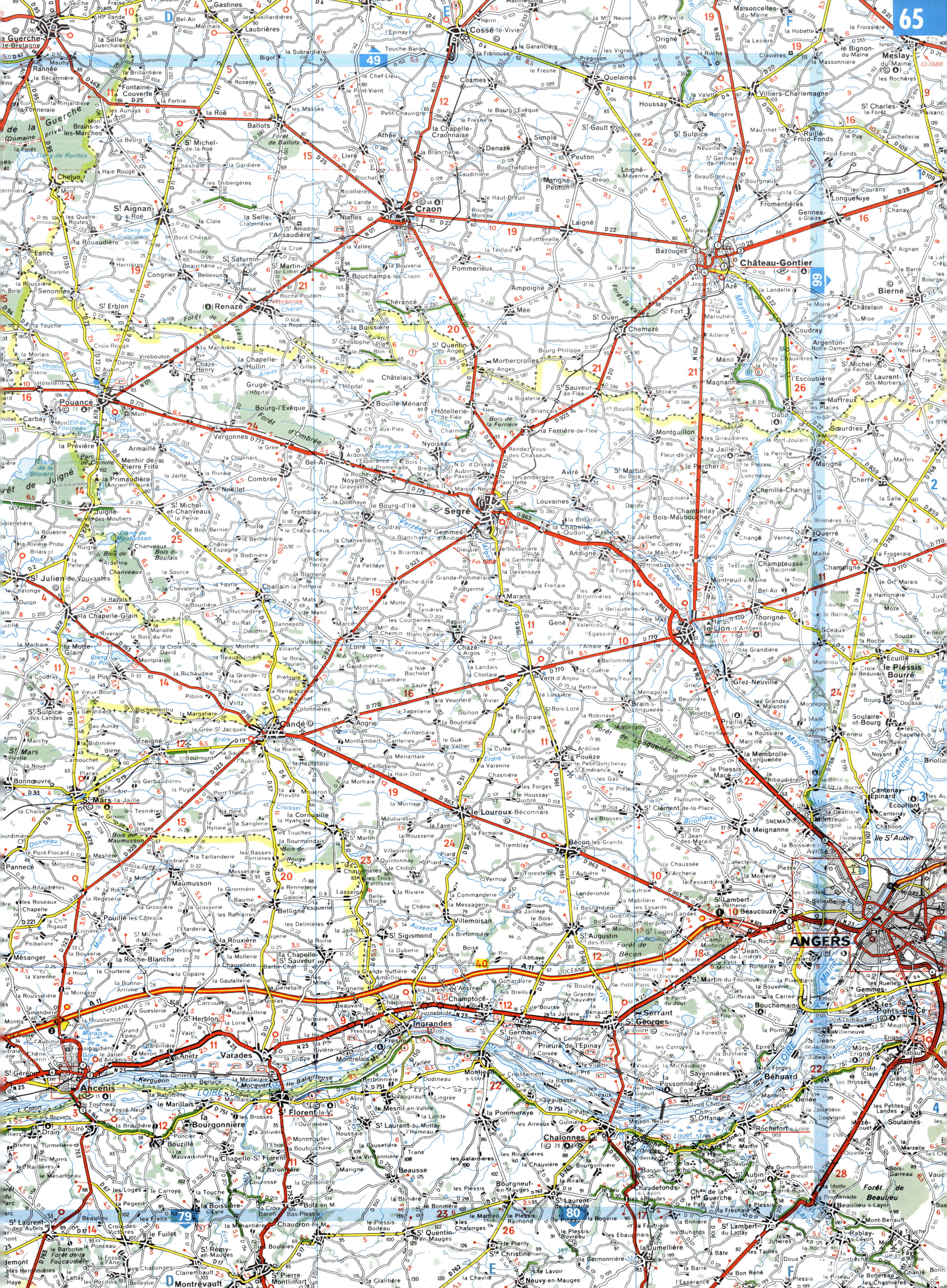

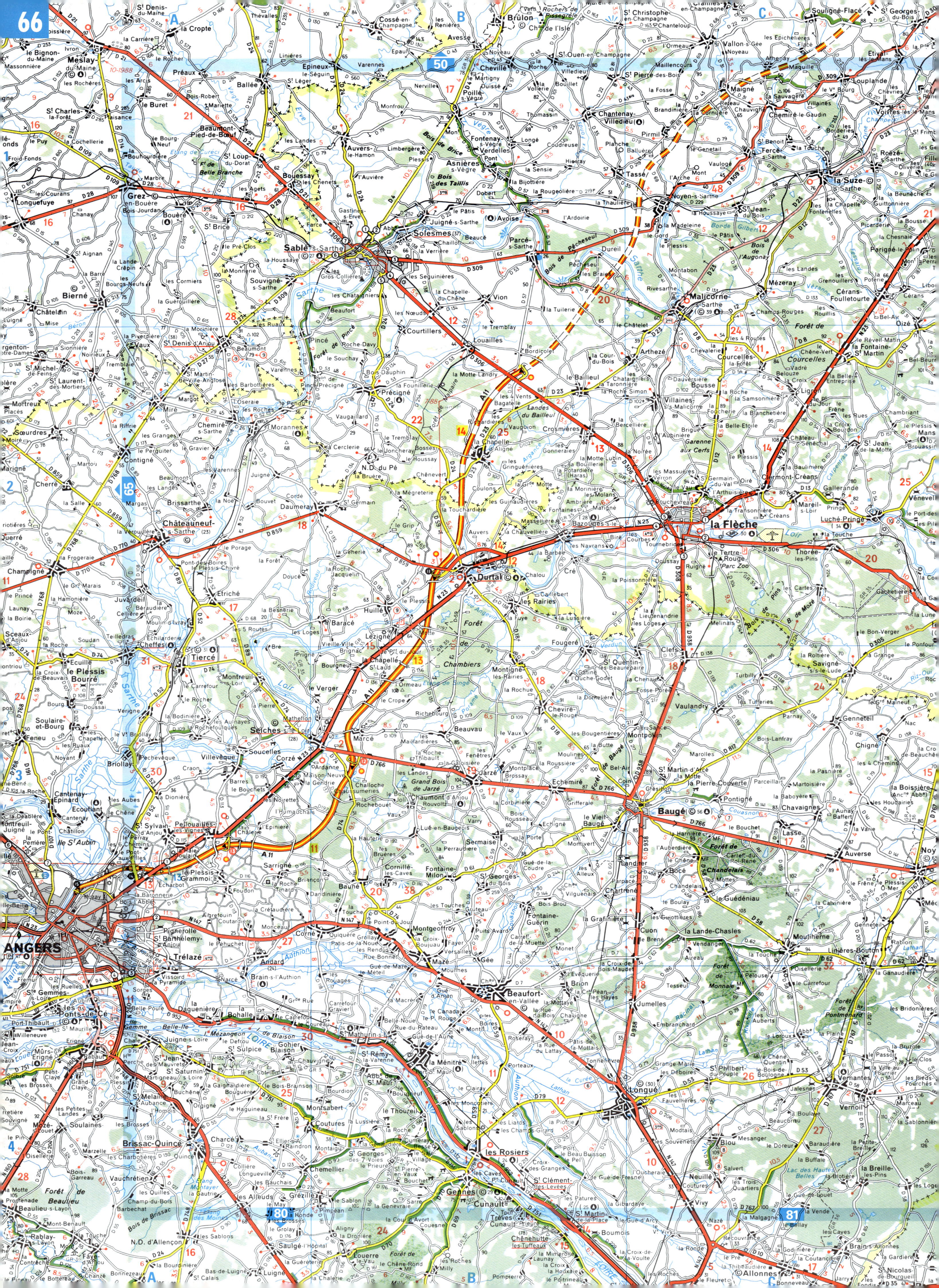

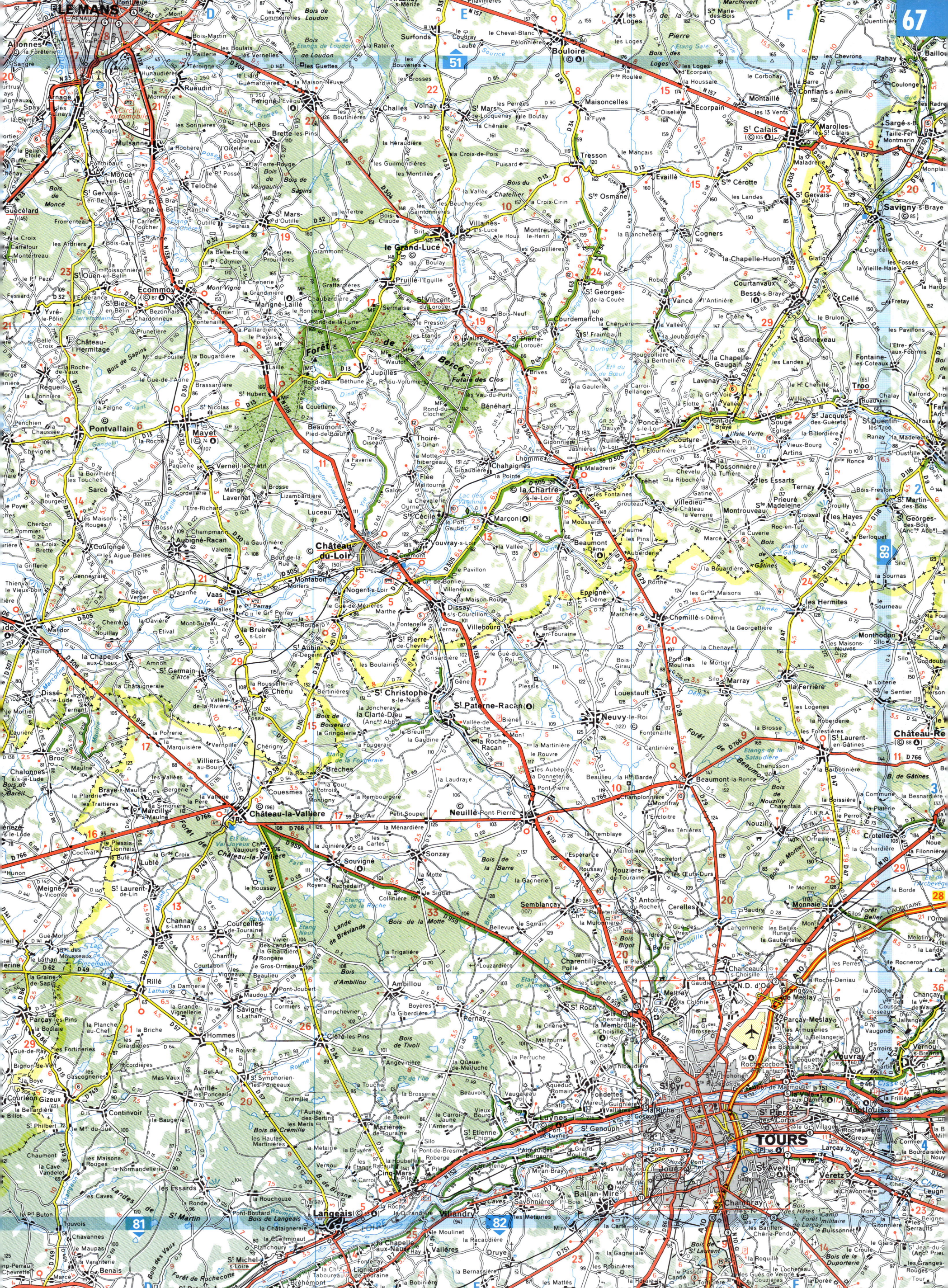

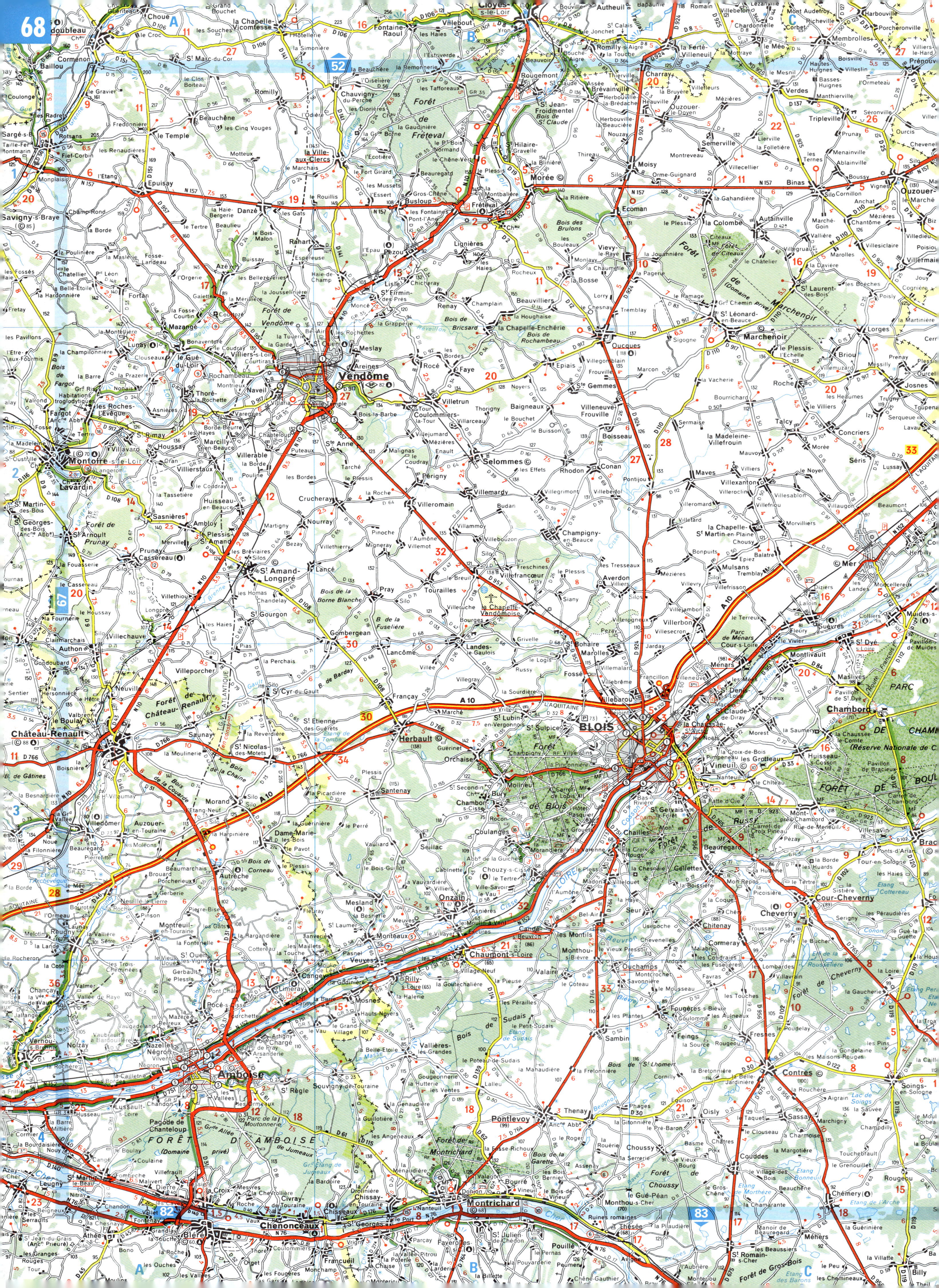
Vendôme
Blois
Amboise
Chenonceaux
Montrichard
Chambord
Cheverny
Château-Renault
Montoire-s-le-Loir
Lavardin
Morée
Fréteval
Forêt de Fréteval
Selommes
Herbault
Onzain
Chaumont-s-Loire
Pontlevoy
Contres
Cour-Cheverny
Mer
Oucques
Marchenoir
Forêt de Marchenoir
Épuisay
Savigny-s-Braye
St Amand-Longpré
Villechauve
Forêt d'Amboise
Forêt de Blois
Forêt de Russy
Forêt de Gros-Bois
Bois des Brulons
Mesland
Montlivault
Ménars
Saint-Gervais
Vineuil
Villebarou
Talcy
Binas
Ouzouer-le-Marché
Verdes
Cloyes-s-le-Loir
Bléré
Sambin
Thenay
Oisly
Chissay-en-Touraine
Sassay

Montargis
Amilly
Bellegarde
Ladon
Nesploy
Quiers
Villemandeur
Lorris
Châteauneuf-s-Loire
St Benoît-s-Loire
Sully-s-Loire
Ouzouer-s-Loire
Dampierre-en-Burly
FORÊT D'ORLÉANS
Gien
Briare
Châtillon-Coligny
Châtillon-s-Loire
Nogent-s-Vernisson
Solterre
La Bussière
Ouzouer-sur-Trézée
Beaulieu
Argent-s-Sauldre
Aubigny-s-Nère
Cerdon
Isdes
Clémont
Brinon-s-Sauldre
Souesmes
Ménétréol-s-Sauldre
Ste Montaine
Blancafort
Concressault
Vailly-s-Sauldre
Autry-le-Châtel
Coullons
Poilly-lez-Gien
St Gondon
Lion-en-Sullias
Viglain
Vannes-s-Cosson
Villemurlin
Presly
la Chapelle-d'Angillon
Ivoy-le-Pré
Henrichemont
Neuvy-s-Barangeon
Nançay
Méry-ès-Bois
Sancerre
St Satur
Léré
Santranges
Belleville
Boulleret
Jars
Sury-ès-Bois
Barlieu
Pierrefitte-ès-Bois
Cernoy-en-Berry
Bonny-s-Loire
Loire
54
69
84
85
A
B
C

Auxerre
Tonnerre
Avallon
Clamecy
Vézelay
Chablis
Noyers
Pontigny
Ligny-le-Châtel
Migennes
Seignelay
Vermenton
Coulanges-la-Vineuse
Coulanges-s-Yonne
Courson-les-Carrières
Tanlay
Flogny-la-Chapelle
Lormes
Quarré-les-Tombes
L'Isle-s-Serein
Montréal
Guillon
Monceaux
Forêt de Pontigny
Forêt de Frétoy
Forêt de Champlive
Bois de la Ville
A6
N6
N65
D965
56
71
86
87

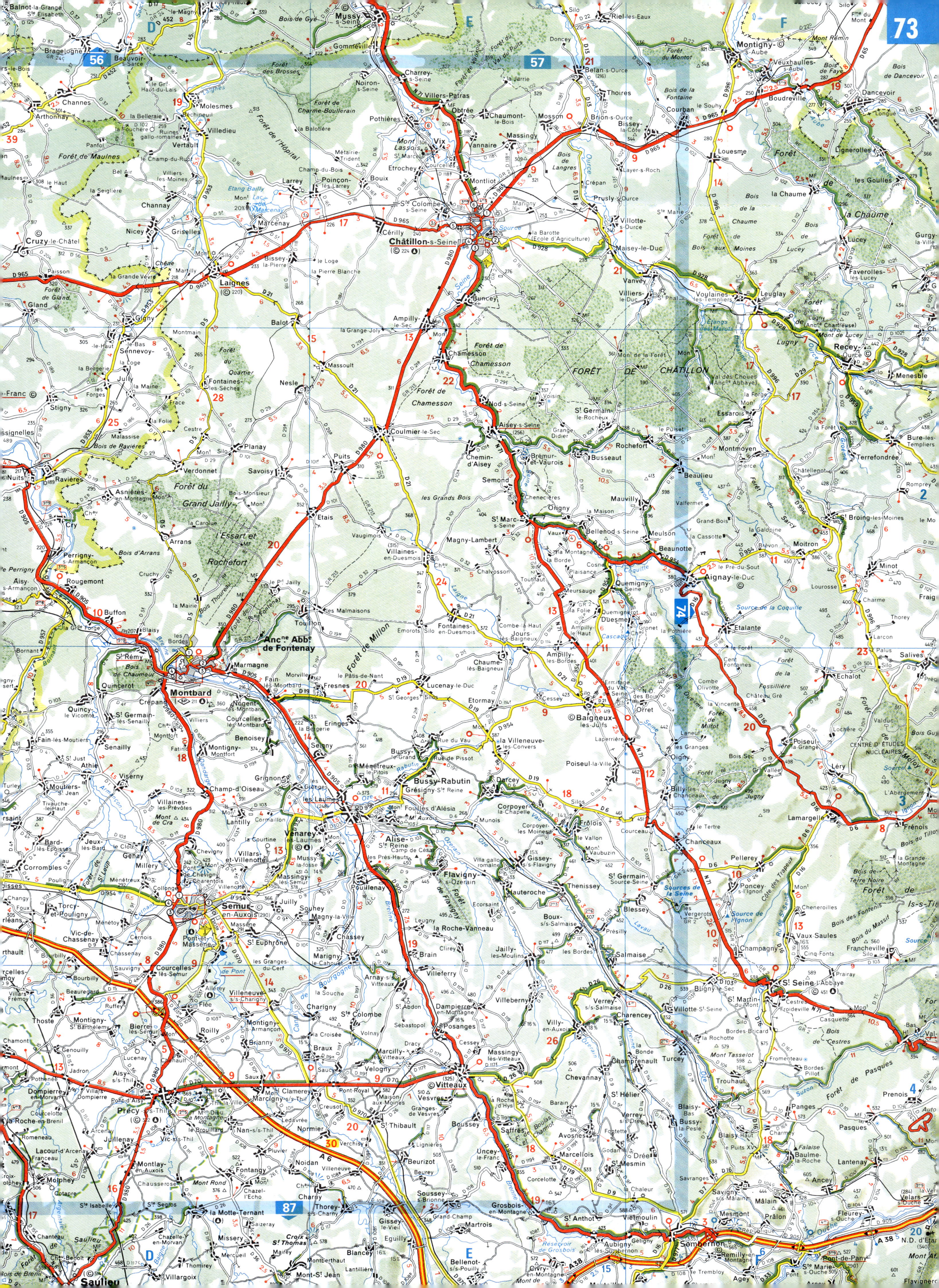
56
57
74
87
Mussy-s-Seine
Gommeville
Charrey-s-Seine
Villers-Patras
Noiron-s-Seine
Pothières
Obtrée
Mont Lassois
Vix
Etrochey
Vannaire
Montliot
Massingy
Mosson
Chaumont-le-Bois
Belan-s-Ource
Riel-les-Eaux
Thoires
Brion-s-Ource
Bissey-la-Côte
Courban
Montigny-s-Aube
Veuxhaulles-s-Aube
Boudreville
Dancevoir
Louesme
Forêt de
Ligneroles
Les Goulles
la Chaume
Gurgy-la-Ville
Lucey
Faverolles-les-Lucey
Leuglay
Voulaines-les-Templiers
Recey-s-Ource
Menesble
Bure-les-Templiers
Terrefondrée
Essarois
Montmoyen
Beaulieu
Moitron
Minot
Beauvoir-s-Sarce
Channes
Arthonnay
Molesmes
Villedieu
Vertault
Forêt de Maulnes
Channay
Nicey
Griselles
Cruzy-le-Châtel
Larrey
Poinçon-lès-Larrey
Bouix
Marcenay
Cérilly
Ste Colombe-s-Seine
Châtillon-s-Seine
Laignes
Gland
Balot
Buncey
Ampilly-le-Sec
Chamesson
Forêt de Chamesson
Villotte-s-Ource
Maisey-le-Duc
Vanvey
Villiers-le-Duc
Forêt de Châtillon
St Germain-le-Rocheux
Nod-s-Seine
Aisey-s-Seine
Rochefort
Busseaut
Chemin-d'Aisey
Bremur-et-Vaurois
Semond
Mauvilly
Meulson
Beaunotte
Aignay-le-Duc
Etalante
Fontaines-les-Sèches
Nesle
Massoult
Coulmier-le-Sec
Planay
Savoisy
Puits
Verdonnet
Ravières
Nuits
Asnières-en-Montagne
Forêt du Grand Jailly
Essart et Rochefort
Etais
Arrans
Perrigny-s-Armançon
Rougemont
Buffon
Villaines-en-Duesmois
Magny-Lambert
St Marc-s-Seine
Bellenod-s-Seine
Quemigny-s-Seine
Duesme
Fontaines-en-Duesmois
Ampilly-les-Bordes
Touillon
Ancne Abbe de Fontenay
Forêt de Millon
Marmagne
Montbard
Fain-lès-Montbard
Fresnes
Lucenay-le-Duc
Baigneux-les-Juifs
Quincerot
Crépand
Nogent-lès-Montbard
Courcelles-lès-Montbard
Benoisey
Eringes
Seigny
Bussy-le-Grand
Darcey
Poiseul-la-Ville
Oigny
Billy-lès-Chanceaux
Chanceaux
Poiseul-la-Grange
Léry
Echalot
Salives
Lamargelle
Villaines-les-Prévôtes
Champ-d'Oiseau
Grignon
Ménétreux-le-Pitois
Bussy-Rabutin
Alise-Ste Reine
Flavigny-s-Ozerain
Corpoyer-la-Chapelle
Frôlois
Thenissey
St Germain-Source-Seine
Pellerey
Poncey-s-l'Ignon
Viserny
Venarey-les-Laumes
Villars-et-Villenotte
Massingy-lès-Semur
Pouillenay
Hauteroche
Boux-s-Salmaise
Blessey
Semur-en-Auxois
Torcy-et-Pouligny
Vic-de-Chassenay
Courcelles-lès-Semur
Chassey
Jailly-les-Moulins
Salmaise
Champagny
Vaux Saules
St Seine-l'Abbaye
Villeneuve-s/s-Charigny
Charigny
Verrey-s/s-Salmaise
Villeberny
Dampierre-en-Montagne
Posanges
Villy-en-Auxois
Blaisy-Bas
Pasques
Prenois
Bierre-lès-Semur
Montigny-s-Armançon
Braux
Marcilly-et-Dracy
Massingy-lès-Vitteaux
Vitteaux
Chevannay
St Hélier
Aisy-s/s-Thil
Précy-s-Thil
Dompierre-en-Morvan
Jadron
Vic-s-Thil
Mont Clamerey
Marcigny-s/s-Thil
Normier
Noidan
St Thibault
Saffres
Marcellois
Avosnes
Drée
Montlay-en-Auxois
Fontangy
Soussey-s-Brionne
Beurizot
Grosbois-en-Montagne
Martrois
St Anthot
Aubigny
Sombernon
Mâlain
Ancey
Lantenay
Velars
Thorey-s-Charny
Charny
Blancey
Saulieu
Thoisy-la-Berchère
Mont-St Jean
Vieux-Château
Sainte-Marie
Le Thil
Missery
Clamerey
St Thomas
La Motte-Ternant
Molphey
Lacour-d'Arcenay
Juillenay
Rouvray
A 38
A 6

Jussey
Combeaufontaine
Scey-s-Saône-et-St-Albin
Port-s-Saône
Vesoul
Gray
Dampierre-s-Salon
Champlitte
Fayl-Billot
Vitrey-s-Mance
Amance
Rioz
Marnay
Pesmes
Gy
Besançon
Montbozon
Vauvillers
Jonvelle
Laferté-s-Amance
Fresne-St-Mamès
Autrey-lès-Gray
Champvans
Noidans-lès-Vesoul
Faverney
Conflandey

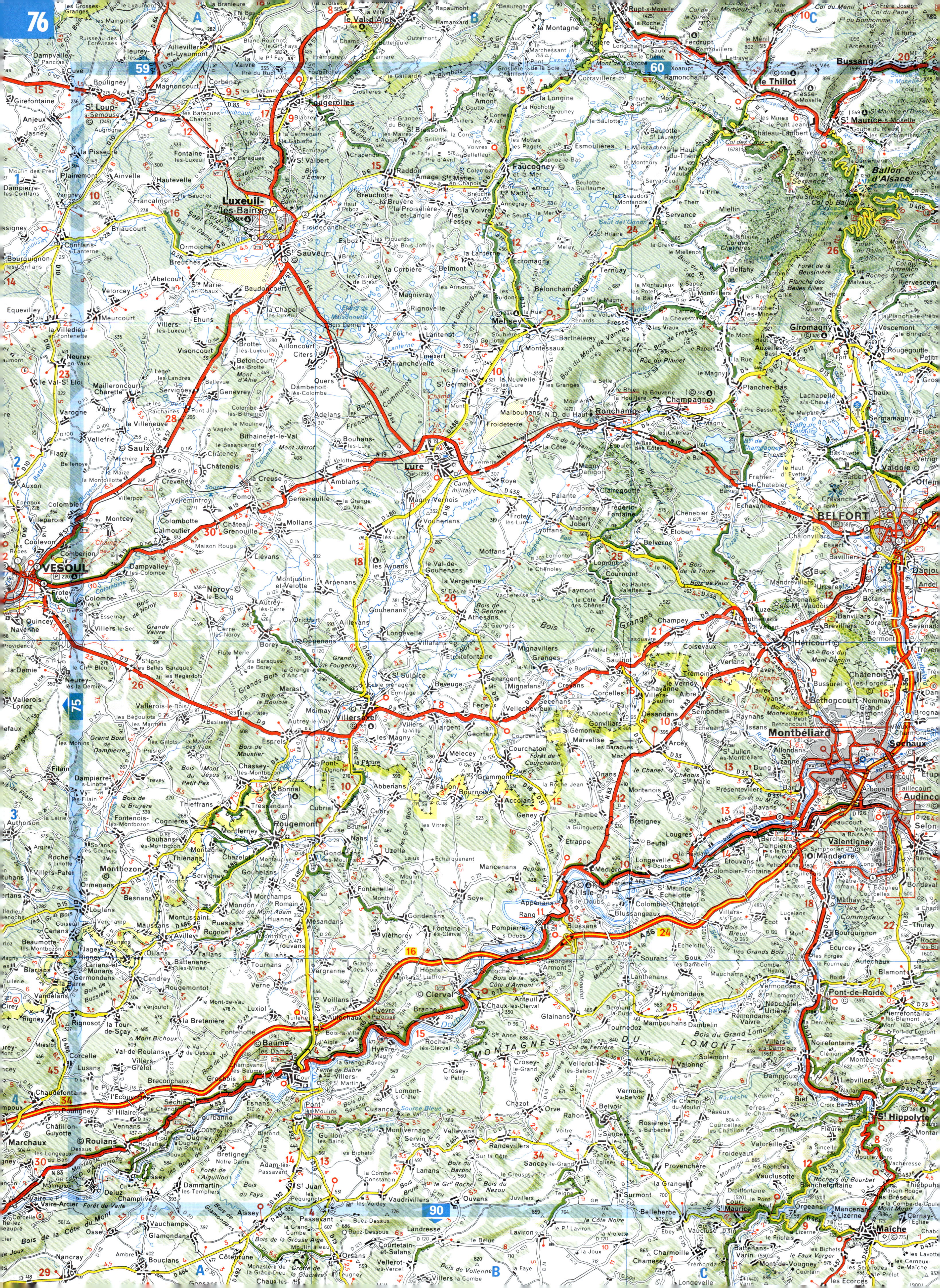

Guebwiller
Grand Ballon
Soultz
Ensisheim
Roggenhouse
Blodelsheim
St Amarin
Vieil Armand
Thann
Cernay
Wittelsheim
Wittenheim
Ottmarsheim
Müllheim
Masevaux
Pfastatt
MULHOUSE
Rixheim
Riedisheim
Habsheim
Chalampé
Neuenburg
Rougemont
Lachapelle
Brunstatt
Zimmersheim
Hochstatt
Dannemarie
Altkirch
Sierentz
Kembs
Kappelen
Hirsingue
St Louis
Huningue
BASEL
(BÂLE)
Binningen
Oberwil
Allschwil
Hésingue
Blotzheim
Folgensbourg
Ferrette
Seppois
Delle
Beaucourt
Boncourt
Porrentruy
Courgenay
St Ursanne
Delémont
Laufen
Breitenbach
Moutier
Tavannes
Tramelan
Saignelégier
Goumois
Solothurn
(Soleure)
Fessevilles
Hérimoncourt
FRANCHES MONTAGNES
Courrendlin
Bassecourt
Glovelier
Lucelle
Reinach
Aesch
Dornach
Therwil
Sondersdorf
Fontaine
Chavannes
Montreux
Grandvillars
Morvillars
Vézelois
Wolschwiller
Kiffis
Charmoille
Rocourt
Fahy
Grandfontaine
Chevenez
Bressaucourt
Asuel
Pleujouse
Miécourt
Alle
Vendlincourt
Bonfol
Damphreux
Beurnevésin
Réclère
Damvant
Montmelon
Epauvillers
Soubey
Montfaucon
Lajoux
Bellelay
Reconvilier
Malleray
Bévilard
Court
Mervelier
Vermes
Courchapoix
Corban
Vicques
Welschenrohr
Balsthal
Grenchenberg
Weissenstein
60
61
91

Pornichet
St Brevin-les-Pins
St Brevin-l'Océan
63
64
St Père-en-Retz
Frossay
Vue
Rouans
le Pellerin
St Michel-Chef-Chef
Tharon-Plage
Pointe de St Gildas
Préfailles
Pornic
Chauvé
Chéméré
Arthon-en-Retz
St Hilaire-de-Chaléons
Ste Pazanne
BAIE DE BOURGNEUF
la Bernerie-en-Retz
les Moutiers
Bourgneuf-en-Retz
Fresnay-en-Retz
Machecoul
ILE DE NOIRMOUTIER
Noirmoutier-en-l'Ile
l'Herbaudière
l'Epine
la Guérinière
Barbâtre
Passage du Gois (Route praticable à basse mer)
Beauvoir-s-Mer
Bois-de-Céné
Paulx
St Etienne-de-Mer-Morte
Fromentine
la Barre-de-Monts
Châteauneuf
la Garnache
Challans
Sallertaine
N.D. de Monts
Marais de Challans
St Christophe-du-Ligneron
Soullans
St Jean-de-Monts
Commequiers
Apremont
PONT D'YEU
ILE D'YEU
Port-Joinville
Port-de-la-Meule
le Vx Château
Côte Sauvage
Pointe des Corbeaux
N.D. de Riez
St Hilaire-de-Riez
St Gilles-Croix-de-Vie
Croix-de-Vie
Coëx
Givrand
St Révérend
l'Aiguillon-s-Vie
la Chapelle-Hermier
la Chaize-Giraud
Landevieille
Brétignolles-s-Mer
St Nicolas-de-Brem
St Martin-de-Brem
92
A
B
C
1
2
3
4

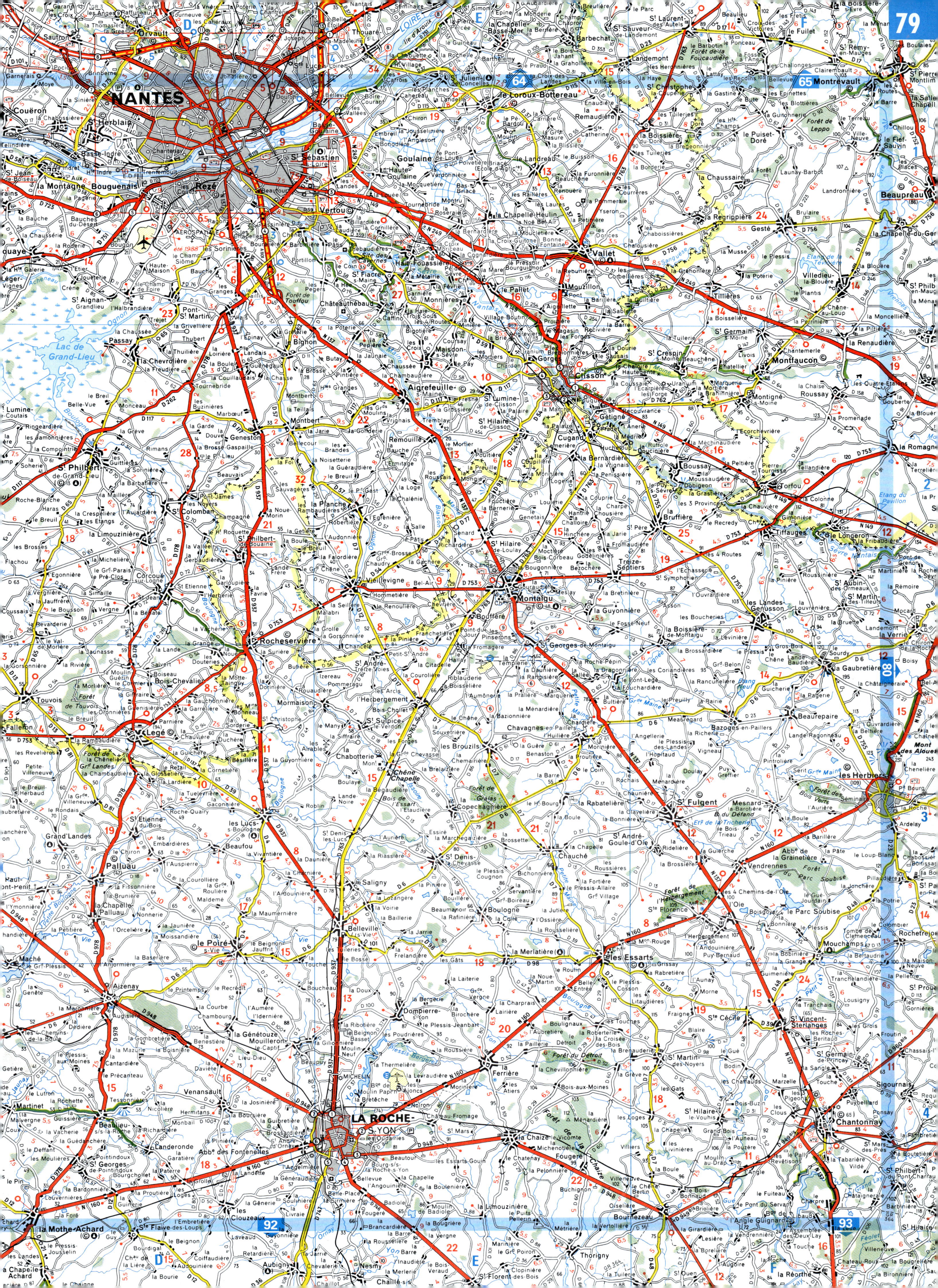
NANTES
Orvault
Couëron
St Herblain
Bouguenais
Rezé
St Sébastien
Vertou
Le Loroux-Bottereau
Goulaine
Vallet
Montrevault
Beaupréau
Lac de Grand-Lieu
Aigrefeuille
Clisson
Gétigné
Cugand
Montfaucon
Tiffauges
Torfou
Montaigu
Rocheservière
Legé
Palluau
Aizenay
Le Poiré-s-Vie
Belleville
LA ROCHE-S-YON
La Mothe-Achard
Les Essarts
St Fulgent
Les Herbiers
Chavagnes-en-Paillers
Mouchamps
Chantonnay
St Vincent-Sterlanges
Bournezeau
Thorigny

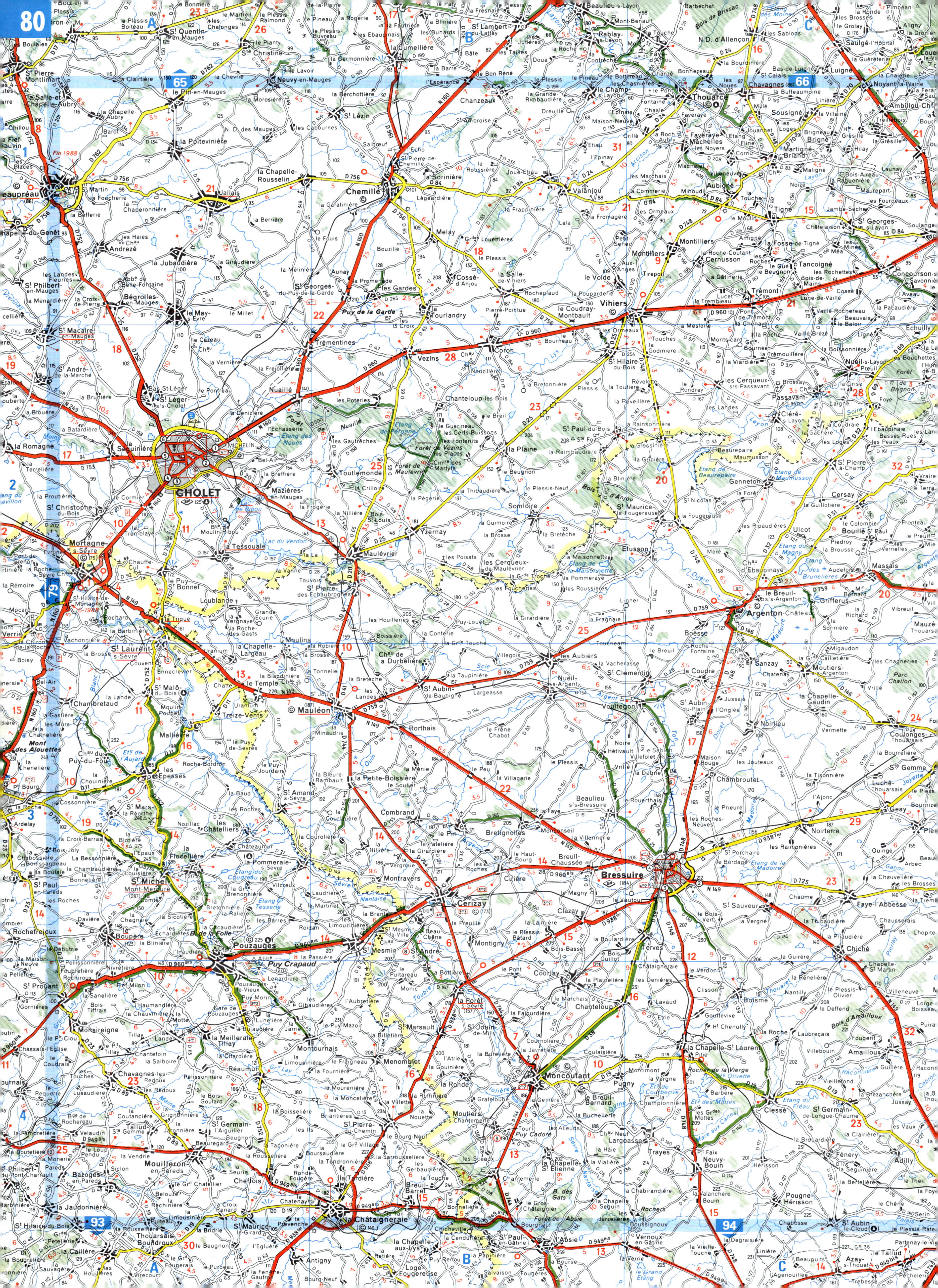
CHOLET
Chemillé
Thouarce
Vihiers
Bressuire
Mauléon
Cerizay
Pouzauges
Moncoutant
La Châtaigneraie
Argenton Château
Mortagne-s-Sèvre
Beaupréau
Coron
Vezins
Maulévrier
Les Aubiers
St Laurent-s-Sèvre
Chanzeaux
Melay
Trémentines
Nuaillé
Yzernay
Somloire
Cléré-s-Layon
Passavant-s-Layon
Nueil-s-Layon
Montilliers
Tigné
Aubigné
Faye-l'Abbesse
Chiché
Clessé
La Chapelle-St Laurent
St Germain-de-Longue-Chaume
Mouilleron-en-Pareds
Chavagnes-les-Redoux
Monsireigne
Les Épesses
Puy-du-Fou
Mallièvre
Treize-Vents
St Amand-s-Sèvre
Courlay
Montravers
La Tessoualle
Toutlemonde
Mazières-en-Mauges
St Hilaire-du-Bois
Les Cerqueux
Étusson
Massais
Bouillé St Paul
Cersay
St Pierre-à-Champ
Genneton
Vernoux-en-Gâtine
L'Absie
St Paul-en-Gâtine
Antigny
Thouarsais-Bouildroux
Puy Crapaud
Puy Cadore
Puy de la Garde
Mont des Alouettes
Forêt de Vezins
Forêt de l'Absie
Forêt de Nuaillé
65
66
93
94
79
N 160
N 149
N 249
D 960
D 759
D 748
D 938
A
B
C

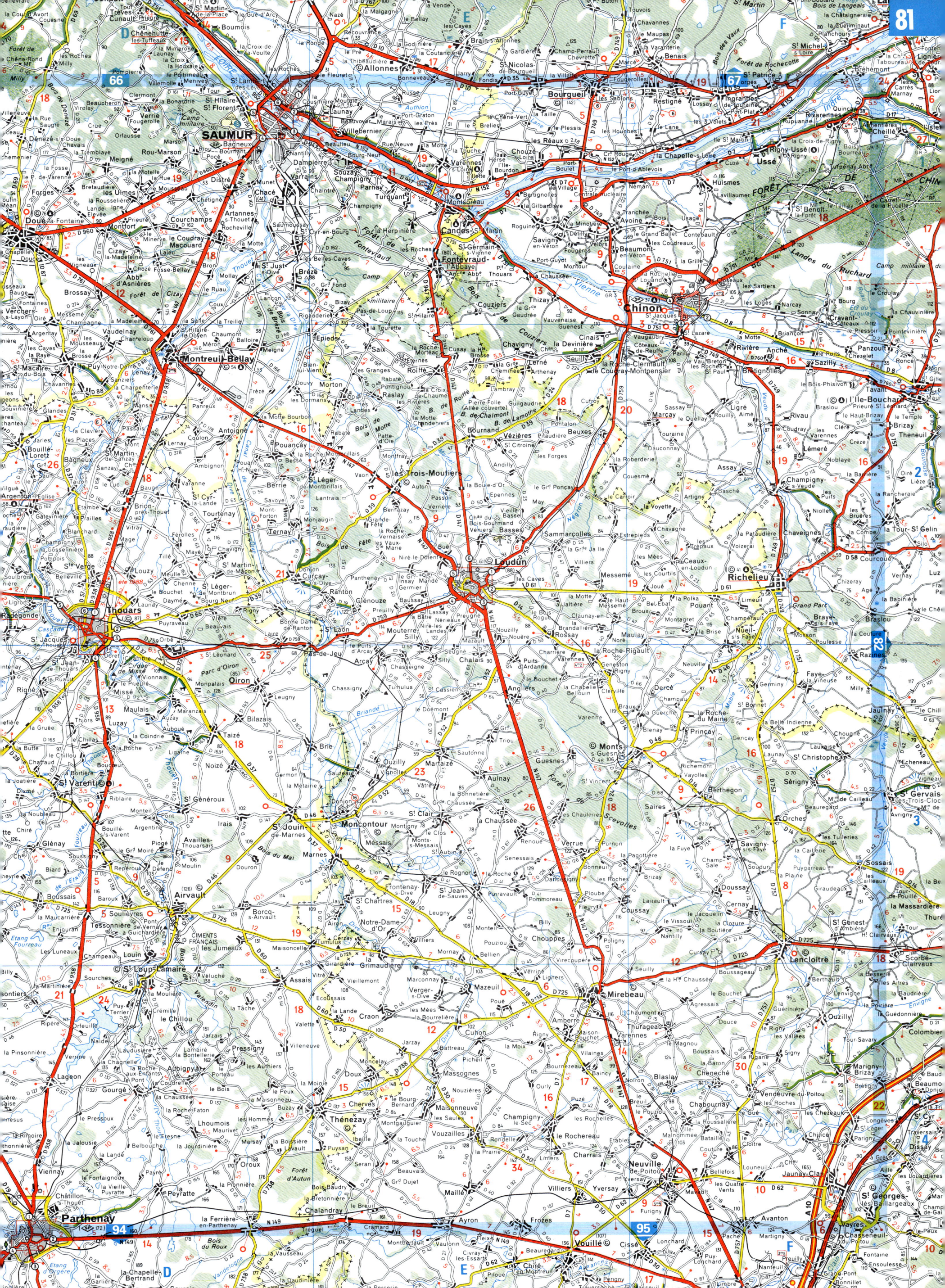

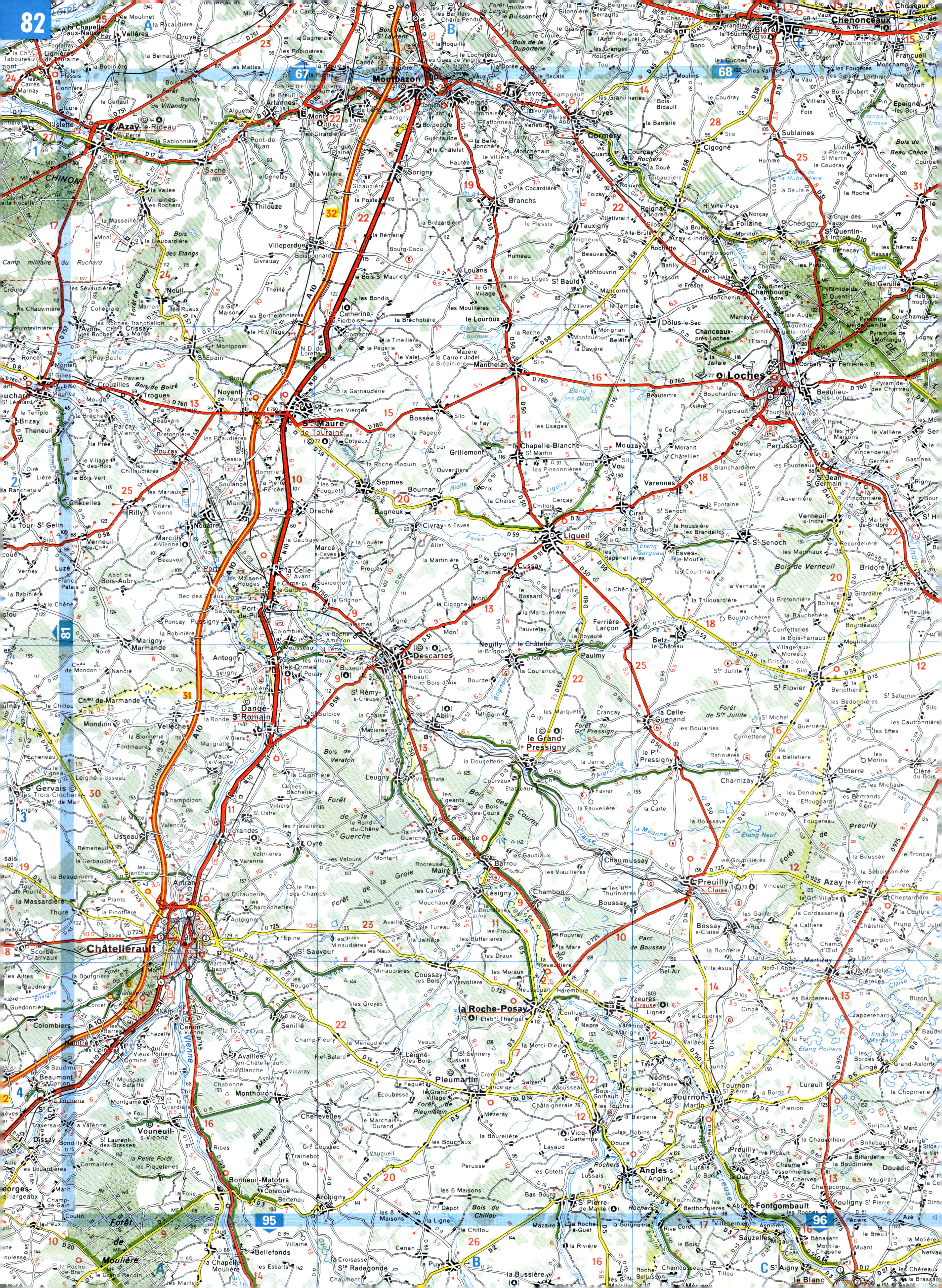

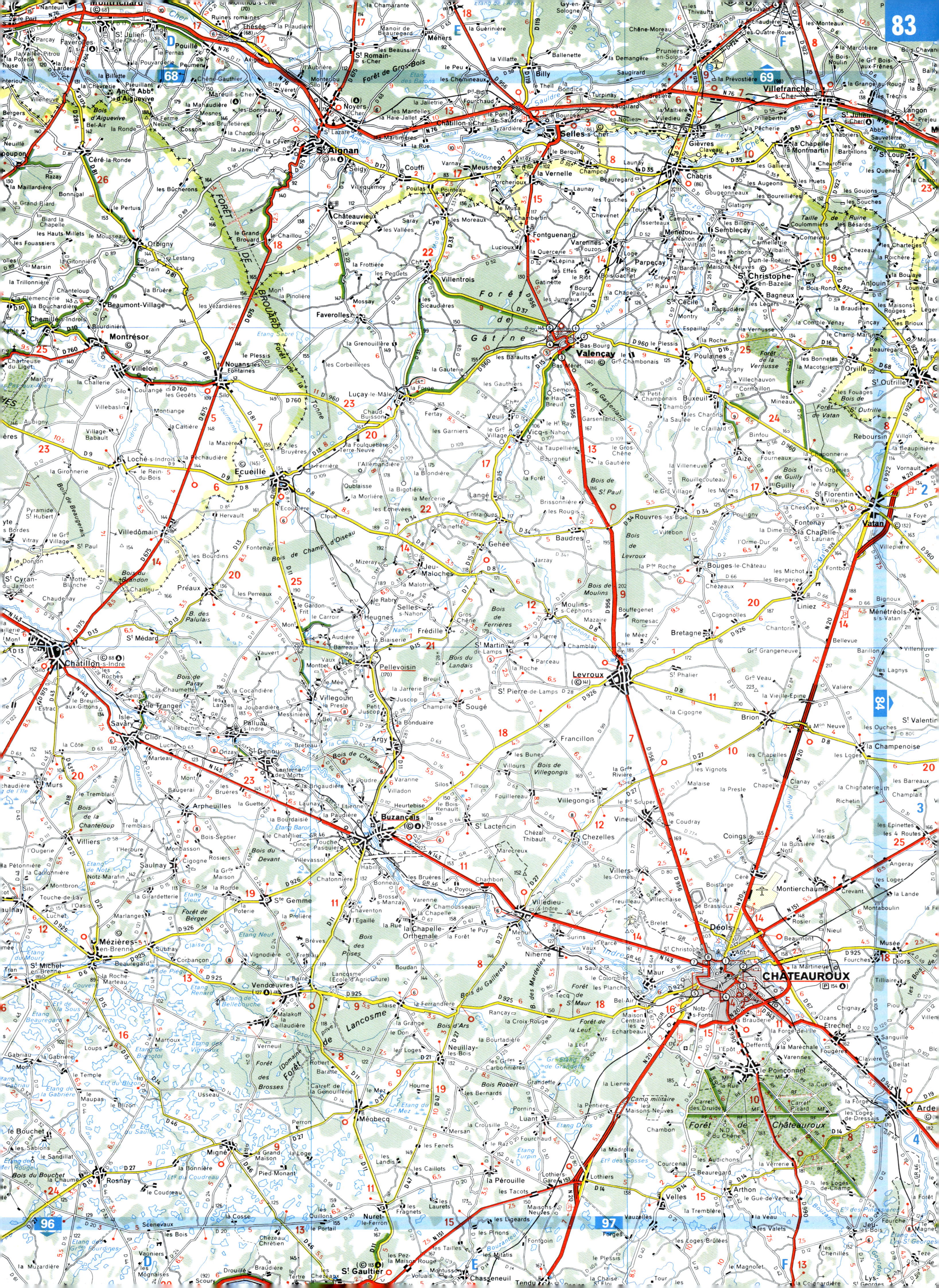
68
69
84
96
97
St Aignan
Montrichard
Selles-s-Cher
Villefranche-s-Cher
Chabris
Valençay
Montrésor
Écueillé
Levroux
Vatan
Châtillon-s-Indre
Buzançais
Pellevoisin
Mézières-en-Brenne
Vendœuvres
Déols
CHÂTEAUROUX
Ardentes
St Gaultier
Forêt de Gros-Bois
Forêt de Gâtine
Forêt de Châteauroux
Forêt de Lancosme
FORÊT DE BROUARD

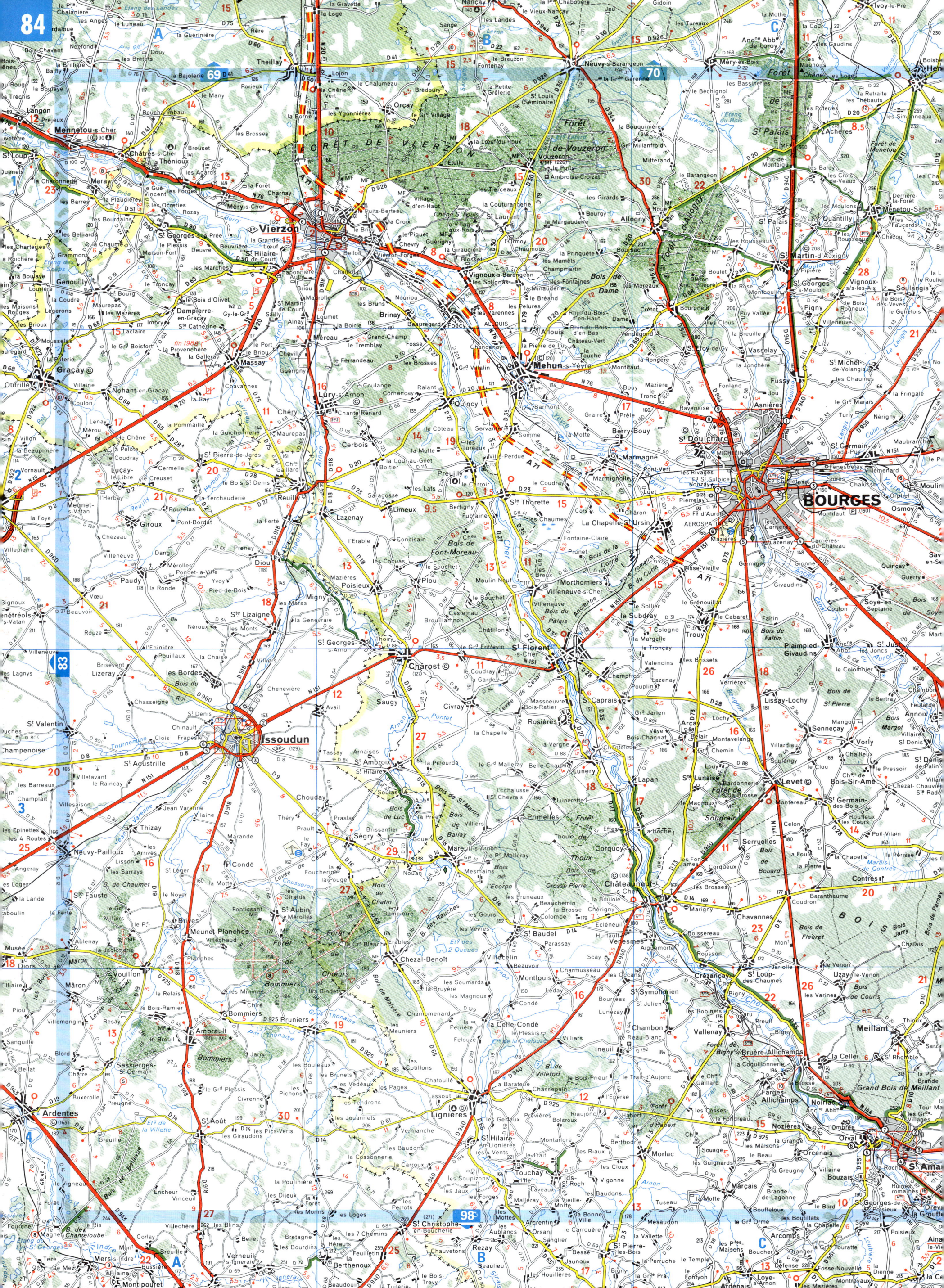

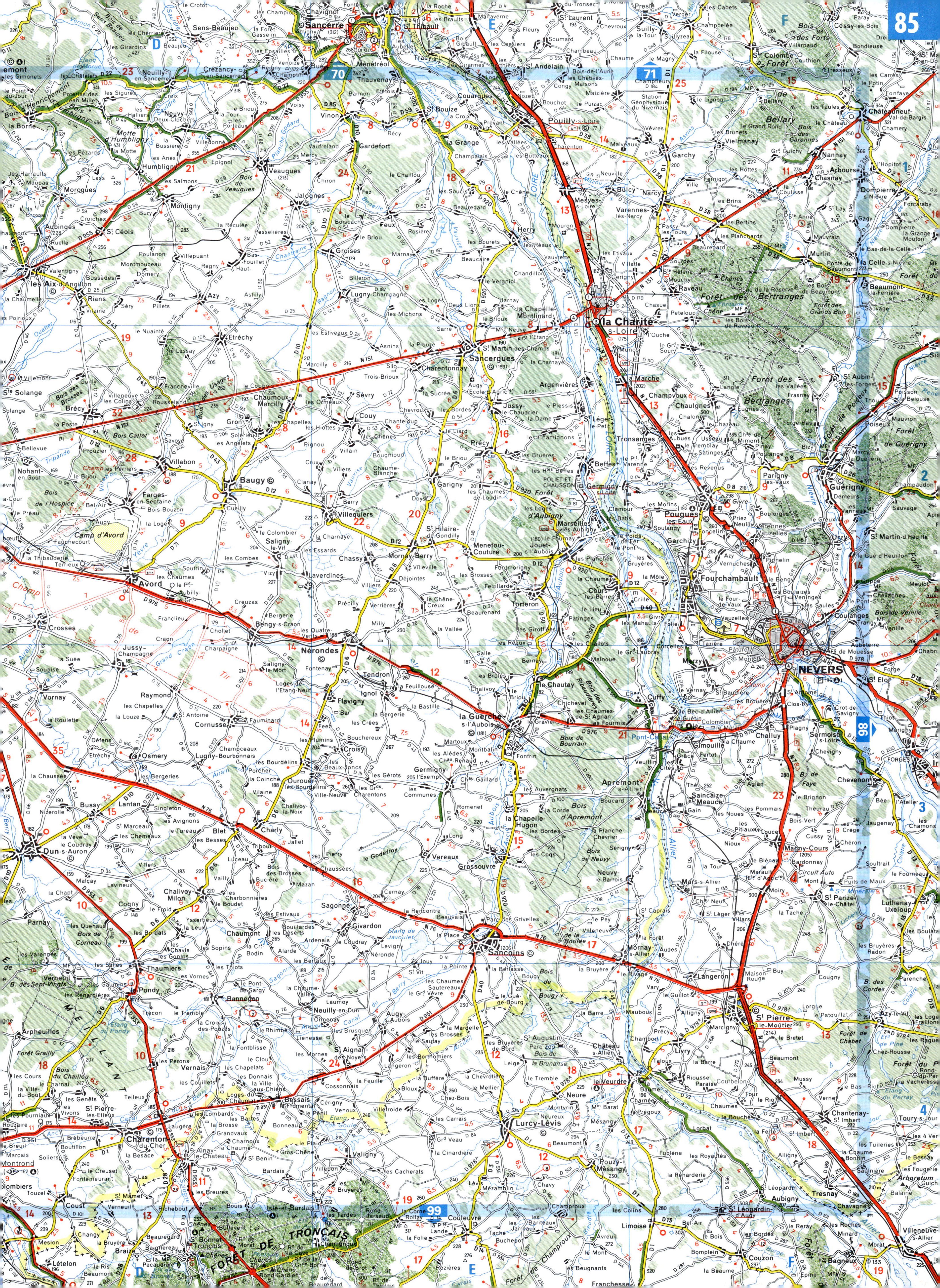

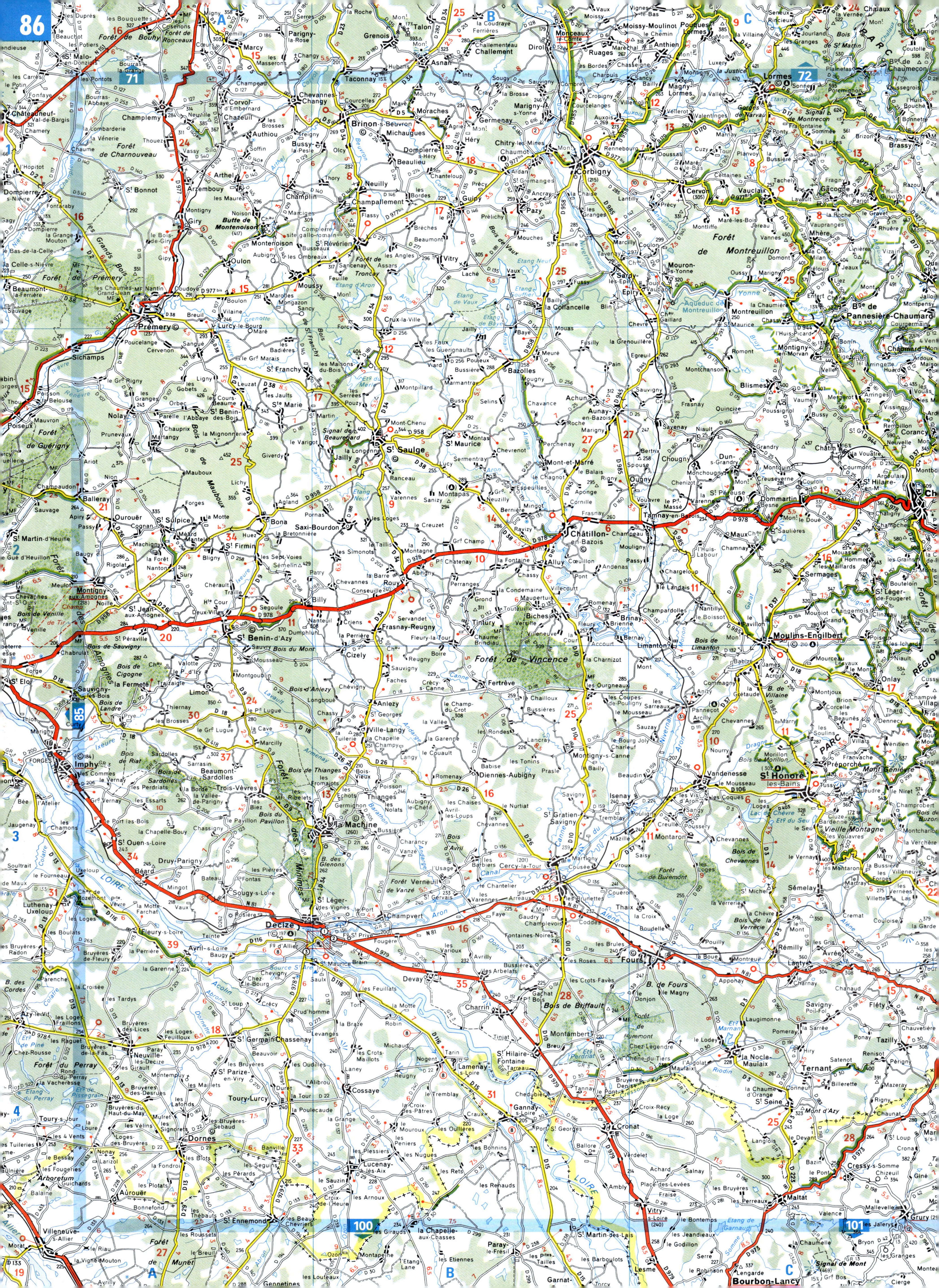

Saulieu
Liernais
Arnay-le-Duc
Pouilly-en-Auxois
Châteauneuf
Commarin
Montsauche
les Settons
MORVAN
Lucenay-l'Évêque
AUTUN
Épinac
Sully
Nolay
Couches
le Creusot
Montcenis
Montchanin
Blanzy
Montceau-les-Mines
Sanvignes-les-Mines
Mesvres
Toulon-s-Arroux
Luzy
Issy-l'Évêque
Château-Chinon
Mont Beuvray
St-Léger
Anost
Forêt de Planoise
Signal d'Uchon
Étang-s-Arroux
Montmort
72
73
88
101
102

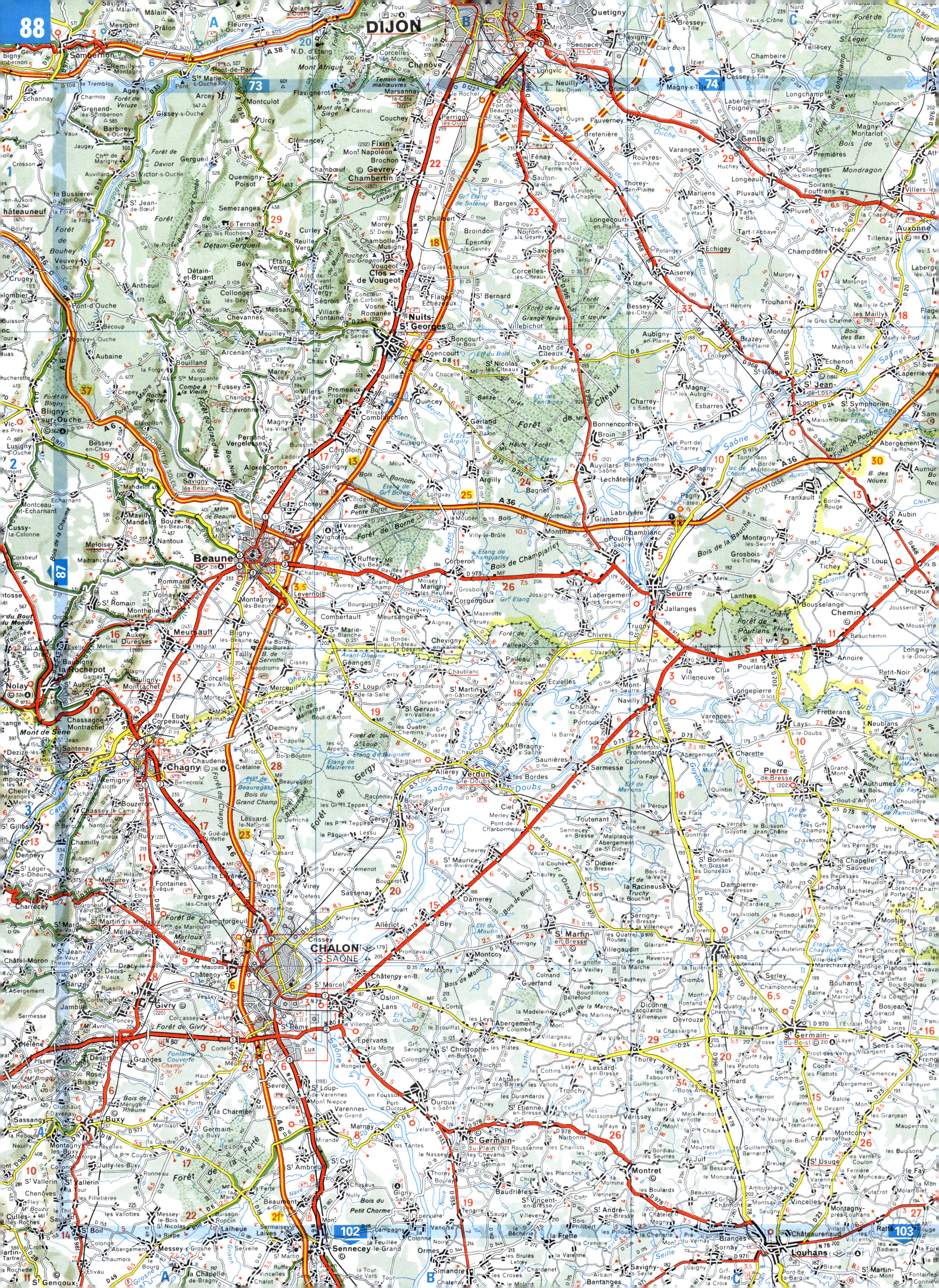

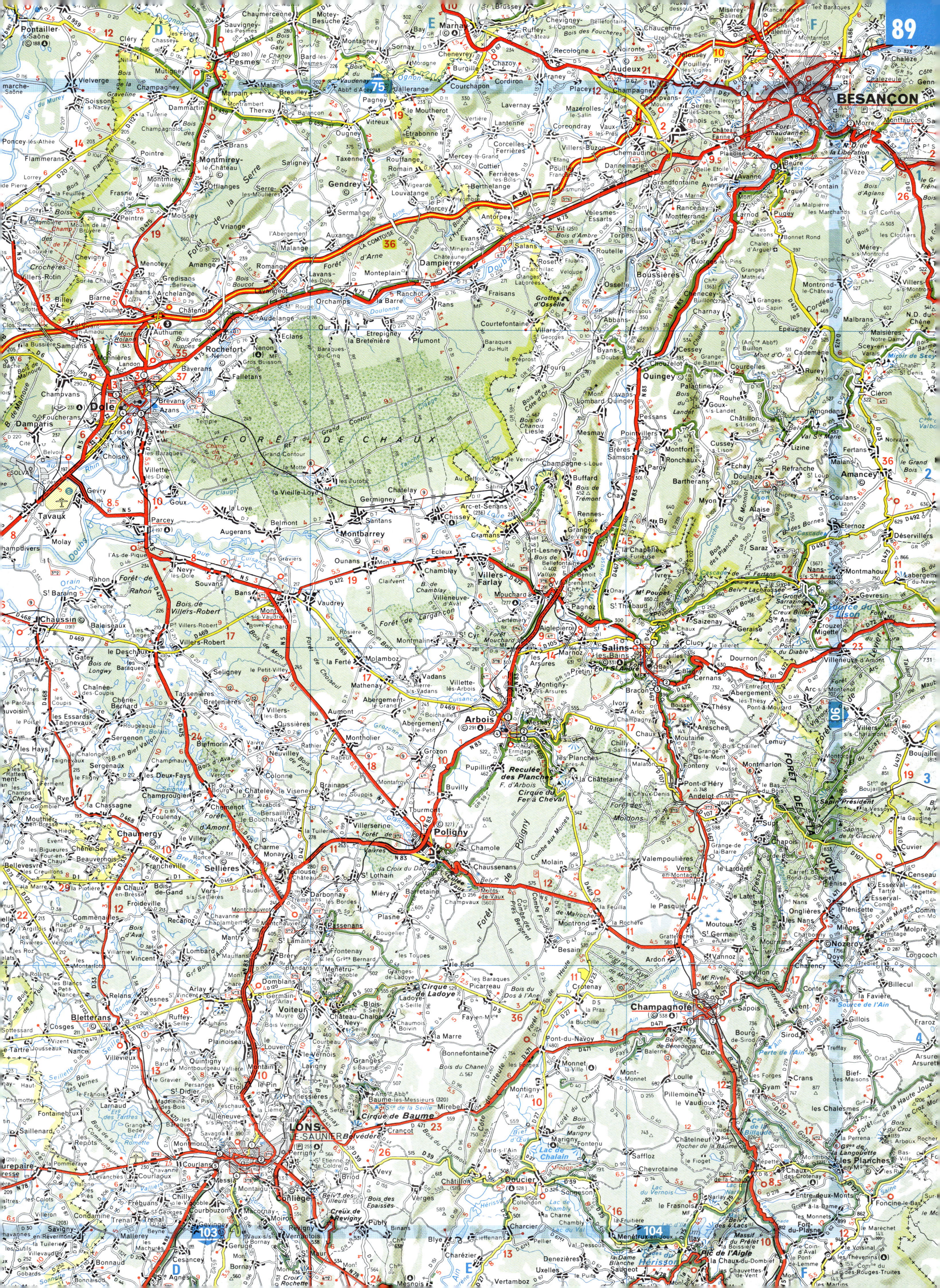

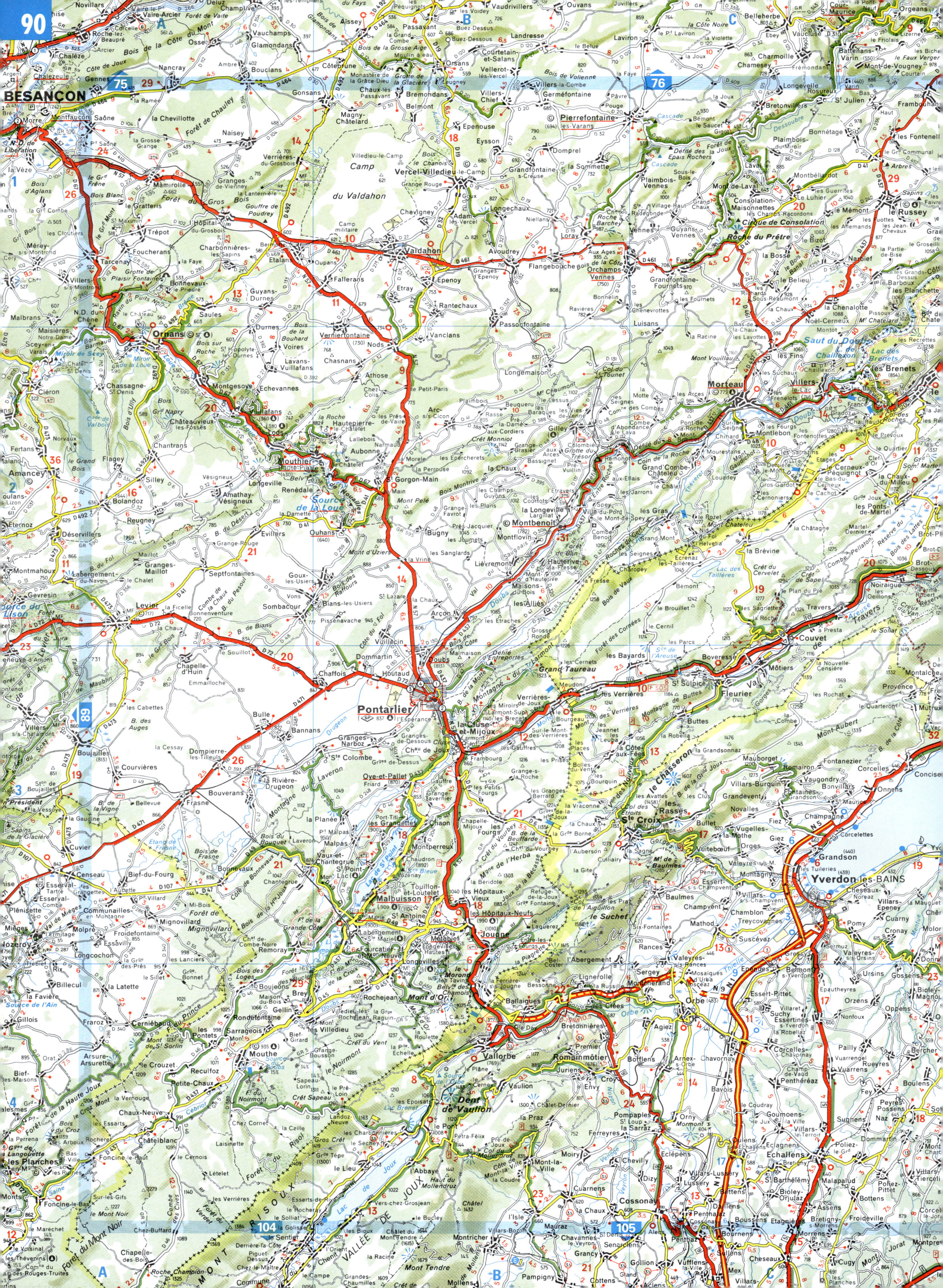

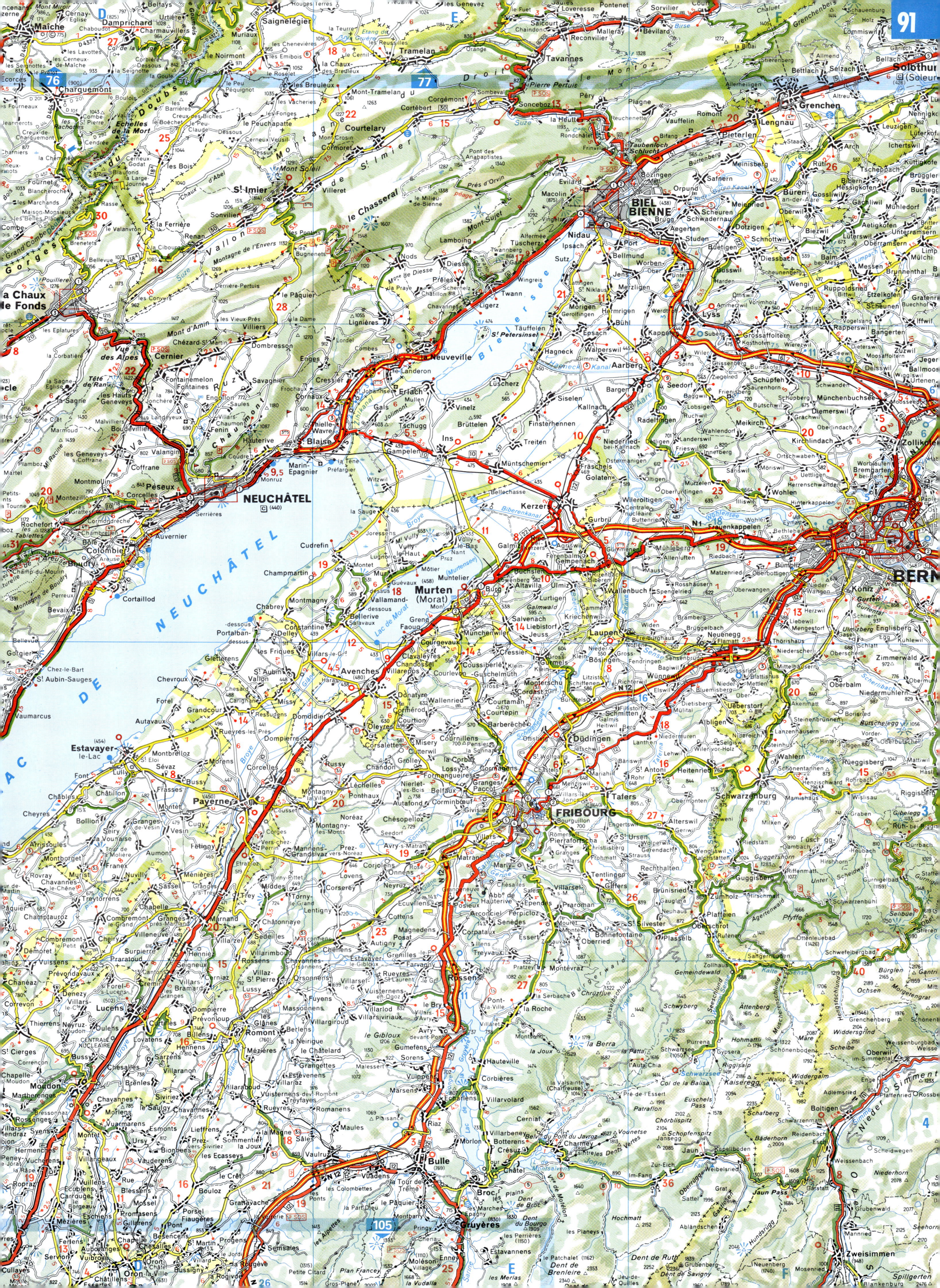

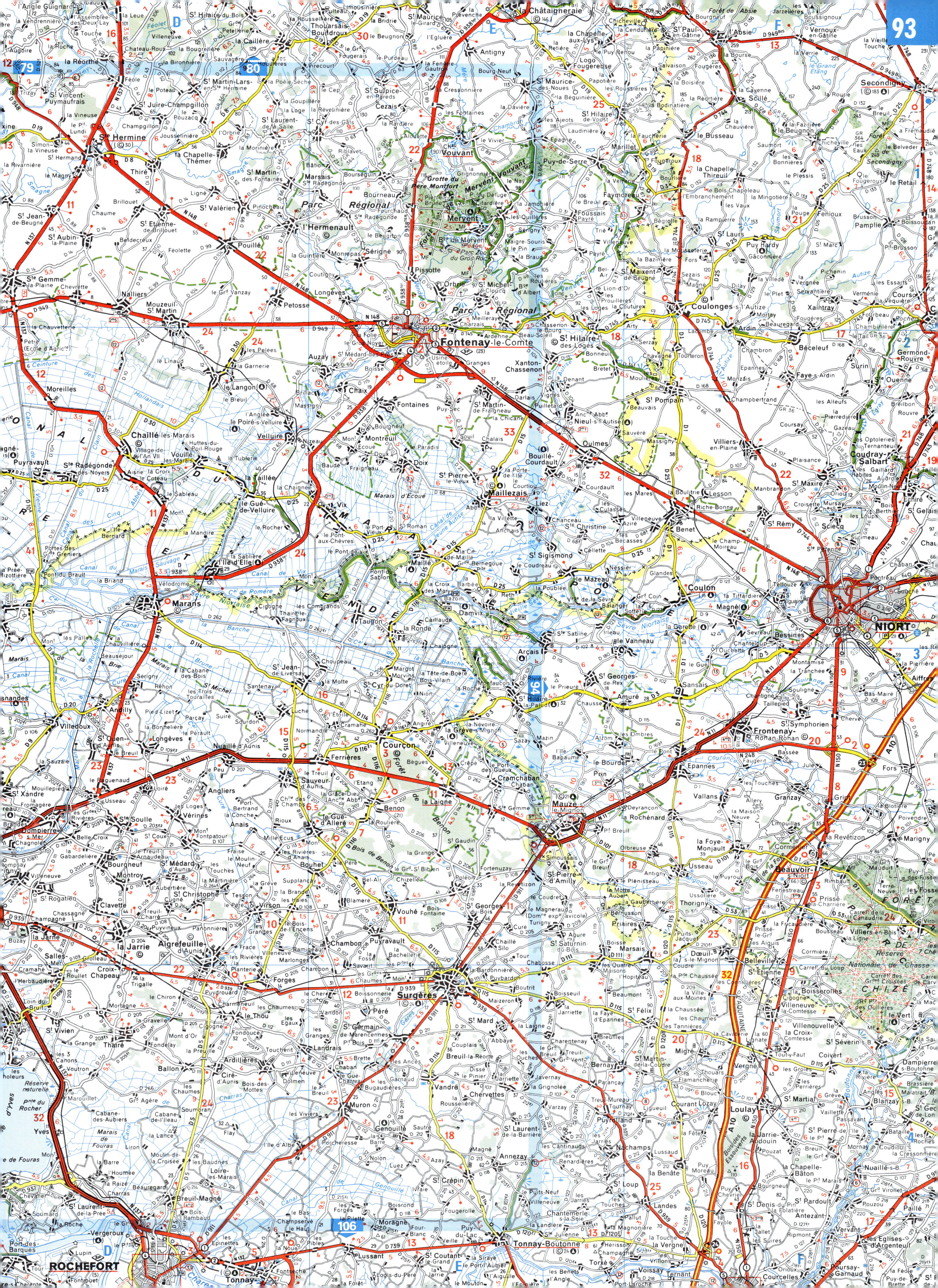

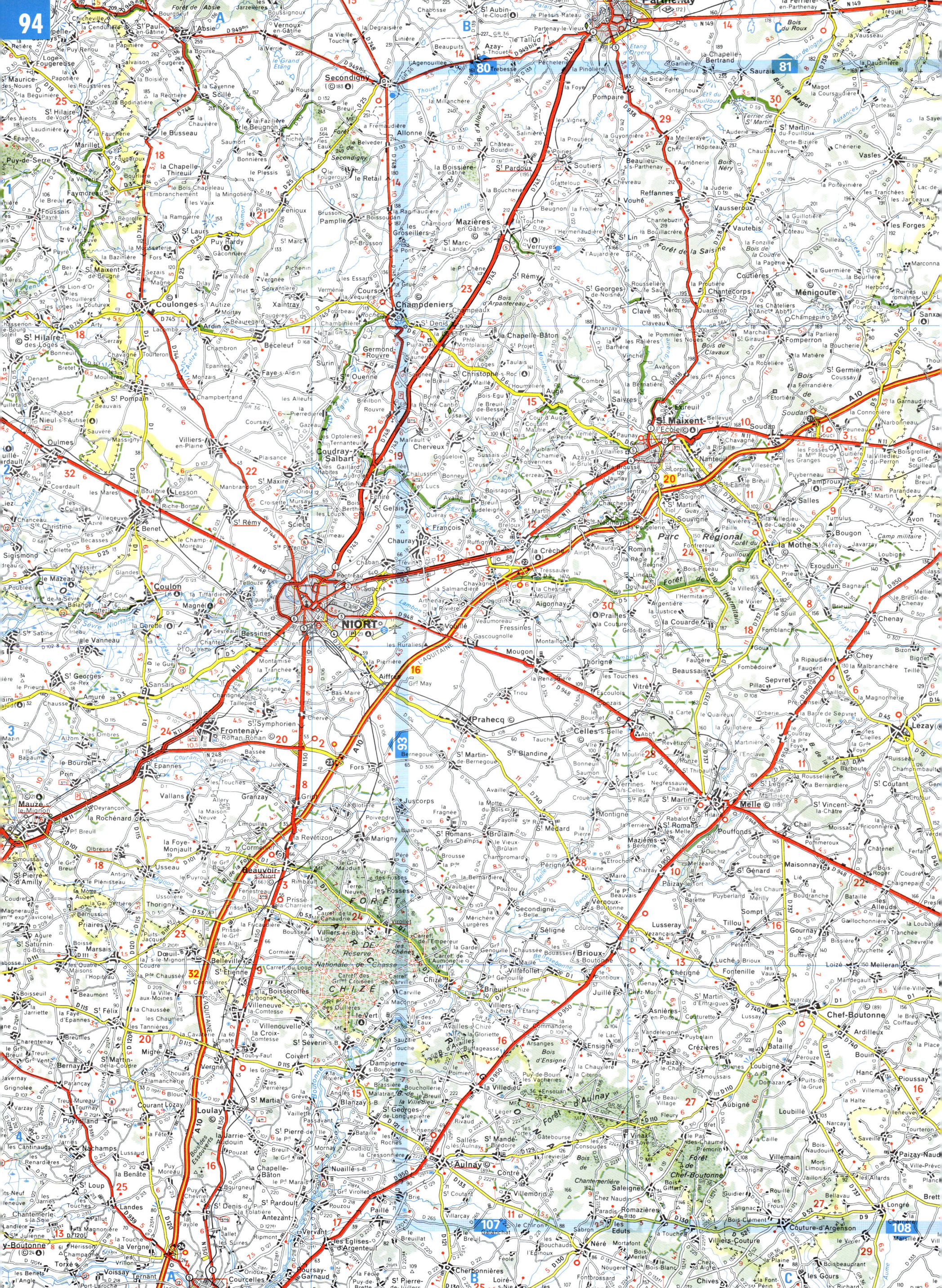

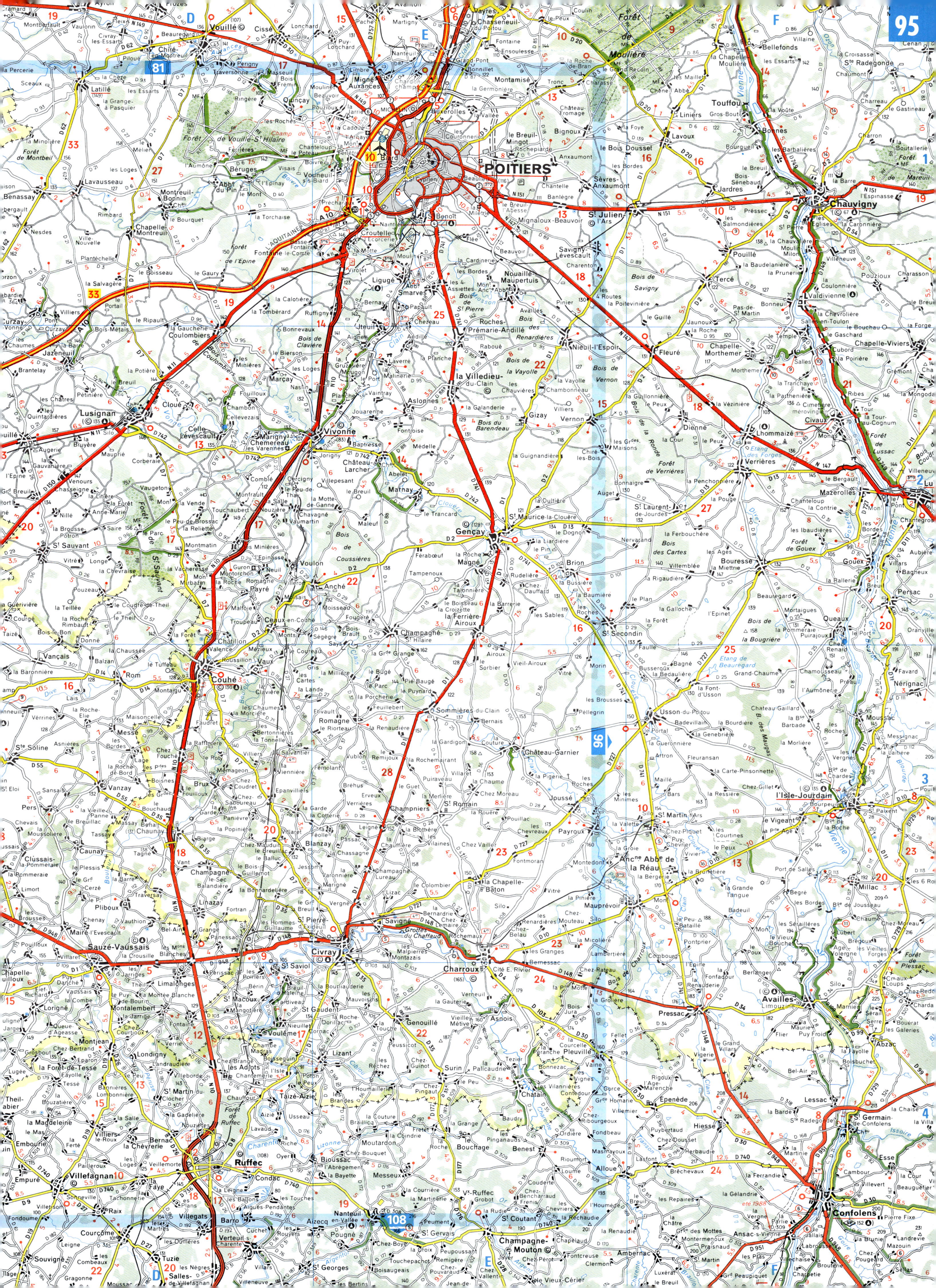

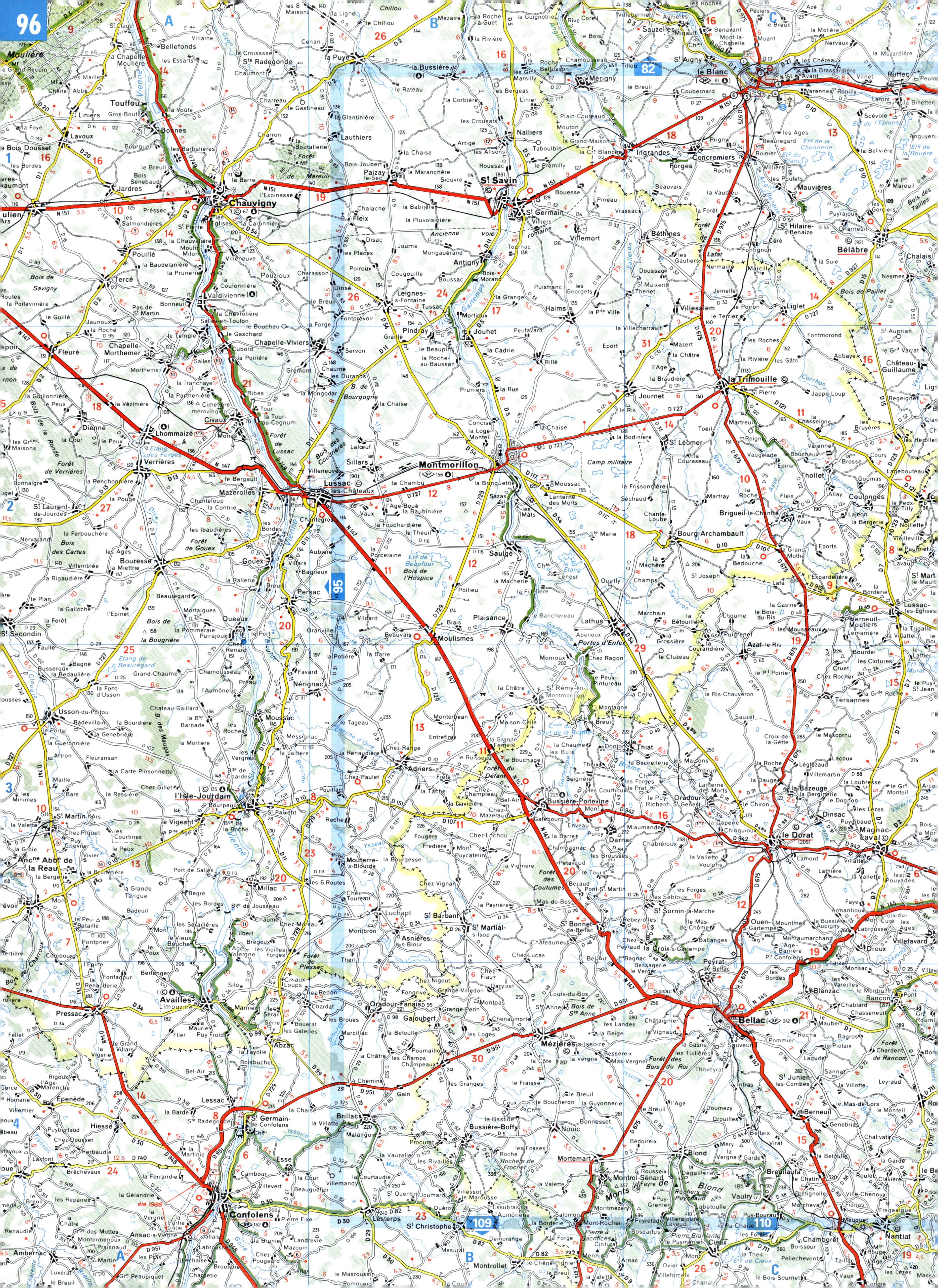
Chauvigny
St Savin
Montmorillon
Lussac-les-Châteaux
la Trimouille
Le Blanc
Bélâbre
l'Isle-Jourdain
Bussière-Poitevine
Le Dorat
Magnac-Laval
Bellac
Mézières-s-Issoire
Confolens
Availles-Limouzine
Moulismes
Adriers
Saulgé
Lathus
Usson-du-Poitou
Civaux
Verrières
Mazerolles
Gouex
Persac
Queaux
Millac
Brillac
Nantiat
Lesterps
Montrollet
Mortemart
Blond
Bussière-Boffy
Oradour-Fanais
St Barbant
Journet
Haims
Jouhet
Antigny
Villesalem
Bourg-Archambault
Azat-le-Ris
Thiat
Darnac
Peyrat-de-Bellac
Blanzac
Berneuil
Pressac
Epenède
Hiesse
Lessac
Esse
Abzac
Mouterre-s-Blourde
Asnières-s-Blour
Luchapt
Nérignac
Moussac
Pindray
Leignes-s-Fontaine
Sillars
Valdivienne
Pouillé
Tercé
Chapelle-Viviers
Chapelle-Morthemer
Fleuré
Dienné
Lhommaizé
Bouresse
Fleix
Paizay-le-Sec
Nalliers
Ingrandes
Concremiers
Mérigny
Béthines
Liglet
Coulonges
Lussac-les-Eglises
Forêt des Coutumes
Bois du Roi
Camp militaire
Forêt de Verrières
Bois des Cartes
Forêt de Mareuil
Forêt de Lussac
Forêt de Plessac
N 147
N 151
D 951
D 675
82
95
109
110
A
B
C
1
2
3
4

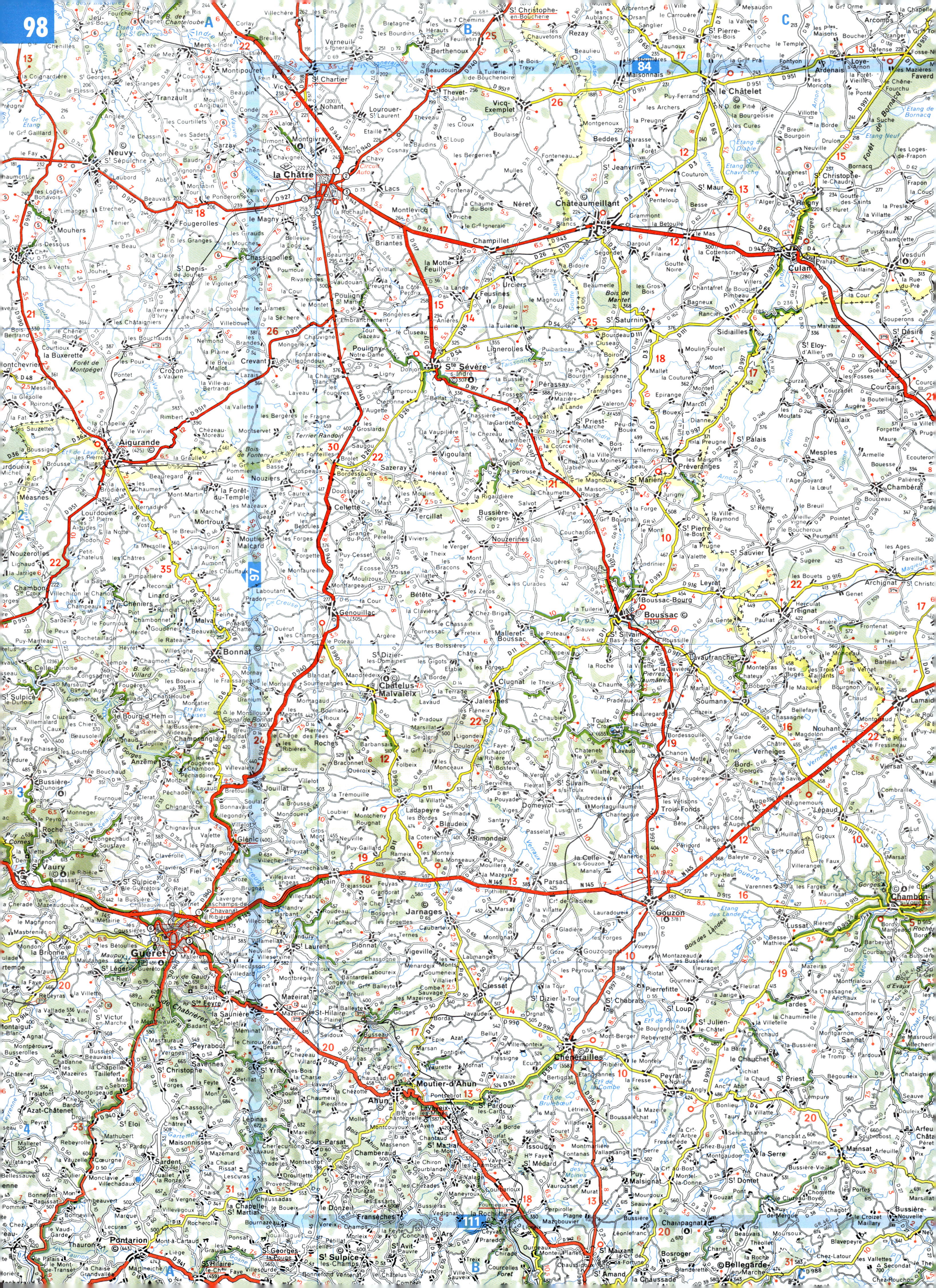

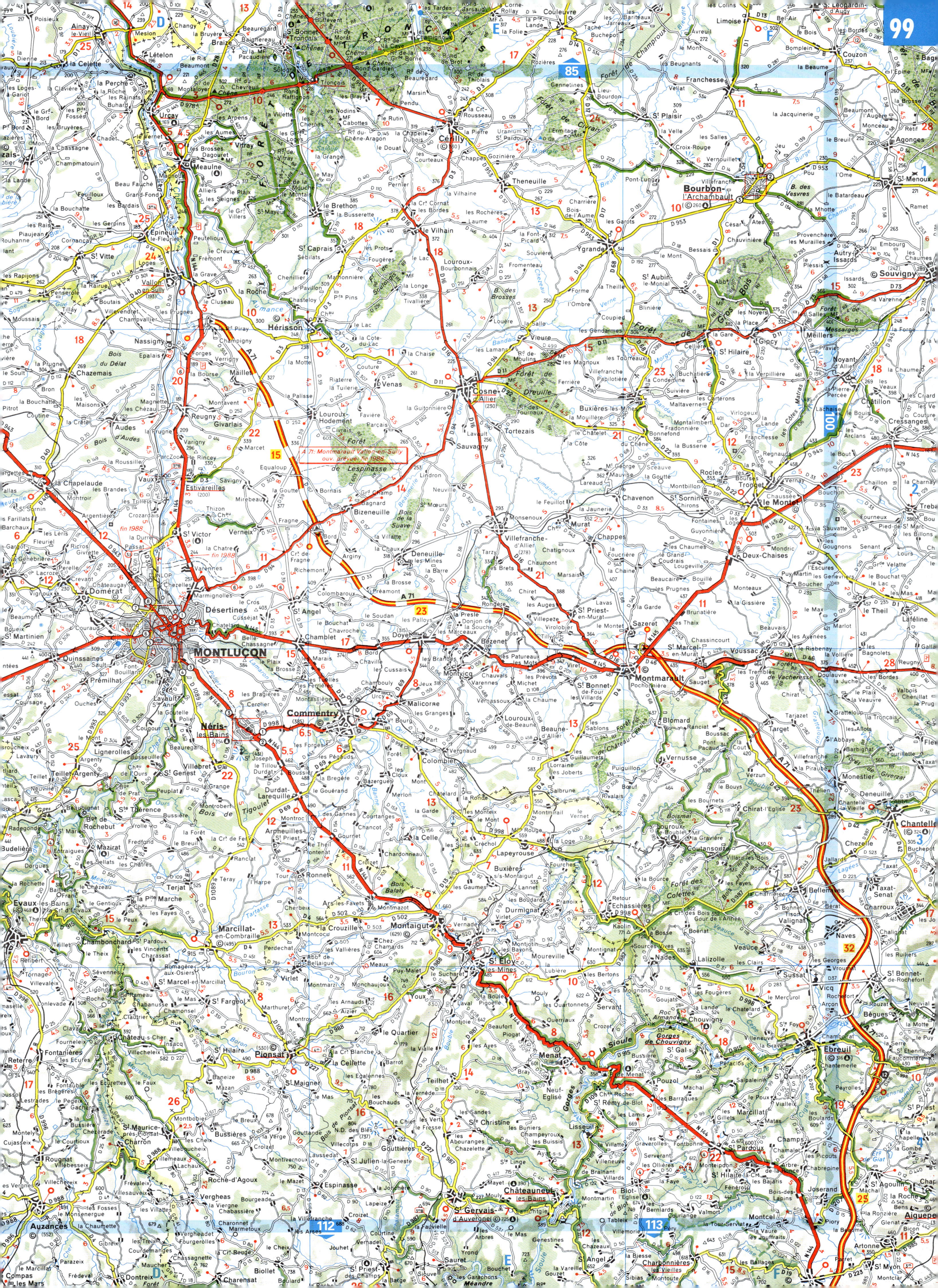
MONTLUÇON
Désertines
Domérat
Commentry
Néris-les-Bains
Montmarault
Cosne-d'Allier
Bourbon-l'Archambault
Cérilly
Hérisson
Meaulne
Urçay
Ainay-le-Vieil
Ygrande
Souvigny
Le Montet
Tronget
Villefranche-d'Allier
Doyet
Montvicq
Hyds
Chantelle
Ebreuil
Menat
St-Eloy-les-Mines
Montaigut
Marcillat-en-Combraille
Pionsat
Evaux-les-Bains
Chambon-sur-Voueize
Auzances
St-Gervais-d'Auvergne
Châteauneuf-les-Bains
St-Pourçain
Forêt de Tronçais
Forêt de Dreuille
Gorges de Chouvigny
A 71: Montmarault-Vallon-en-Sully ouv. prévue fin 1988
fin 1988
A 71
85
100
112
113

Gueugnon
Digoin
Paray-le-Monial
Charolles
Palinges
Génelard
St Vallier
Gourdon
Mont-St-Vincent
La Guiche
St Bonnet-de-Joux
Marcigny
Semur-en-Brionnais
La Clayette
Chauffailles
Charlieu
Pouilly-s-C.
ROANNE
Le Coteau
Thizy
Cours
Belmont
Lamure-s-Azergues
Amplepuis
Renaison
Ambierle
Le Crozet
St Haon-le-Châtel
St Germain-Lespinasse
Briennon
Iguerande
Anzy
Dompierre-s-Besbre
Marcilly
Matour
Dyo
Sivignon
Monsols
Perreux
Régny
Pradines
Chassenard
Molinet
Yan
Vitry-en-Charollais
Baugy
Chandon
Cuinzier
Sevelinges
Villers
Vougy
Mably
Riorges
Chambilly
Artaix
Melay
Avrilly
Luneau
Neuilly-en-Donjon
Bois-Ste-Marie
Dompierre-les-Ormes
Ozolles
Verosvres
Chevagny
Trivy
86
87
114
115
201

103

107

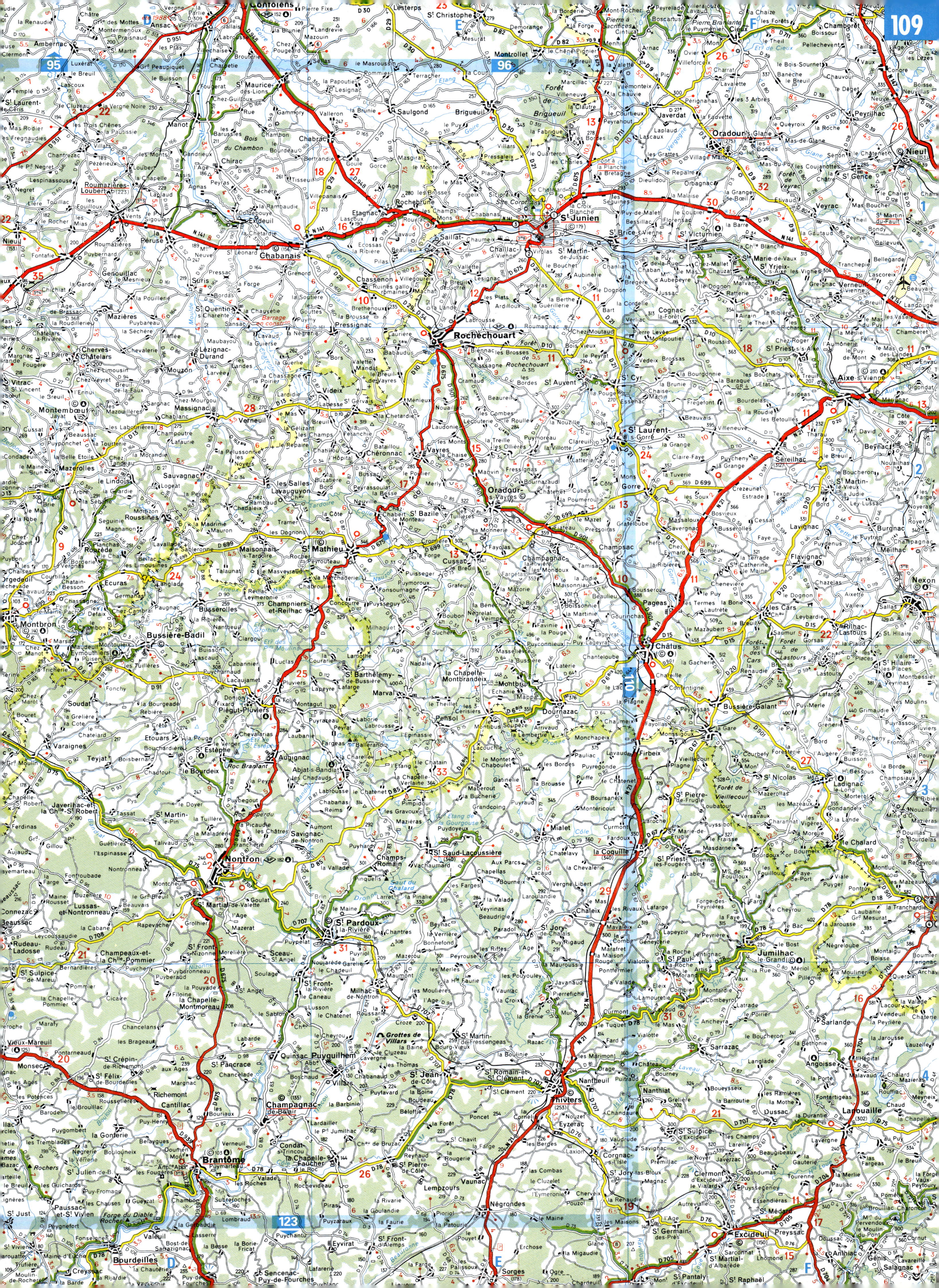
95
96
123
Confolens
St Junien
Chabanais
Rochechouart
Oradour-sur-Glane
Aixe-s-Vienne
Nieul
Châlus
St Mathieu
Nontron
Brantôme
Thiviers
Excideuil
Jumilhac-le-Grand
Bussière-Galant
Piégut-Pluviers
Bussière-Badil
Montbron
Mareuil
Bourdeilles
La Coquille
Champagnac-de-Belair
St Pardoux-la-Rivière
Lanouaille
Nexon
Sorges
Rilhac-Lastours
St Laurent-s-Gorre
Cussac
Vayres
Verneuil
Chéronnac

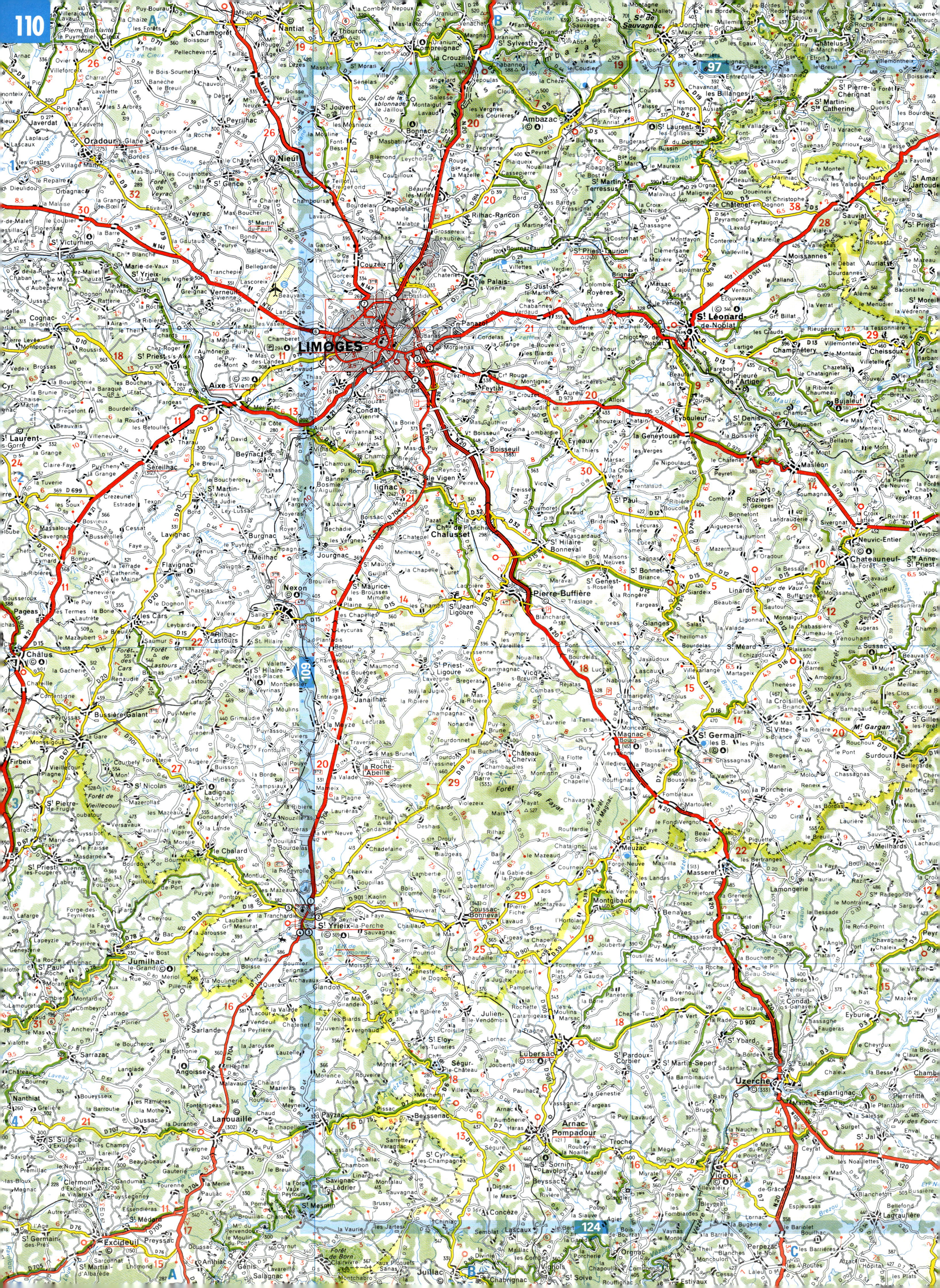

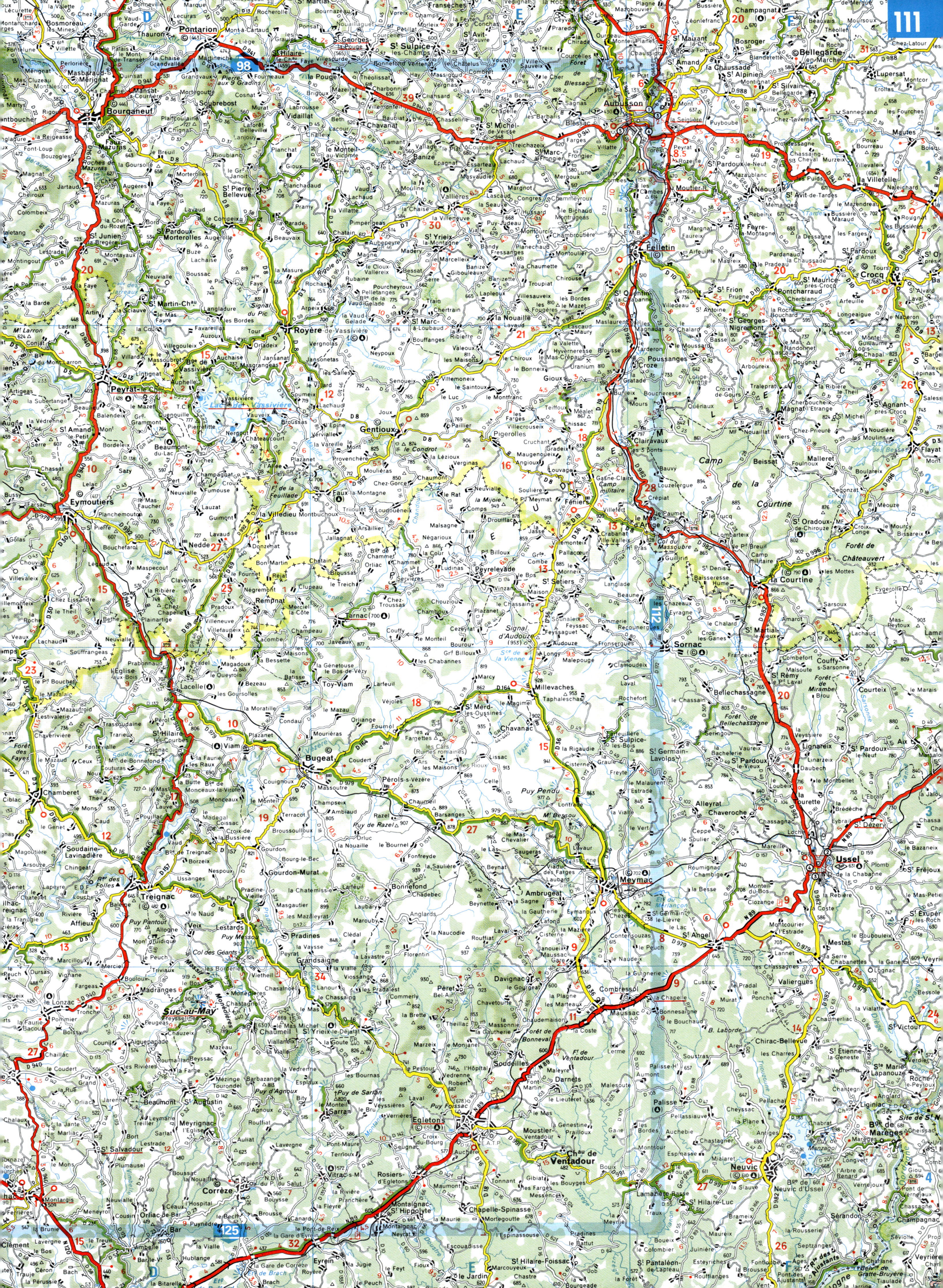

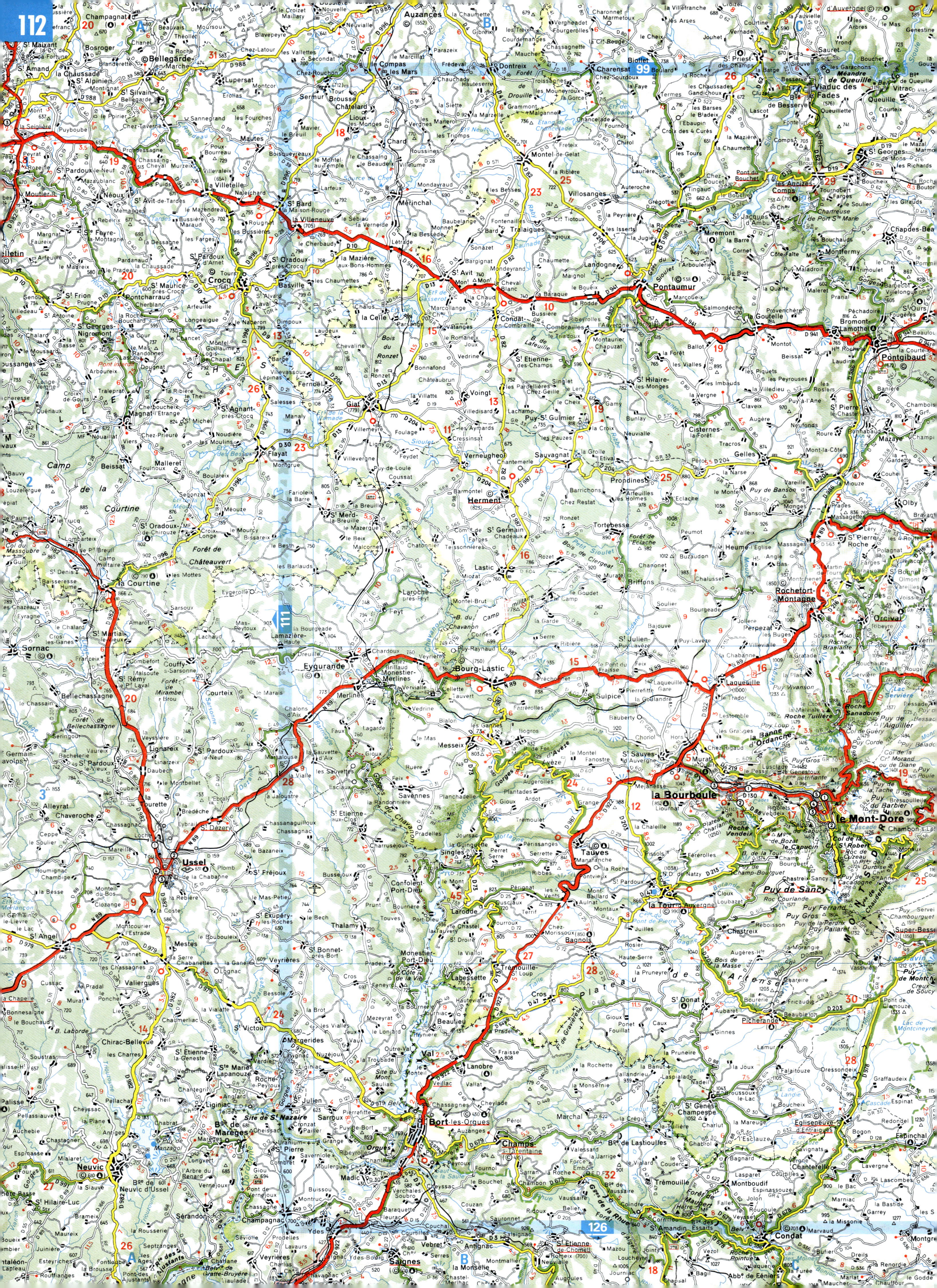

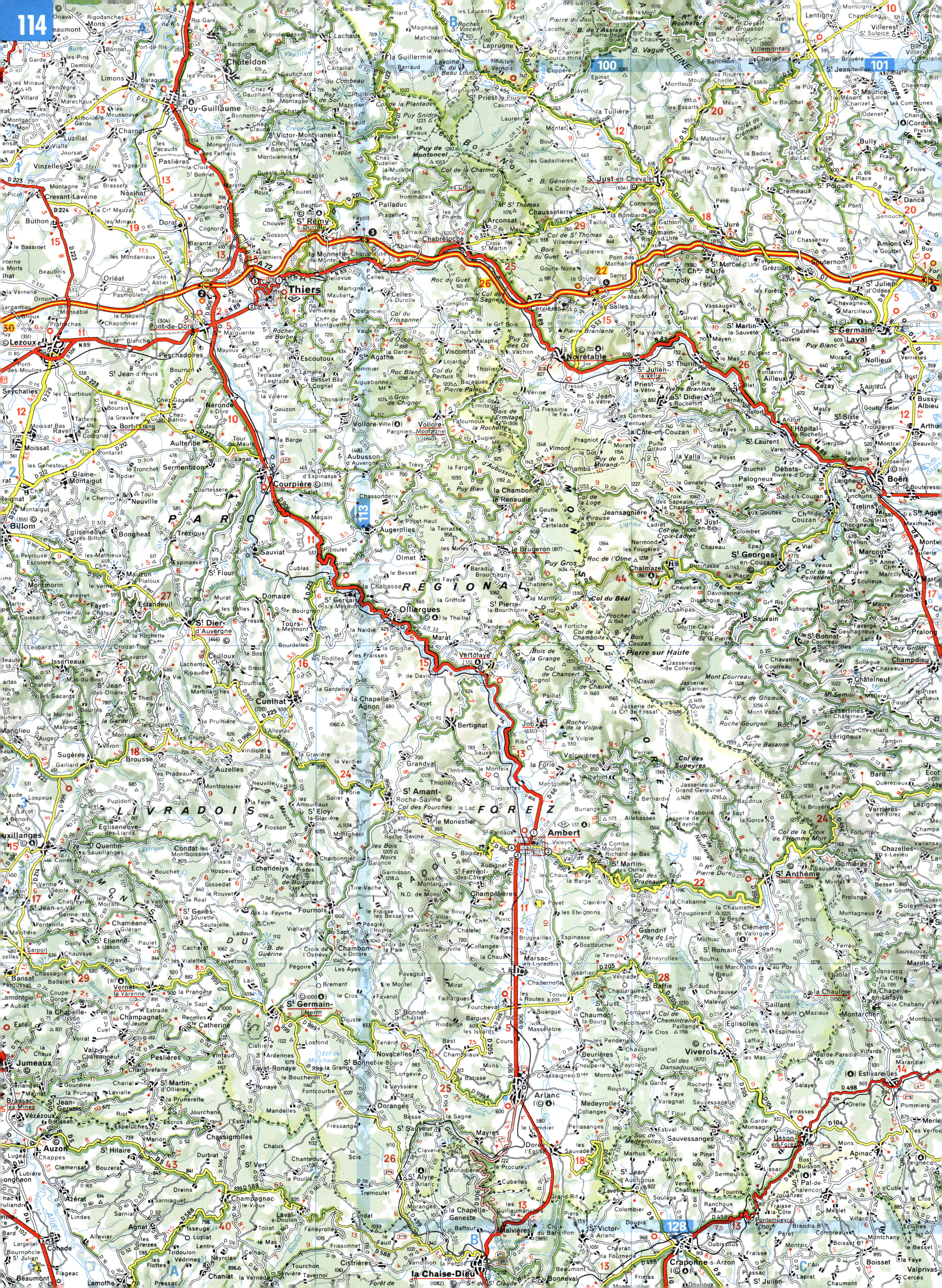

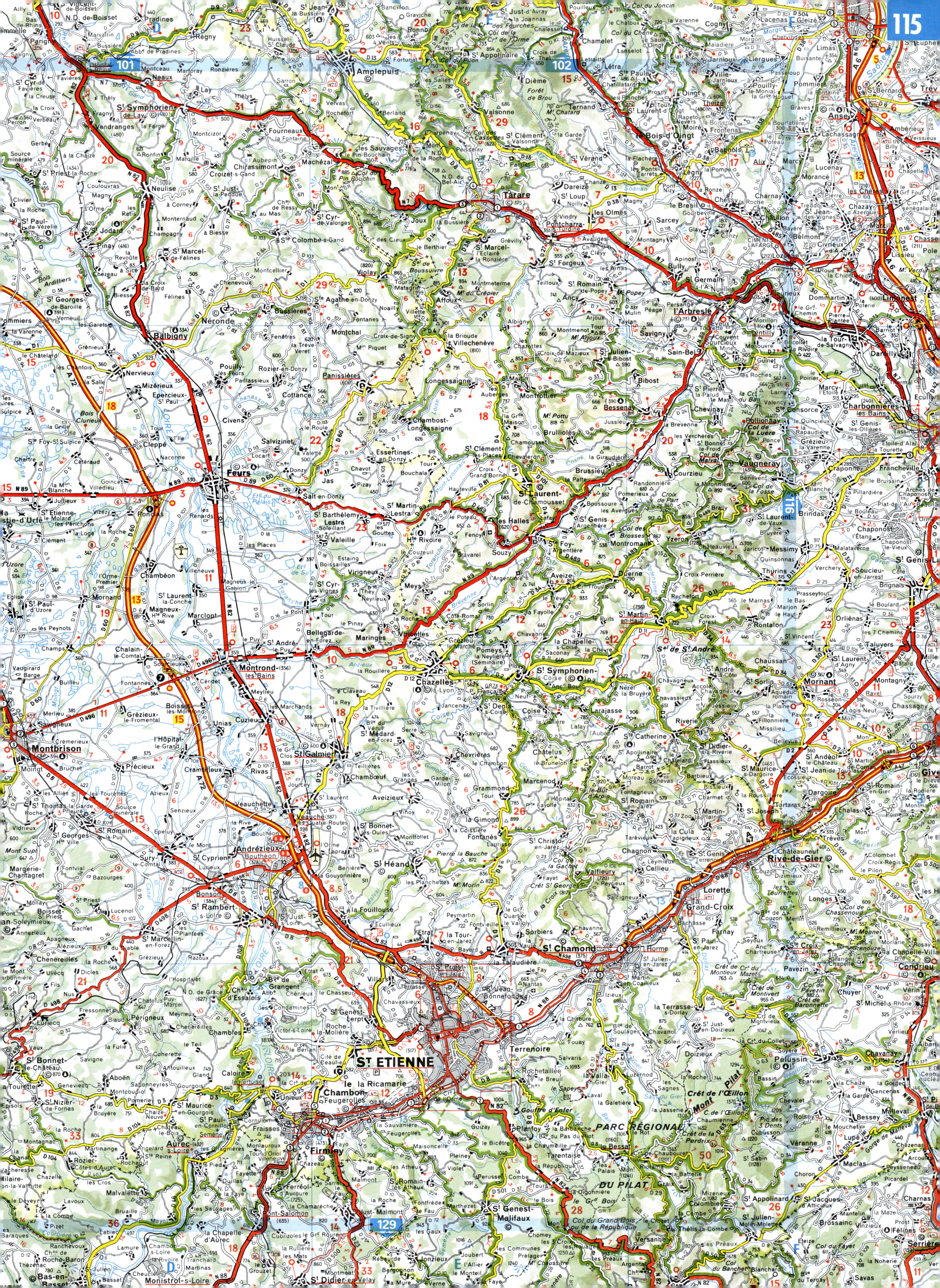

LYON
Villeurbanne
Caluire
Vaulx-en-Velin
Bron
Vénissieux
St Priest
St Fons
Oullins
Décines-Charpieu
Meyzieu
Neuville-s-Saône
Trévoux
Anse
Pérouges
Meximieux
Montluel
Miribel
Beynost
Pont-de-Chéruy
Crémieu
Villefontaine
La Verpillière
L'Isle d'Abeau
Bourgoin-Jallieu
Heyrieux
Givors
VIENNE
Condrieu
Roussillon
Le Péage-de-Roussillon
Beaurepaire
La Côte-St André
St Jean-de-Bournay
St Symphorien-d'Ozon
Mornant
Feyzin
Chasse
Serrières
Lyon-Satolas
Camp de la Valbonne
Parc de Miribel-Jonage
Forêt de Bonnevaux
A 43
A 42
A 7
Fin 1988

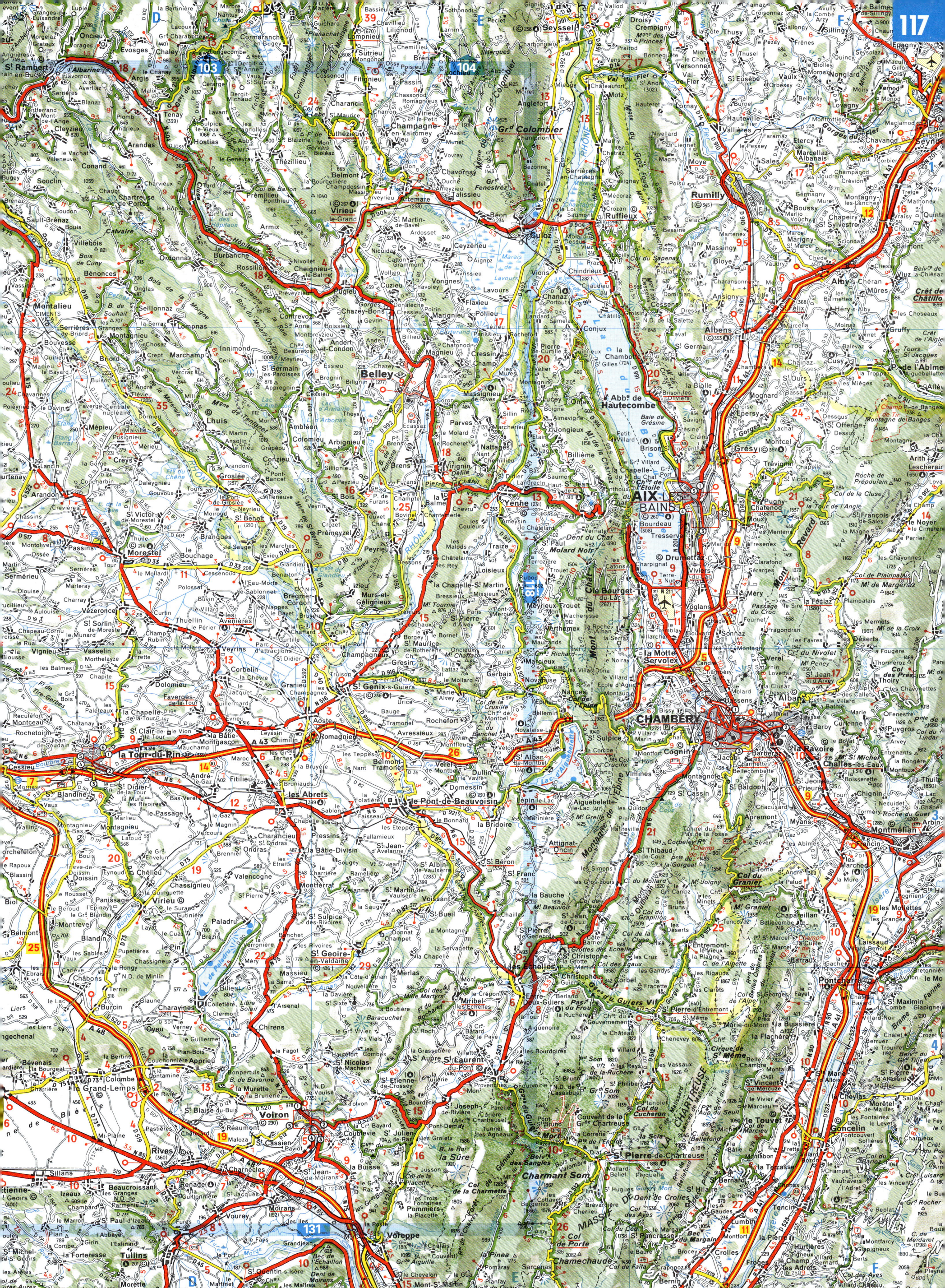

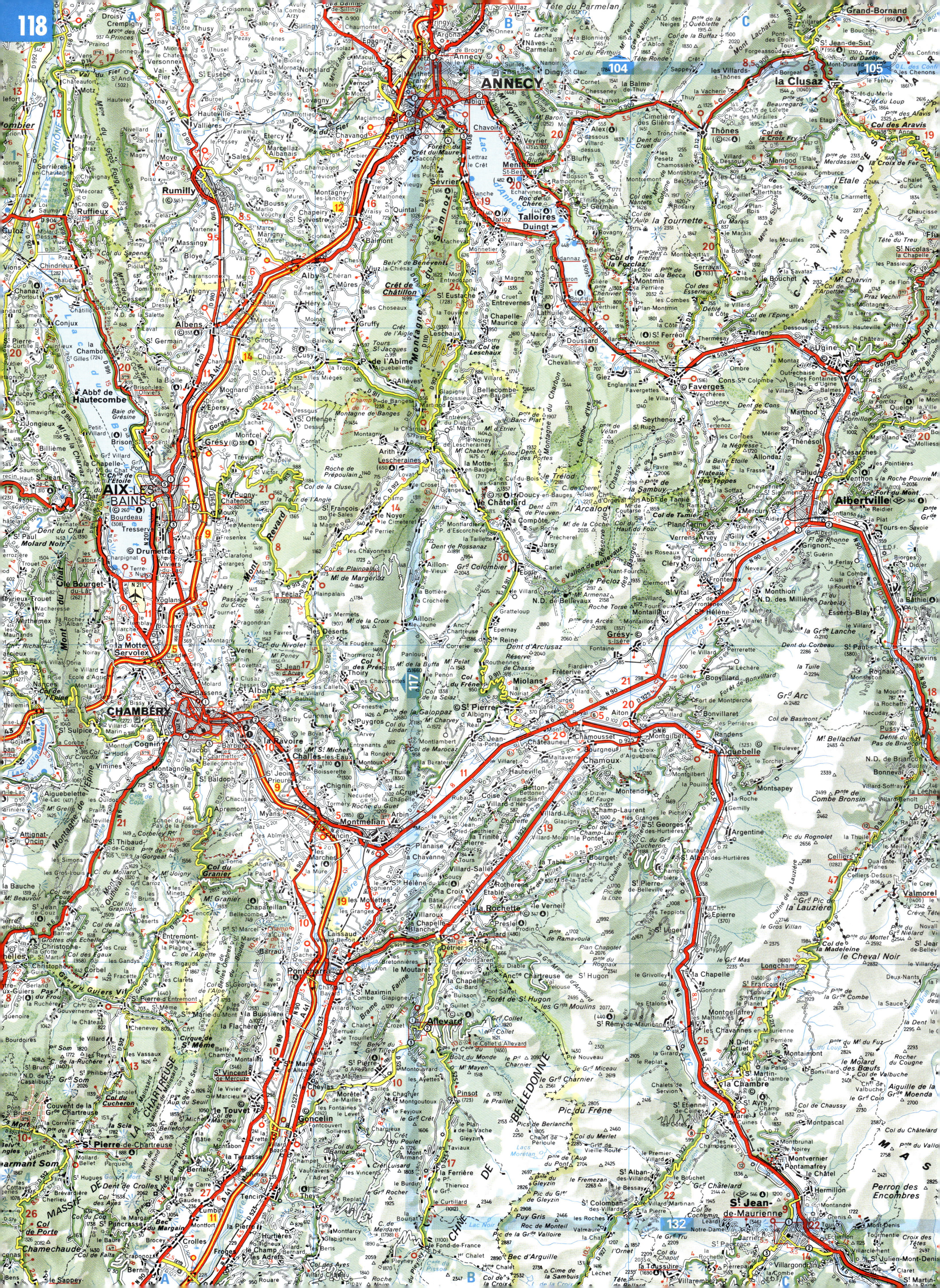

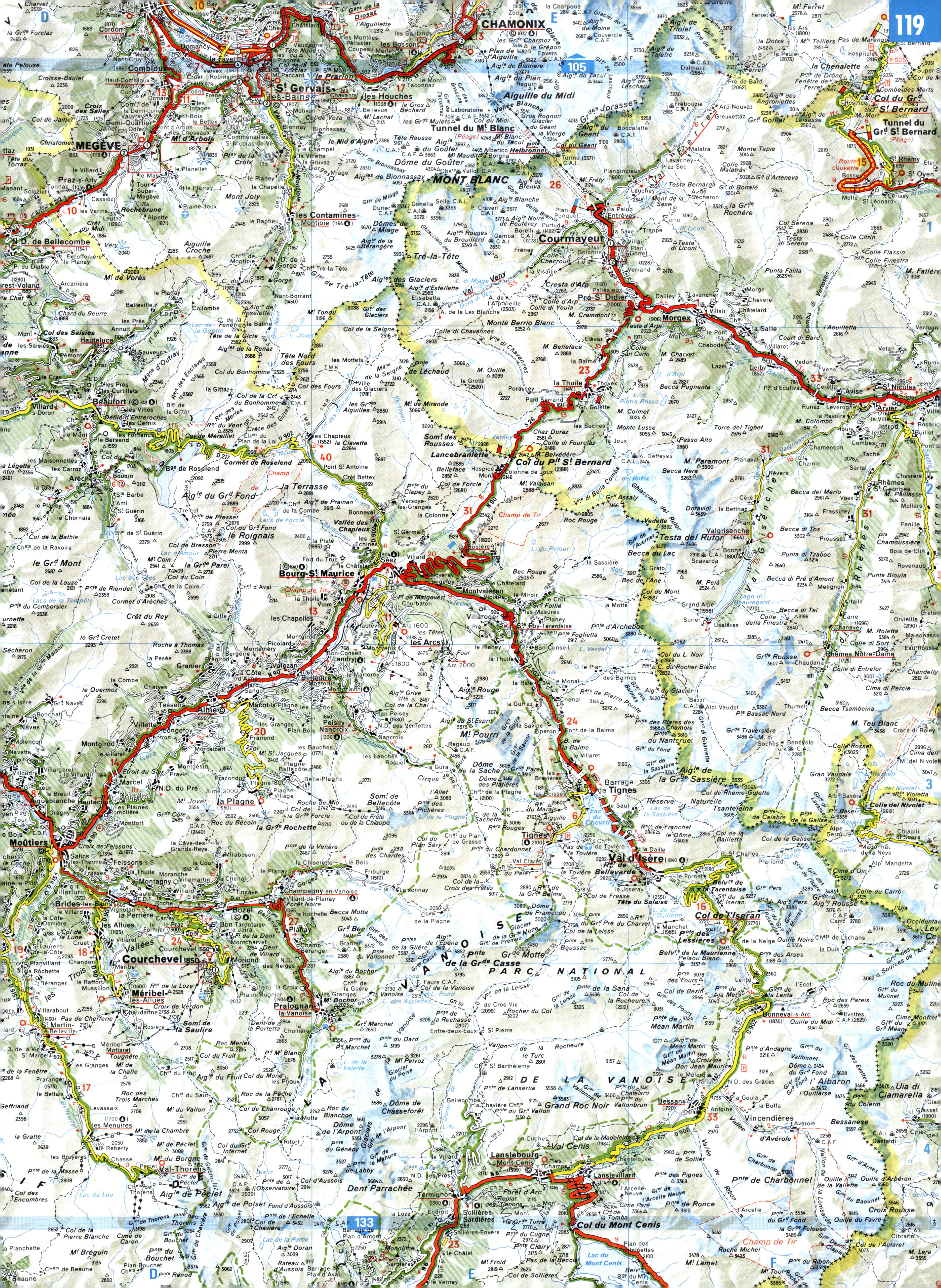
CHAMONIX
Tunnel du Mt Blanc
Aiguille du Midi
MONT BLANC
Courmayeur
MEGÈVE
St Gervais-les-Bains
les Houches
les Contamines-Montjoie
N.D. de Bellecombe
Tunnel du Grd St Bernard
Col du Grd St Bernard
Pré St Didier
Morgex
la Thuile
Col du Pt St Bernard
Beaufort
Bourg-St Maurice
les Arcs
Aime
la Plagne
Moûtiers
Courchevel 1850
Méribel
Val-Thorens
Pralognan-la-Vanoise
Tignes
Val d'Isère
Col de l'Iseran
PARC NATIONAL
DE LA VANOISE
Bonneval-s-Arc
Bessans
Lanslebourg-Mont-Cenis
Col du Mont Cenis
Testa del Rutor

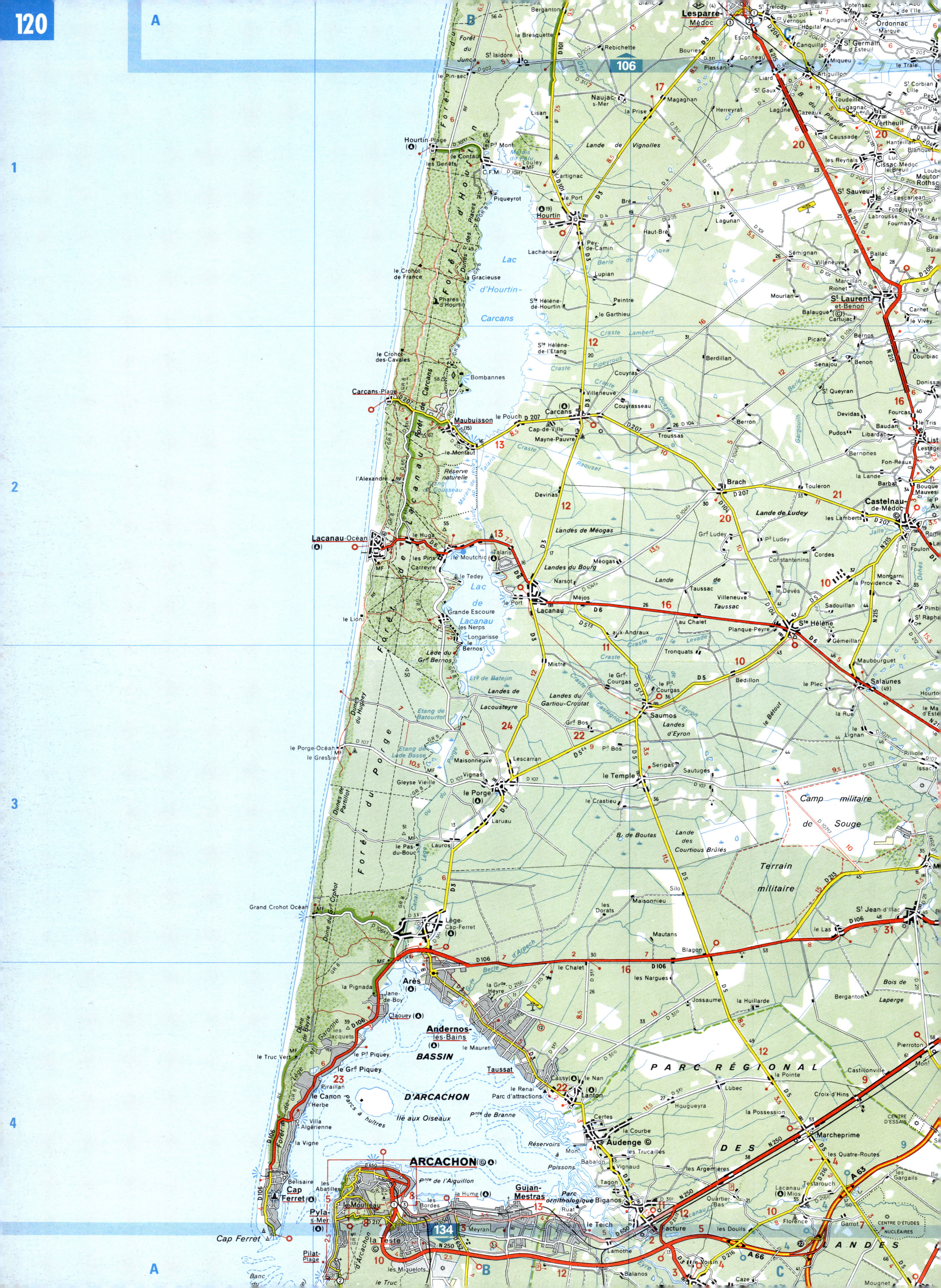

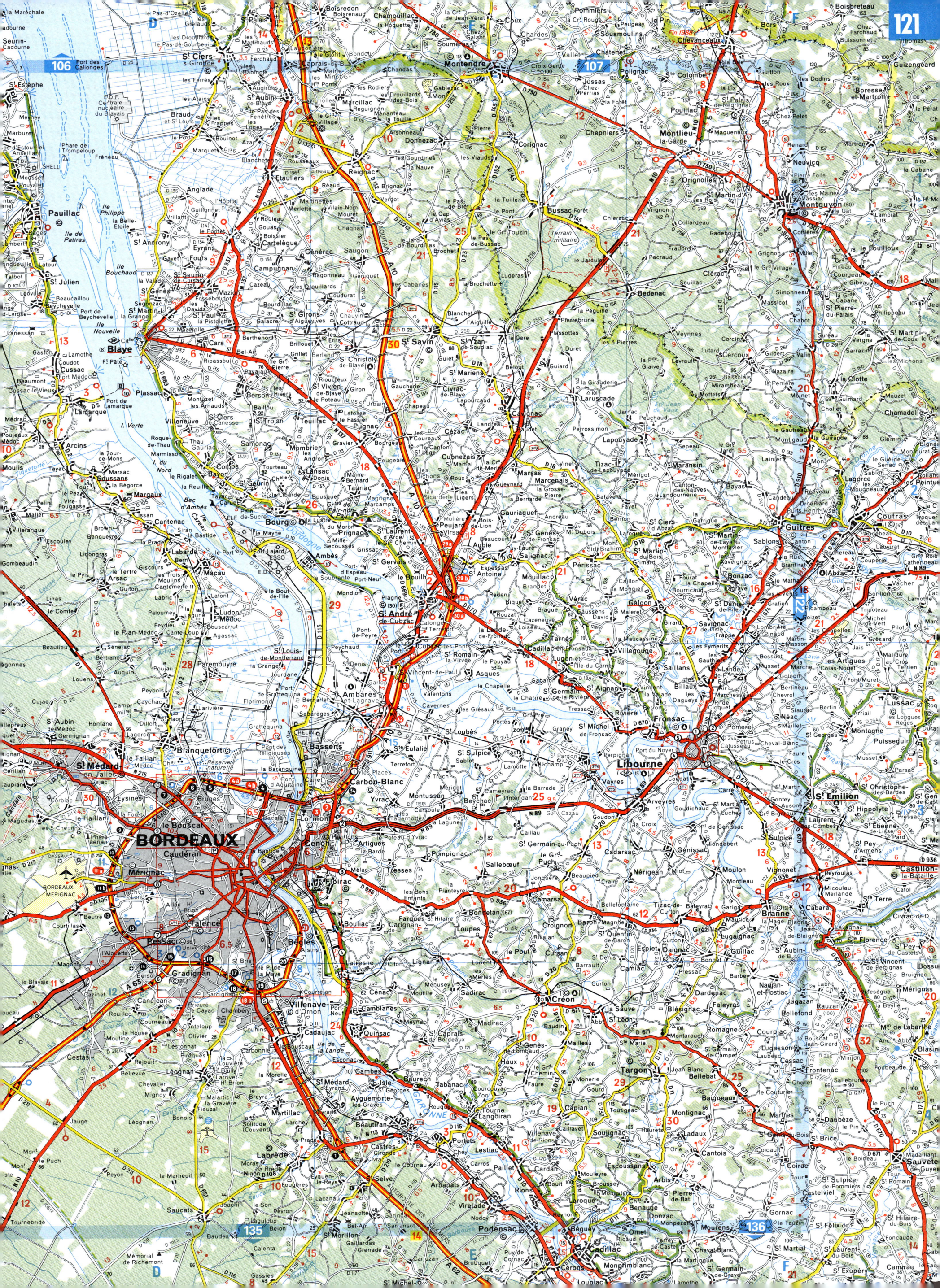

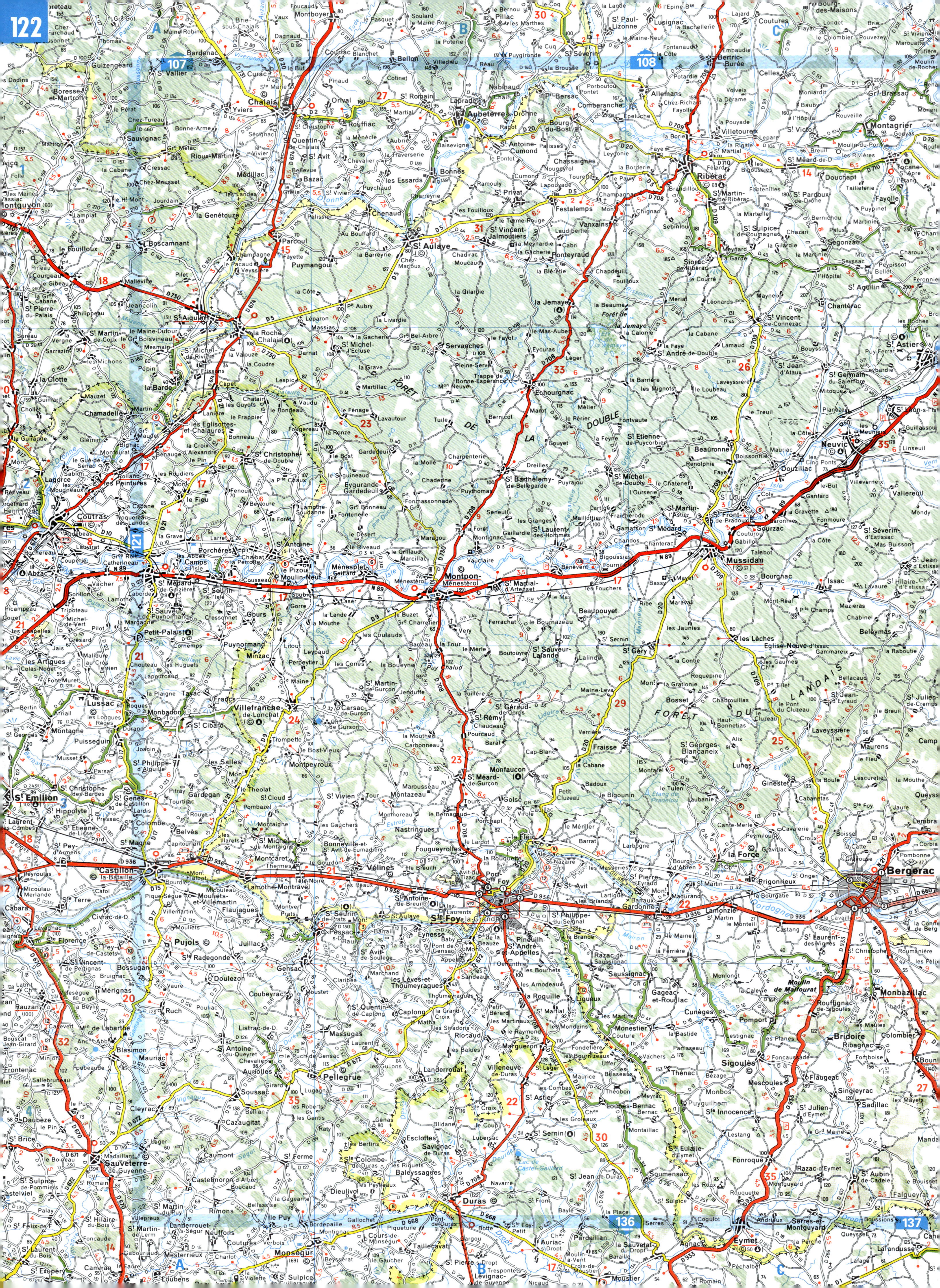

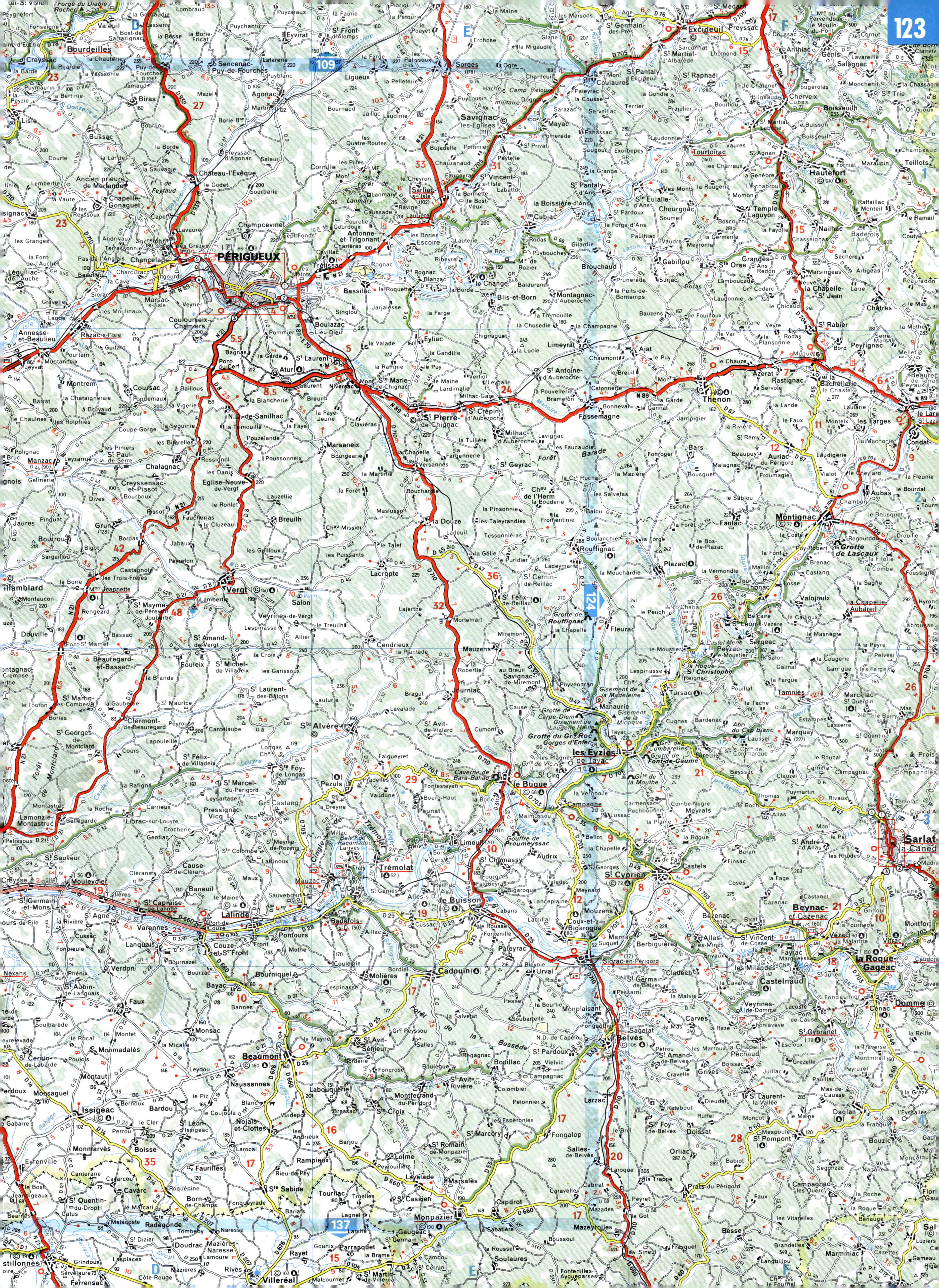

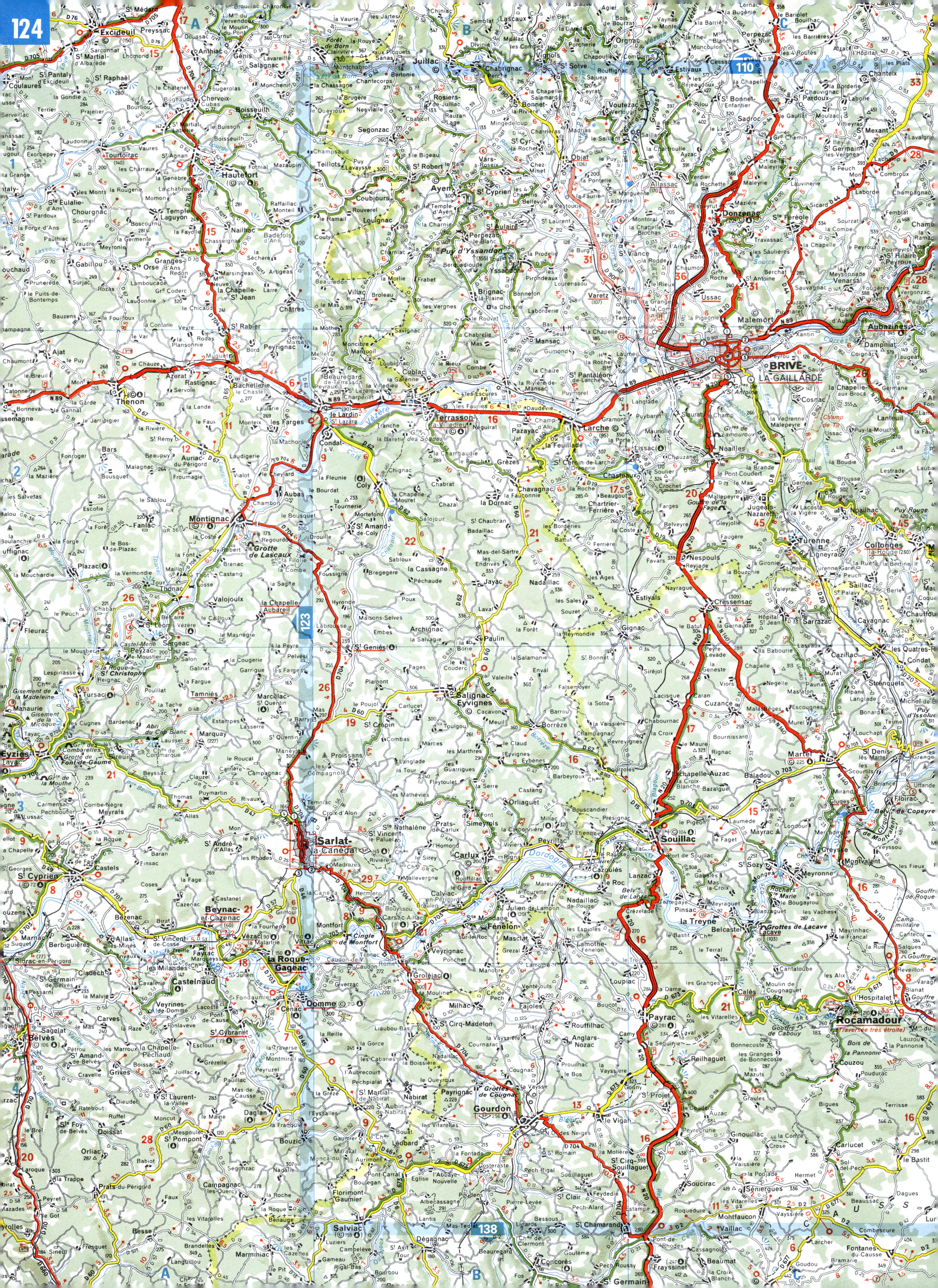

Tulle
Naves
Gimel
Laguenne
Clergoux
Marcillac-la-Croisille
Lapleau
Bort-les-Orgues
B^ge de l'Aigle
Mauriac
Salins
Drignac
la Roche-Canillac
St Privat
Servières-le-Ch^au
Pleaux
Argentat
St Chamant
Beynat
Neuville
Monceaux-s-Dordogne
Tours de Merle
St Geniez-Ô-Merle
B^ge d'Enchanet
Mercœur
Sexcles
Beaulieu-s-Dordogne
Vayrac
Laroquebrou
St Étienne-Cantalès
St Paul-des-Landes
Bretenoux
Castelnau
Gouffre de Padirac
Sousceyrac
St Céré
Autoire
Montal
Latronquière
St Mamet-la-Salvetat
Cayrols
Gramat
Lacapelle-Marival
Assier
Maurs
Boisset
Marcolès
Calvinet
Livernon
Bagnac
St Constant
Dordogne
Cère
111
126
139
N 120
N 140
D
E
F

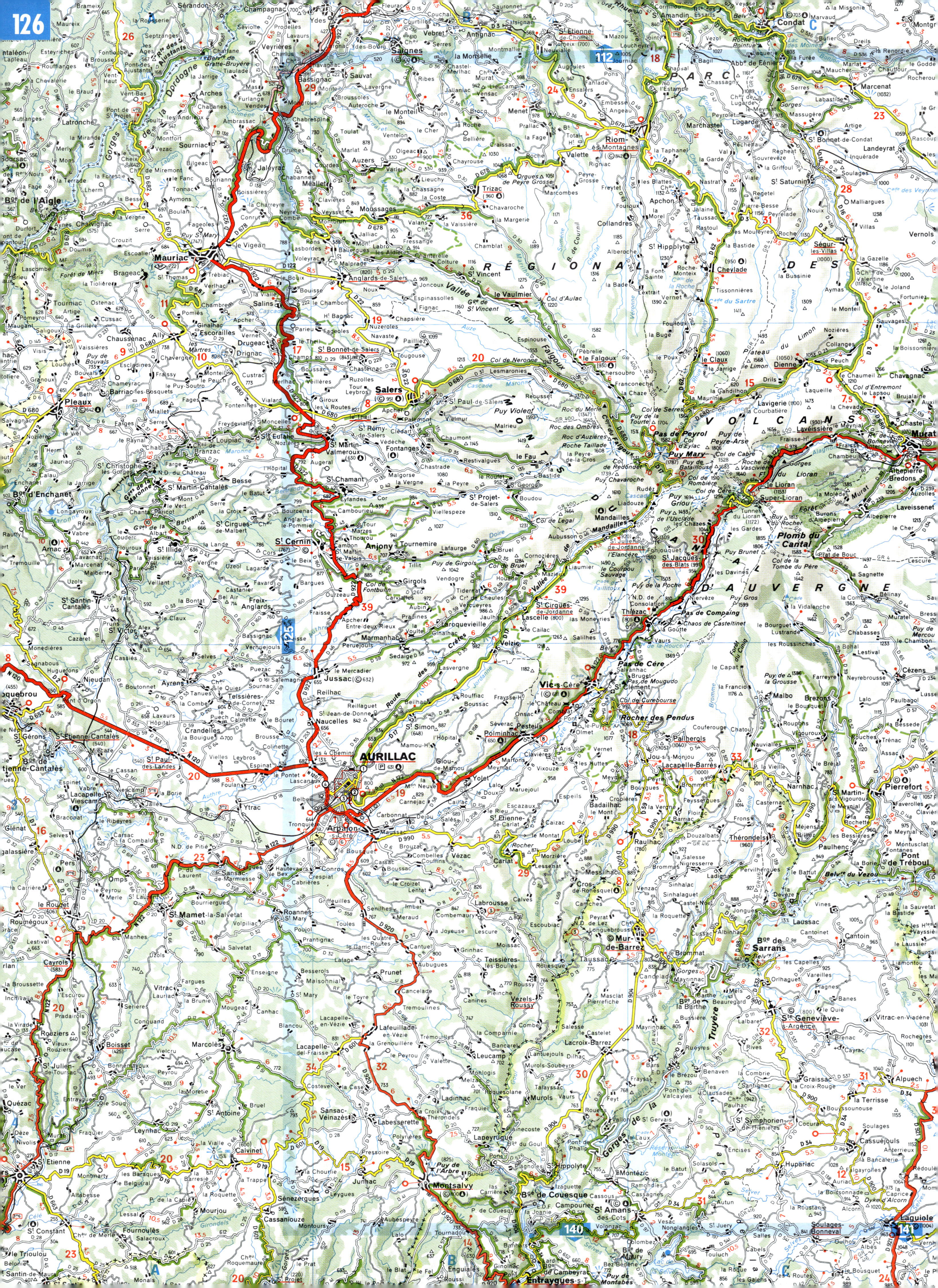

127

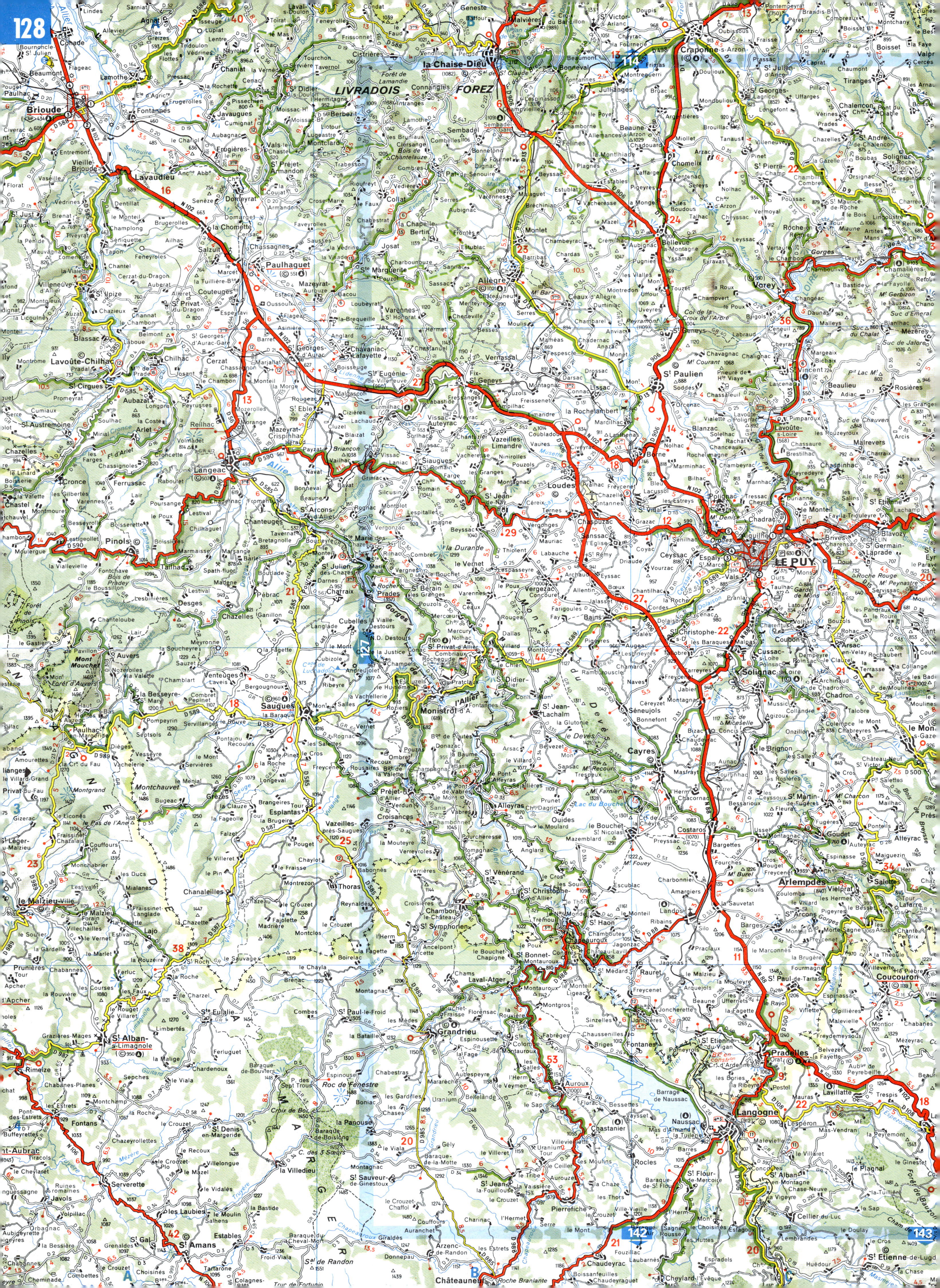

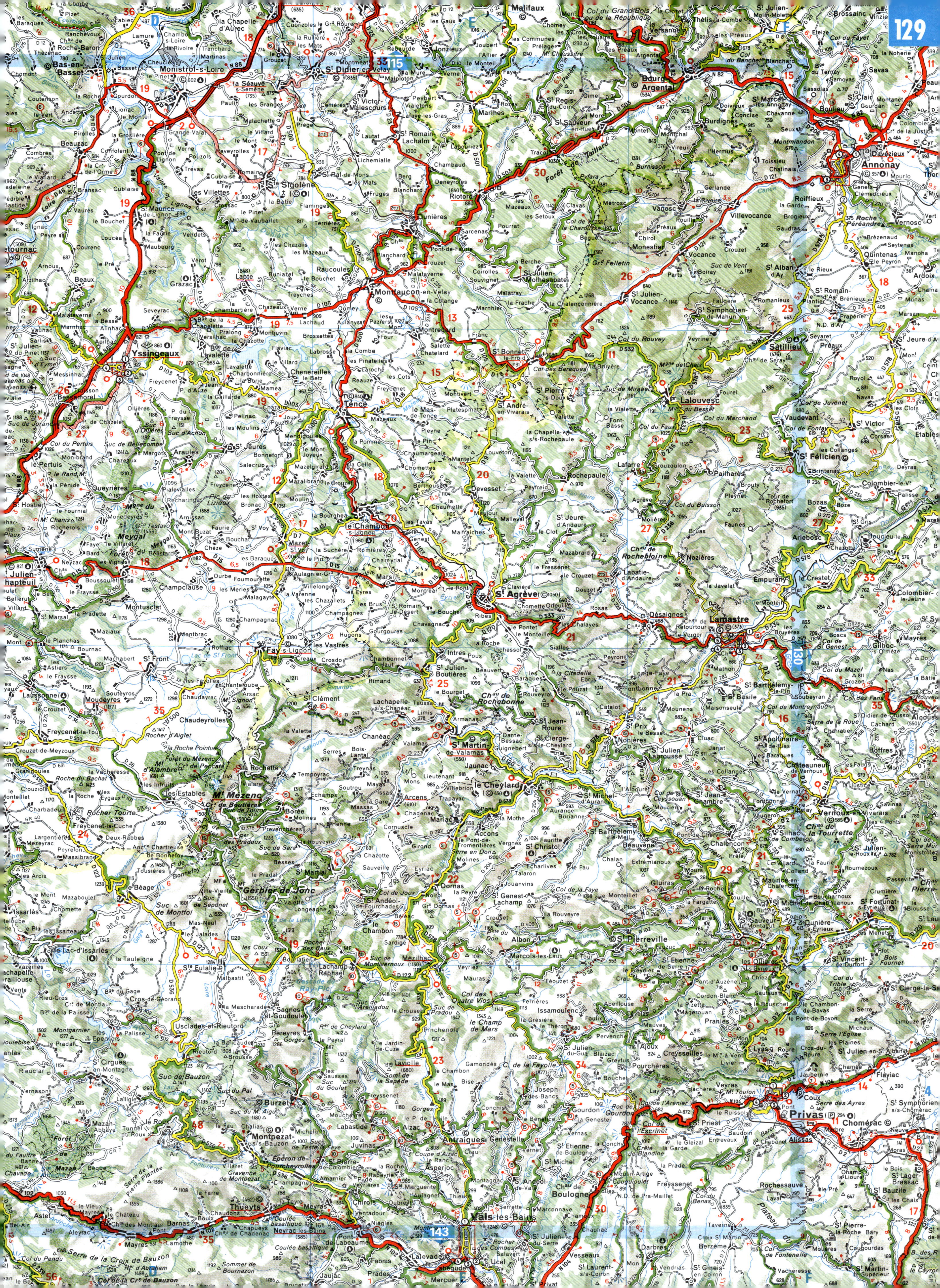

130

131

133

A
B
C
1
2
3
4
120
148
149
Cap Ferret
Pilat-Plage
la Teste
Banc du Toulinguet
Dune du Pilat
Pointe d'Arcachon
Forêt usagère de la Teste
Cazaux
Champ de Tir
Etang de Cazaux et de Sanguinet
Sanguinet
Biscarrosse-Plage
Biscarrosse
CENTRE D'ESSAIS DES LANDES
Etang de Biscarrosse et de Parentis
Parentis-en-Born
Zone militaire interdite
Forêt de Ste Eulalie
Ste Eulalie-en-Born
Pontenx-les-Forges
Mimizan-Plage
Mimizan
Aureilhan
St Paul-en-Born
Forêt de Mimizan
Bias
Forêt de St Julien-en-Born
Contis-Plage
St Julien-en-Born
Mézos
Lit-et-Mixe
Forêt de Lit-et-Mixe
Lévignacq
Lesperon
St Girons-Plage
Vielle-St Girons
Mios
Salles
Belin-Béliet
Lugos
Forêt de Lugos
Forêt de Salles
Gare de Lugos
CENTRE D'ESSAIS
Saugnacq-et-Muret
Ychoux
Liposthey
Pissos
Forêt de Ligautenx
Labouheyre
Commensacq
Escource
Sabres
Solférino
Onesse-et-Laharie
Morcenx
Sindères
Arjuzanx
Arengosse
Ygos-St Saturnin
Ousse-Suzan
LANDES DE GASCOGNE

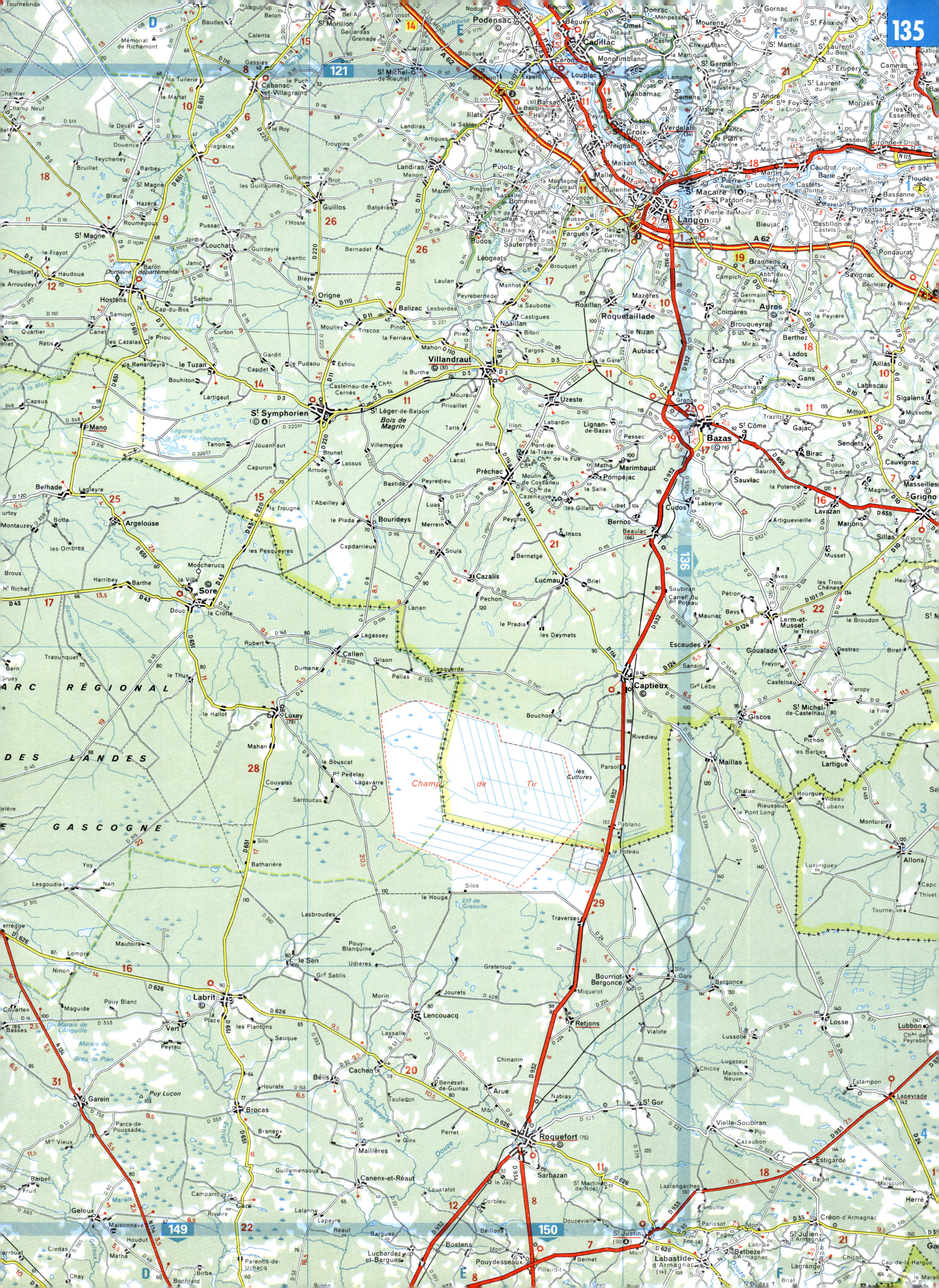

136

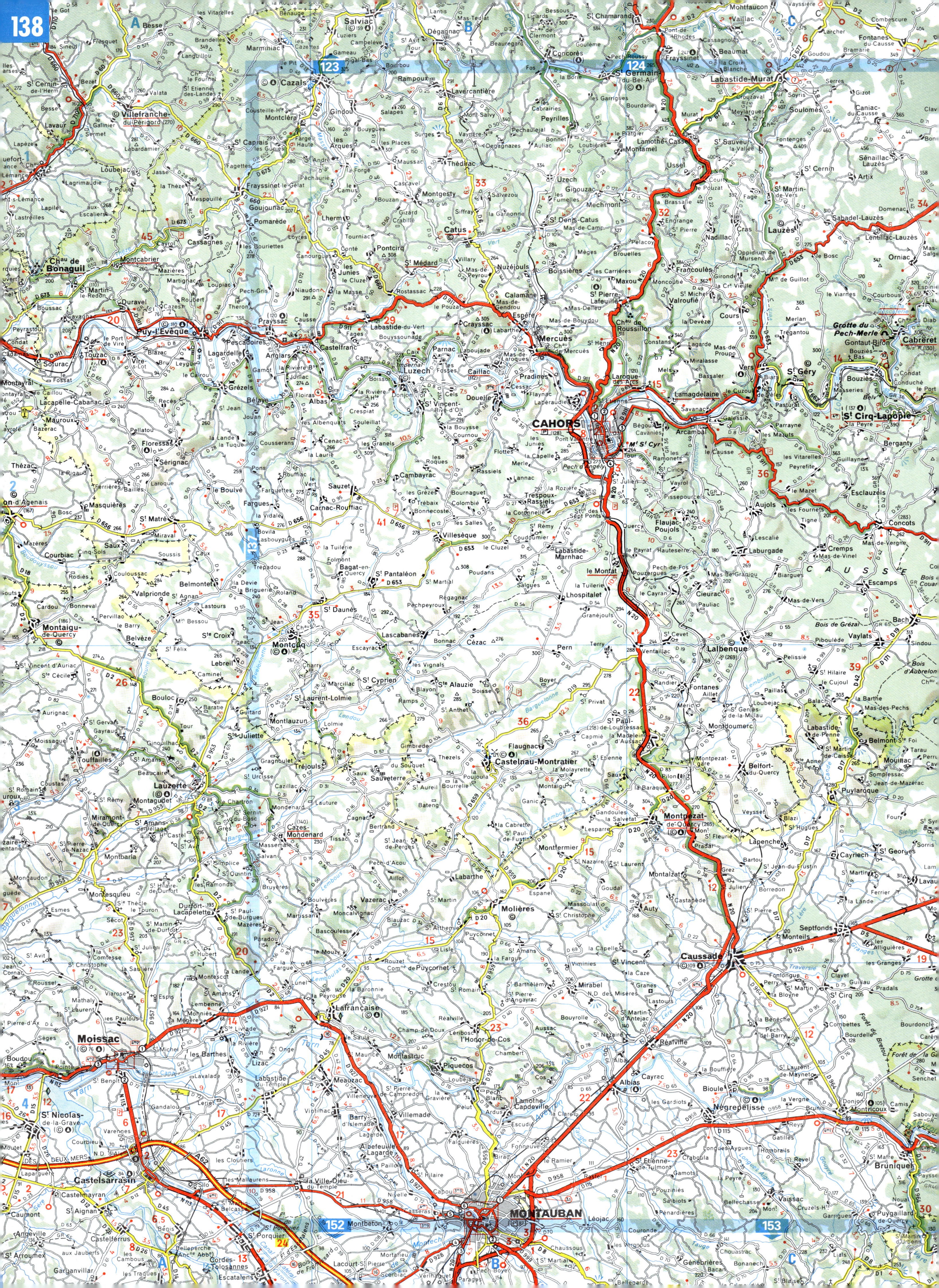

Figeac
Capdenac
Decazeville
Aubin
Cransac
Montbazens
Rignac
Villeneuve
Villefranche-de-Rouergue
Cajarc
Limogne
Caylus
St Antonin-Noble-Val
Najac
Laguépie
Rieupeyroux
La Salvetat-Peyralès
Naucelle
Pampelonne
Carmaux
Cordes
Monestiés
Valderiès
Conques
Viaduc du Viaur
Forêt de Grésigne
Causse de Limogne
Livernon
Assier
Sauliac-s-Célé
Marcillac
Bournazel
Vaour
Labarthe-Bleys
Mirandol-Bourgnounac
Tanus
Lunac
Sauveterre-de-Rouergue
125
140
153

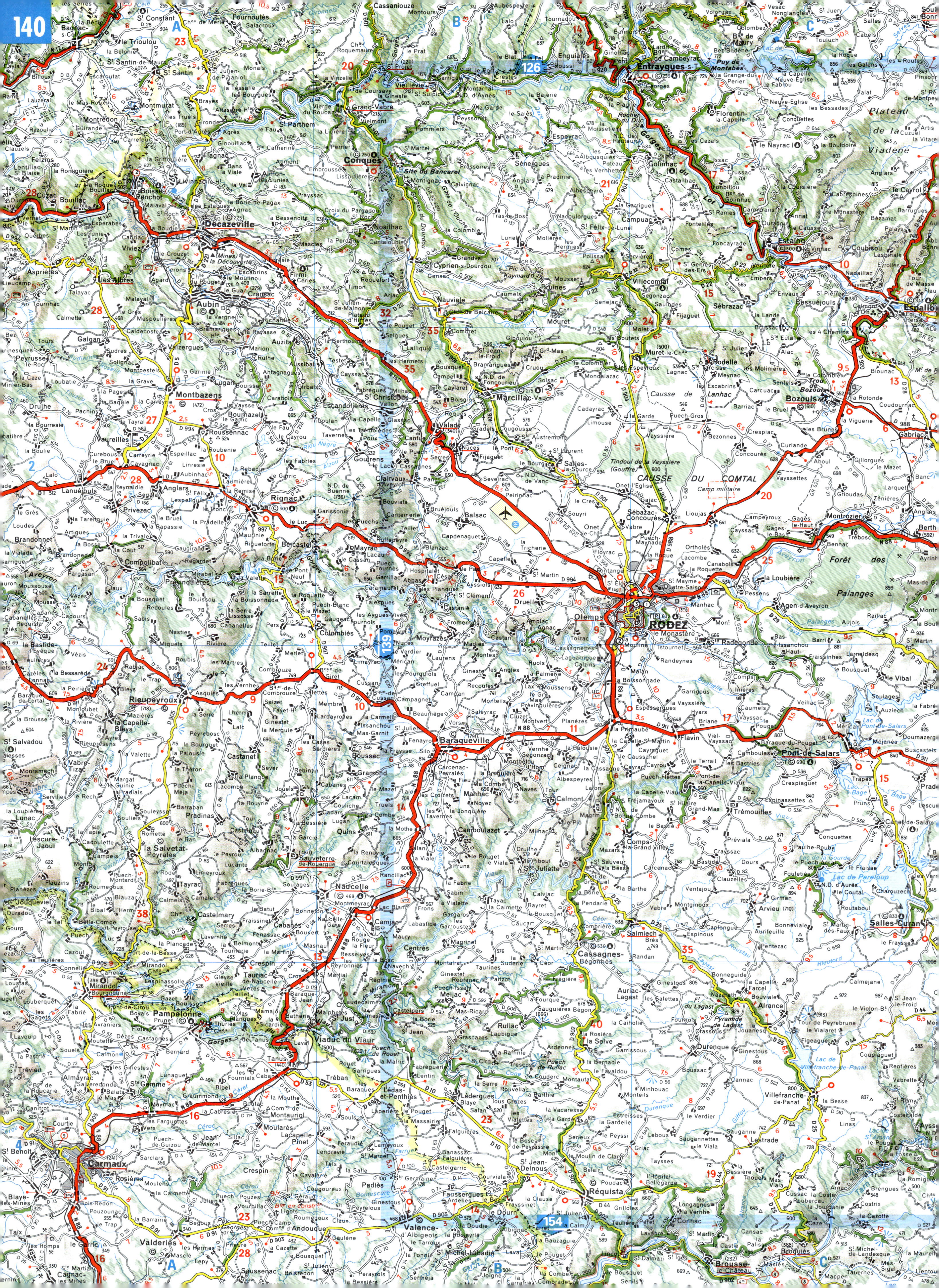

Laguiole
Nasbinals
Aubrac
St Chély-d'Aubrac
Marvejols
Chanac
Signal de Mailhebiau
Aubrac
St Geniez-d'Olt
Campagnac
la Canourgue
St Germain-du-Teil
Sévérac-le-Château
Laissac
Causse de Sévérac
Causse de Sauveterre
Ste Enimie
le Massegros
Point Sublime
Gorges du Tarn
Causse Méjean
Aven Armand
Meyrueis
le Rozier
Peyreleau
Chaos de Montpellier-le-Vieux
Millau
Causse Noir
Causse du Larzac
la Cavalerie
Nant
Trèves
St Rome-de-Tarn
St Beauzély
Vézins-de-Lévézou
Lévézou
Plateau
Grotte de Dargilan
Gorges de la Jonte
St Jean-du-Bruel
Mende
Balsièges
St Amans
Prinsuéjols
Marchastel
Sauveterre
Roquefort
127
142
155

127
128
Châteauneuf-de-Randon
Chaudeyrac
Truc de Fortunio
Plateau du Palais du Roi
Lac de Charpal
Mende
Badaroux
Balsièges
Chanac
Bagnols-les-Bains
Le Bleymard
Laubert
Montbel
Causse de Montbel
Montagne du Goulet
Villefort
St Étienne-du-Valdonnez
Col de Montmirat
Sauveterre
Causse de Sauveterre
Parc National
Mont Lozère
Col de Finiels
Le Pont-de-Montvert
Florac
Ispagnac
Quézac
Ste Enimie
Gorges du Tarn
La Malène
Cocurès
Bédouès
Vialas
Génolhac
Montagne du Bougès
Cévennes
Cassagnas
Causse Méjean
141
Meyrueis
Barre-des-Cévennes
St Germain-de-Calberte
St Jean-du-Gard
Aven Armand
Gorges de la Jonte
Grotte de Dargilan
Causse Noir
Mont Aigoual
Observatoire
L'Espérou
Valleraugue
St André-de-Valborgne
St Jean-du-Bruel
Trèves
Lanuéjols
Le Vigan
156
Sumène
St Hippolyte-du-Fort
Lasalle
St Martin-de-Lansuscle
Le Pompidou
Corniche des Cévennes
Rieutort-de-Randon
Les Laubies
Grèzes
Barjac
Le Collet-de-Dèze

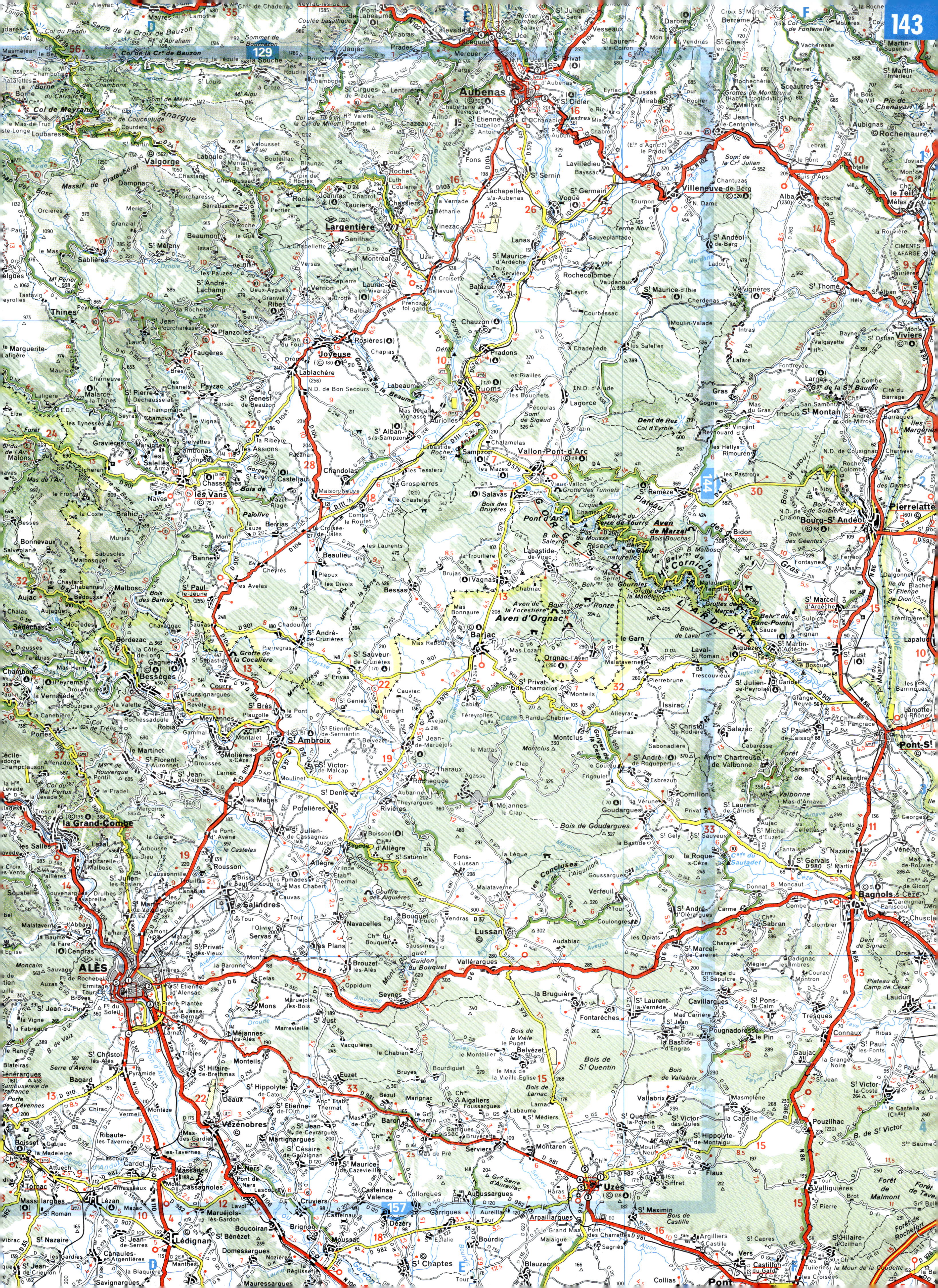

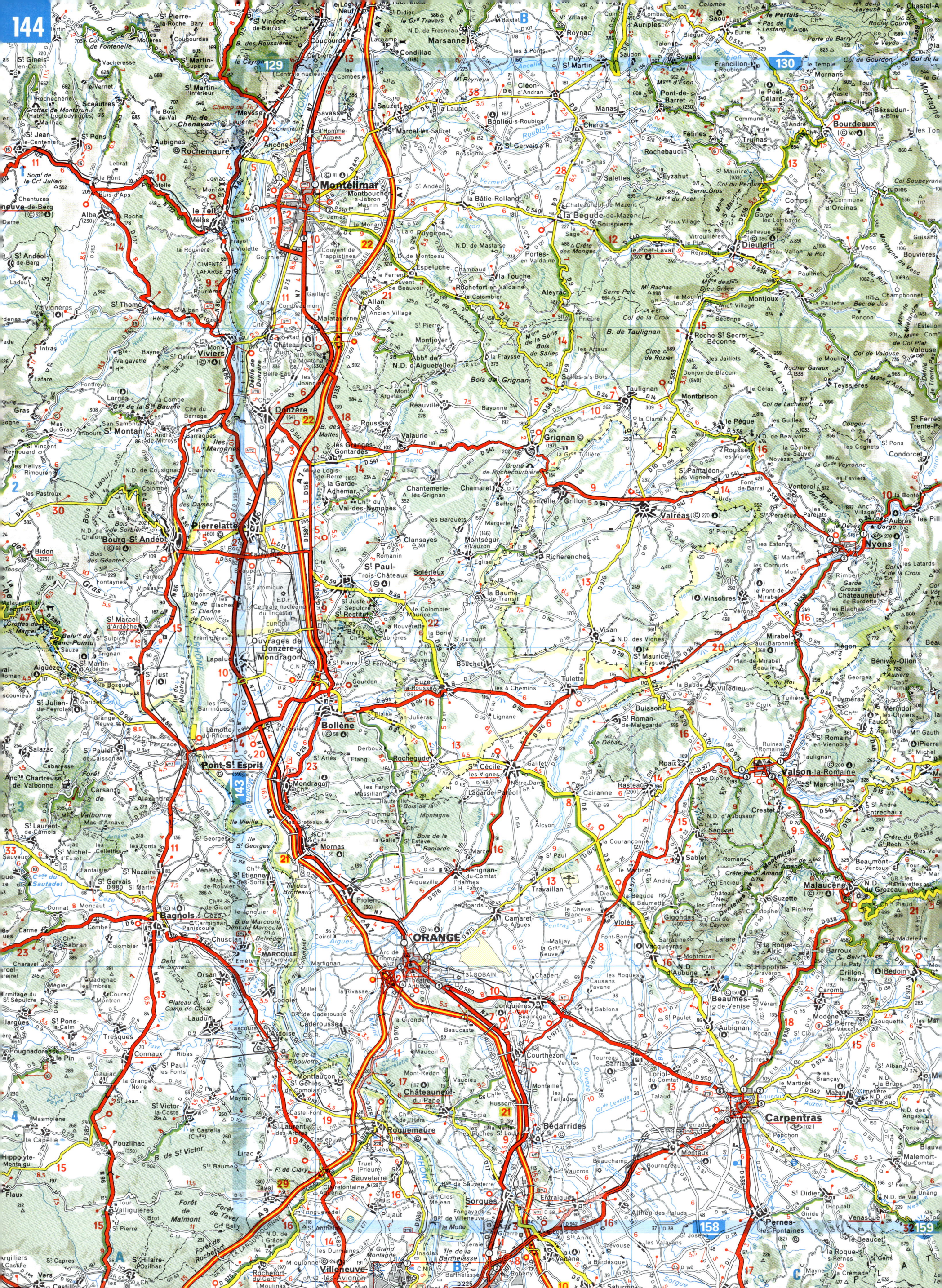

A
B
C
132
133
145
162
164
GAP
Col Bayard
Pic de Bure
Veynes
Serre-Ponçon
Savines-le-Lac
Chorges
Tallard
La Bâtie-Neuve
Barcillonnette
Laragne-Montéglin
Sisteron
Turriers
Seyne
Barles
La Javie
DIGNE
Château-Arnoux
Volonne
St Auban
Les Mées
Rochers des Mées
Peyruis
Forcalquier
Mézel
Barrême
Montagne de Lure
Montfort
Malijai
Route Napoléon
Ribiers
Noyers-s-Jabron
St Étienne
Montmaur
Le Sauze
Remollon
Espinasses
La Motte
Bayons
Clamensane
Valavoire
Les Monges
Blayeul Somt
Chateaufort
Thèze
Sigoyer
Upaix
Valernes
Mison
Vaumeilh
Ventavon
Monêtier-Allemont
Lettret
Châteauvieux
Jarjayes
Rambaud
Valserres
Théus
Rochebrune
Piégut
Venterol
Bréziers
Gigors
Bellaffaire
Selonnet
Montclar
St Vincent-les-Forts
Le Vernet
Verdaches
Thoard
Courbons
Champtercier
Aiglun
Mallemoisson
Le Chaffaut-St Jurson
Châteauredon
Entrages
Col de Corobin
Chaudon-Norante
St Jacques
Puimichel
Fontienne
Sigonce
Lurs
Prieuré
Ganagobie
Mallefougasse
Cruis
Montlaux
Revest-St Martin
Pierrerue

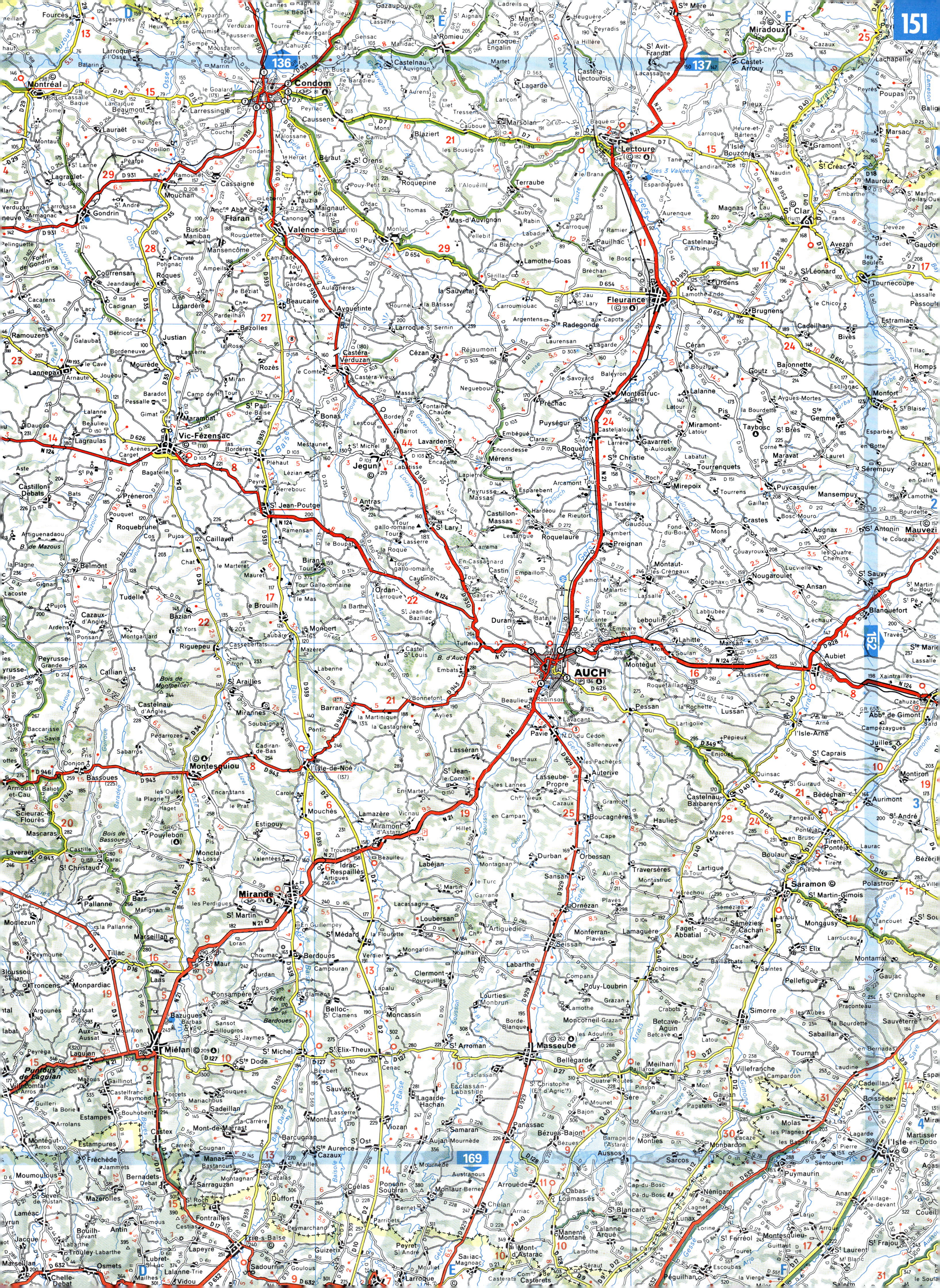

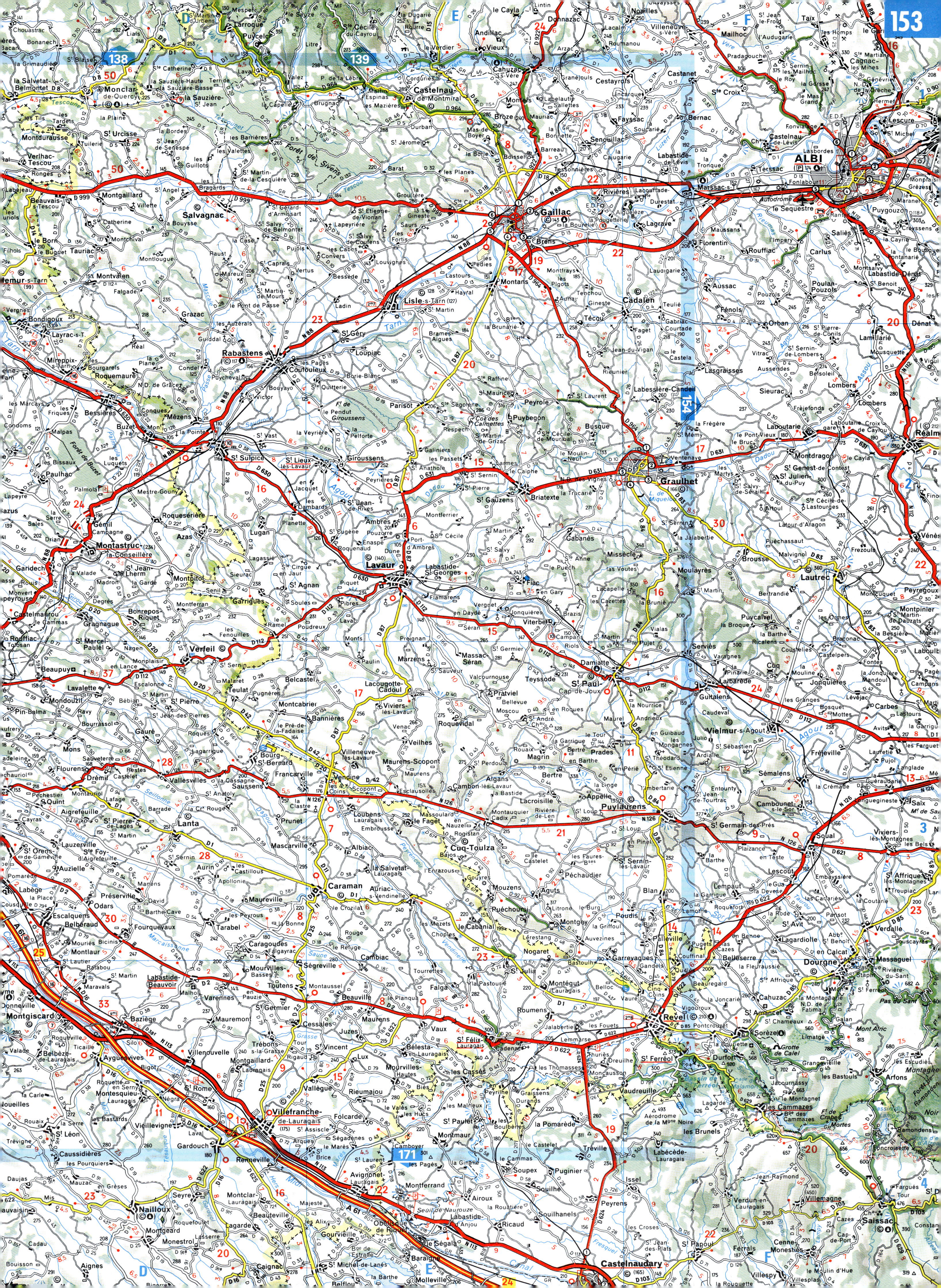

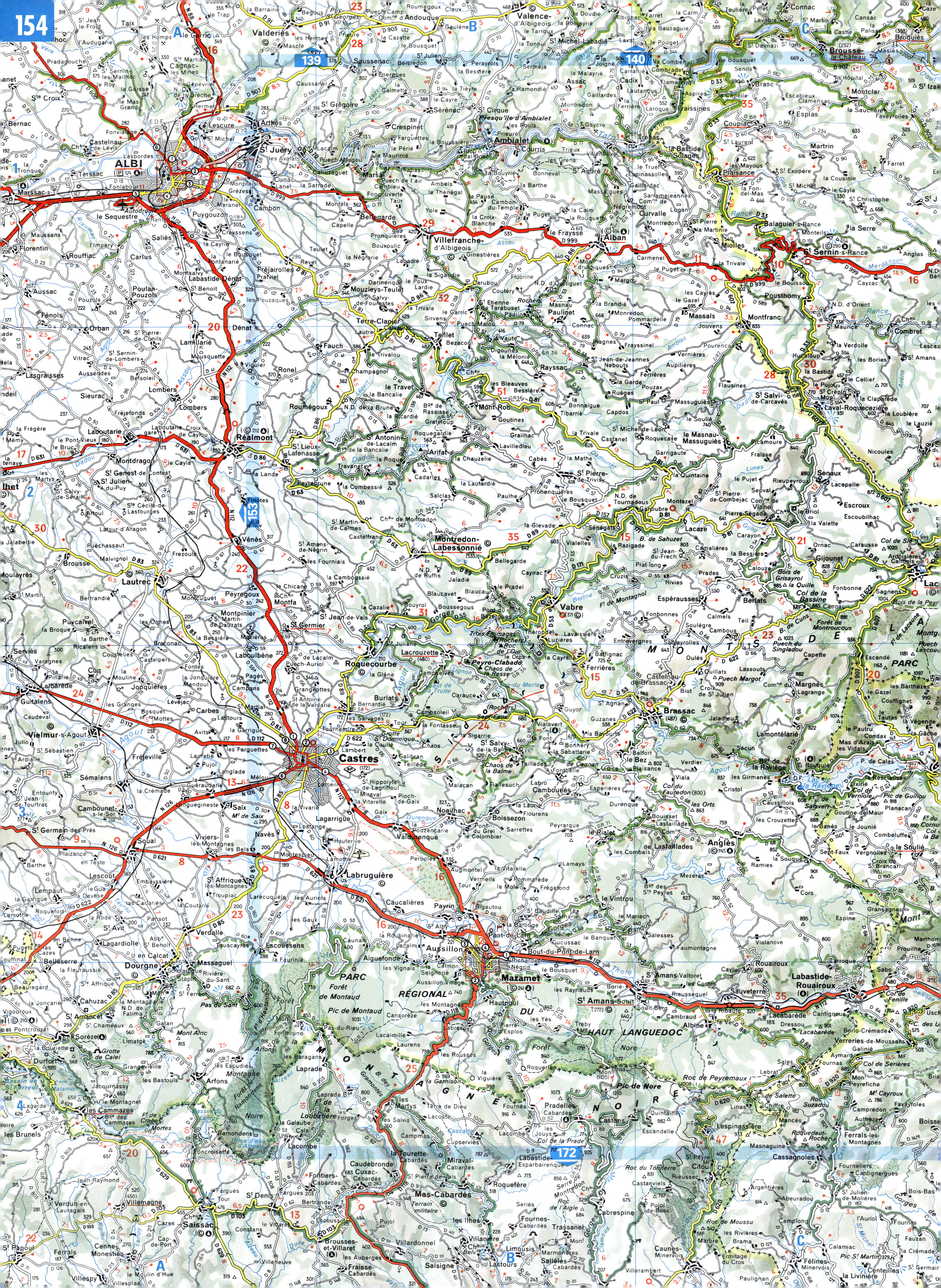

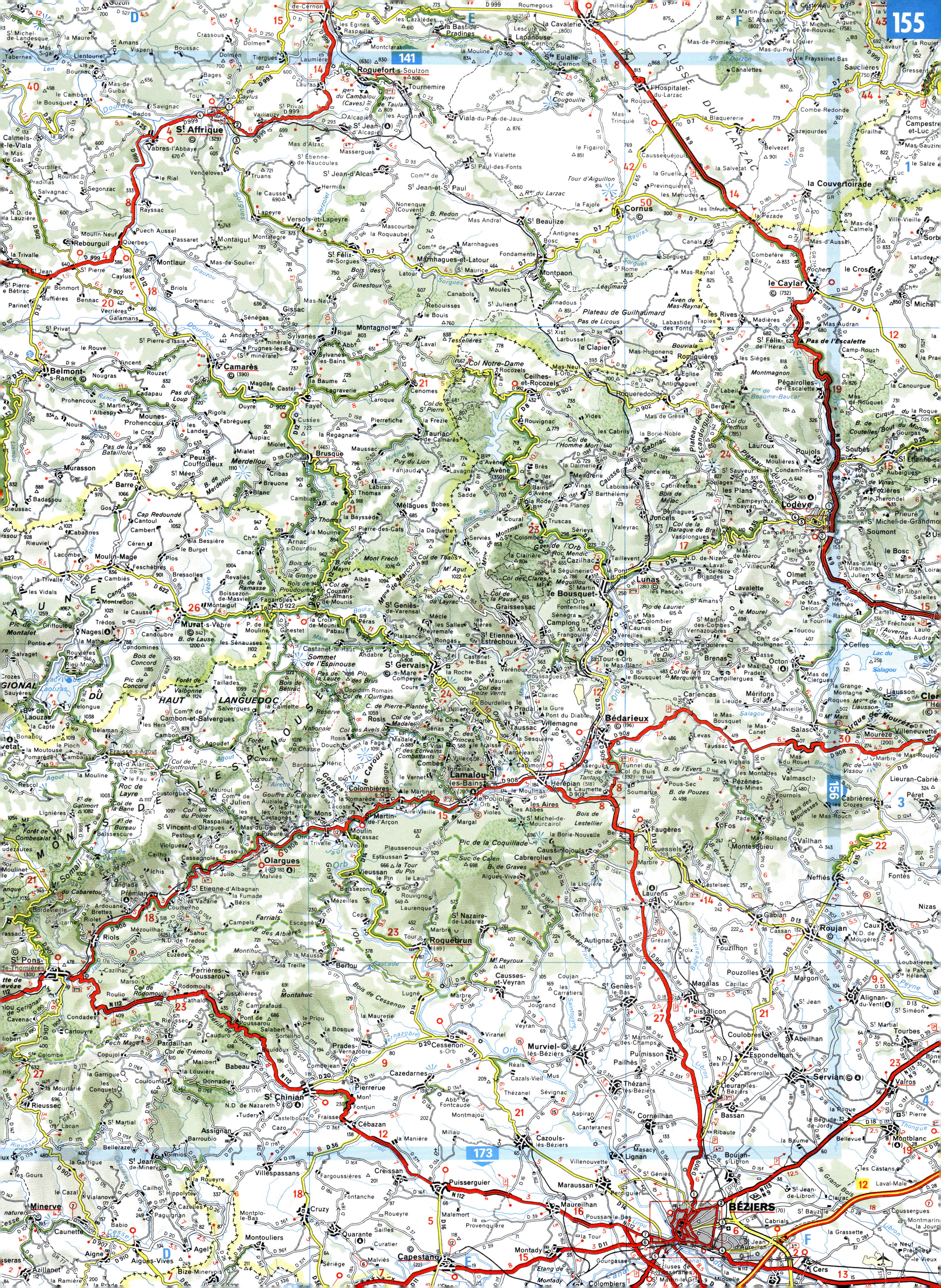

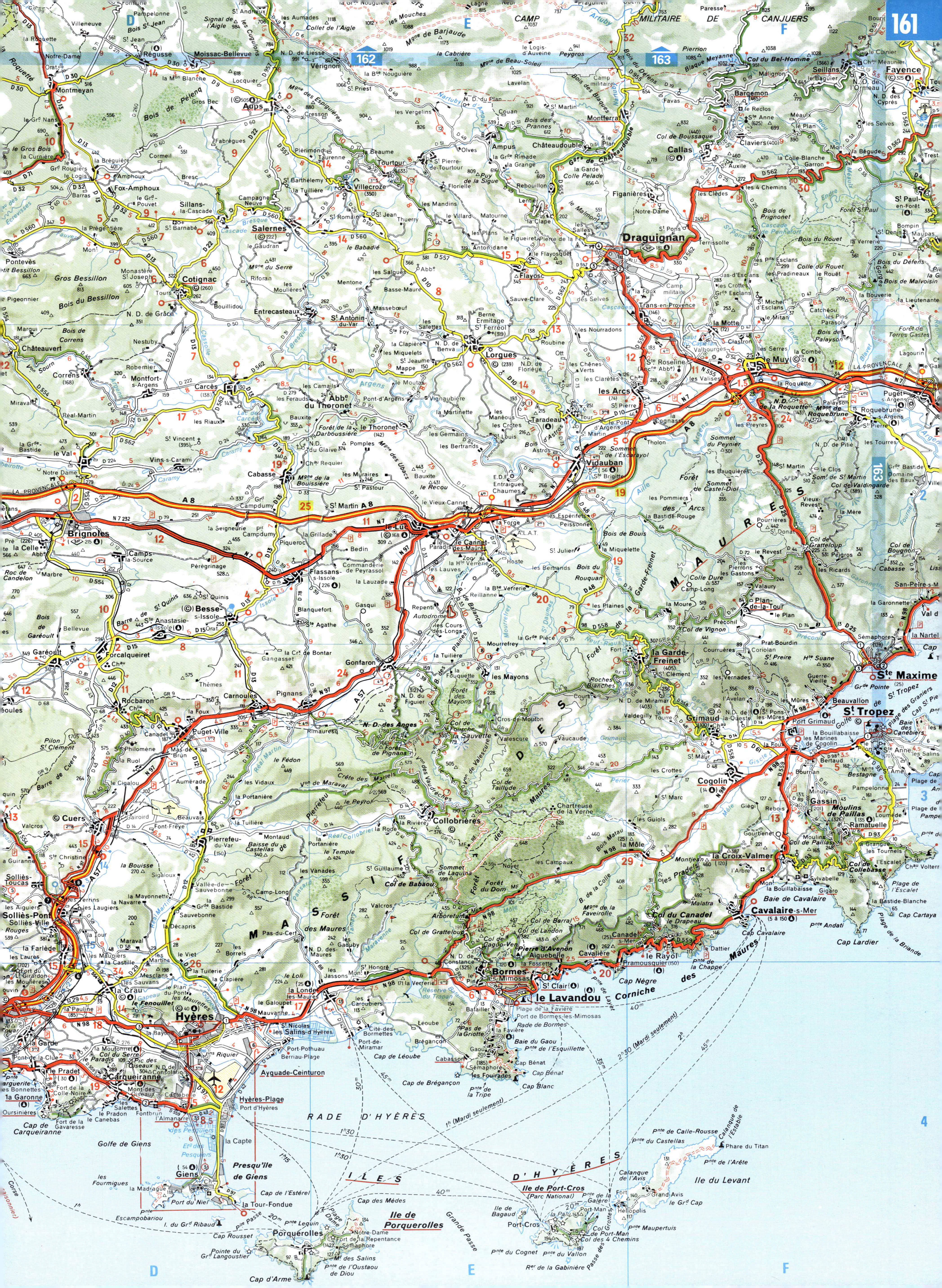

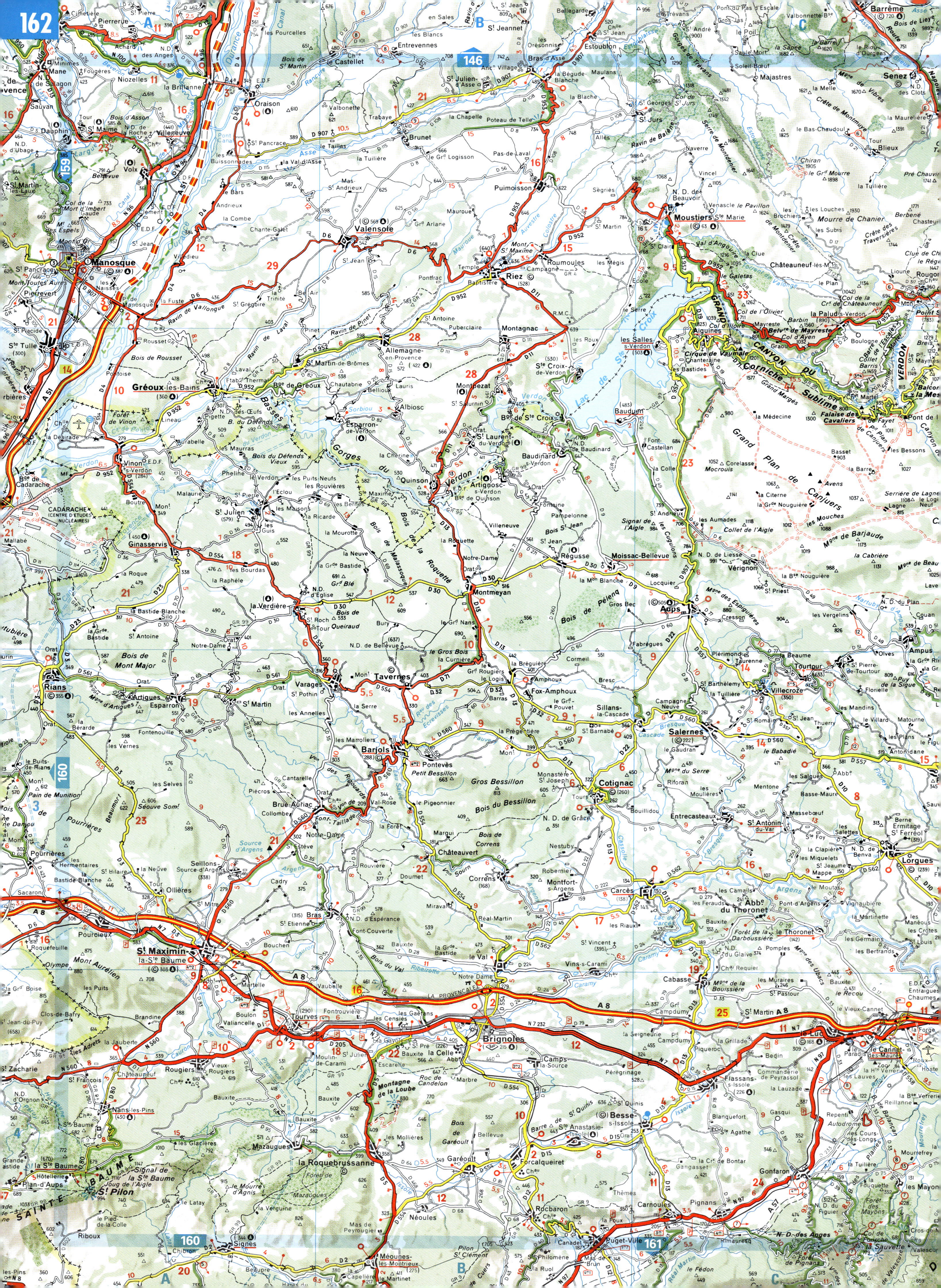

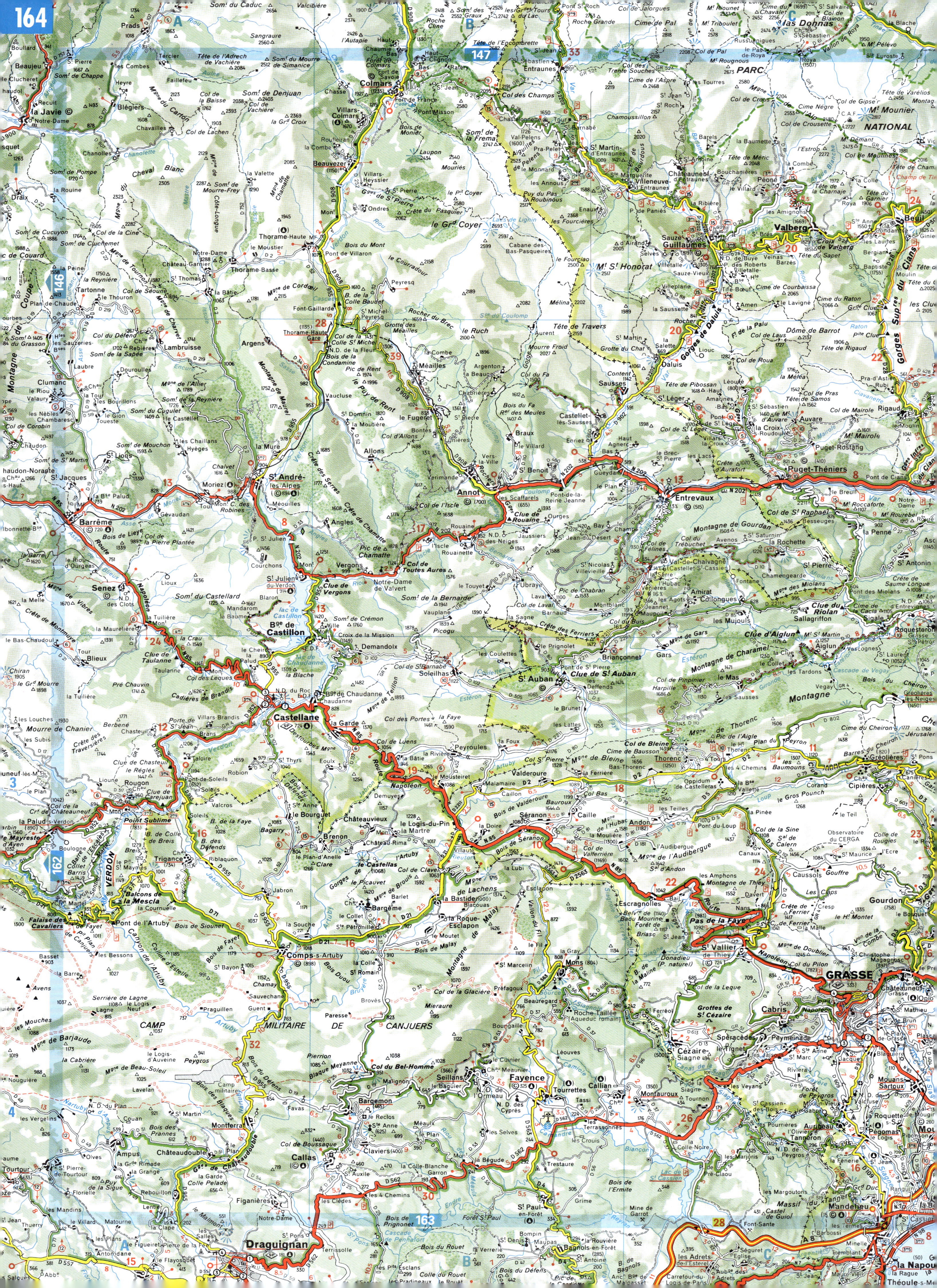

166

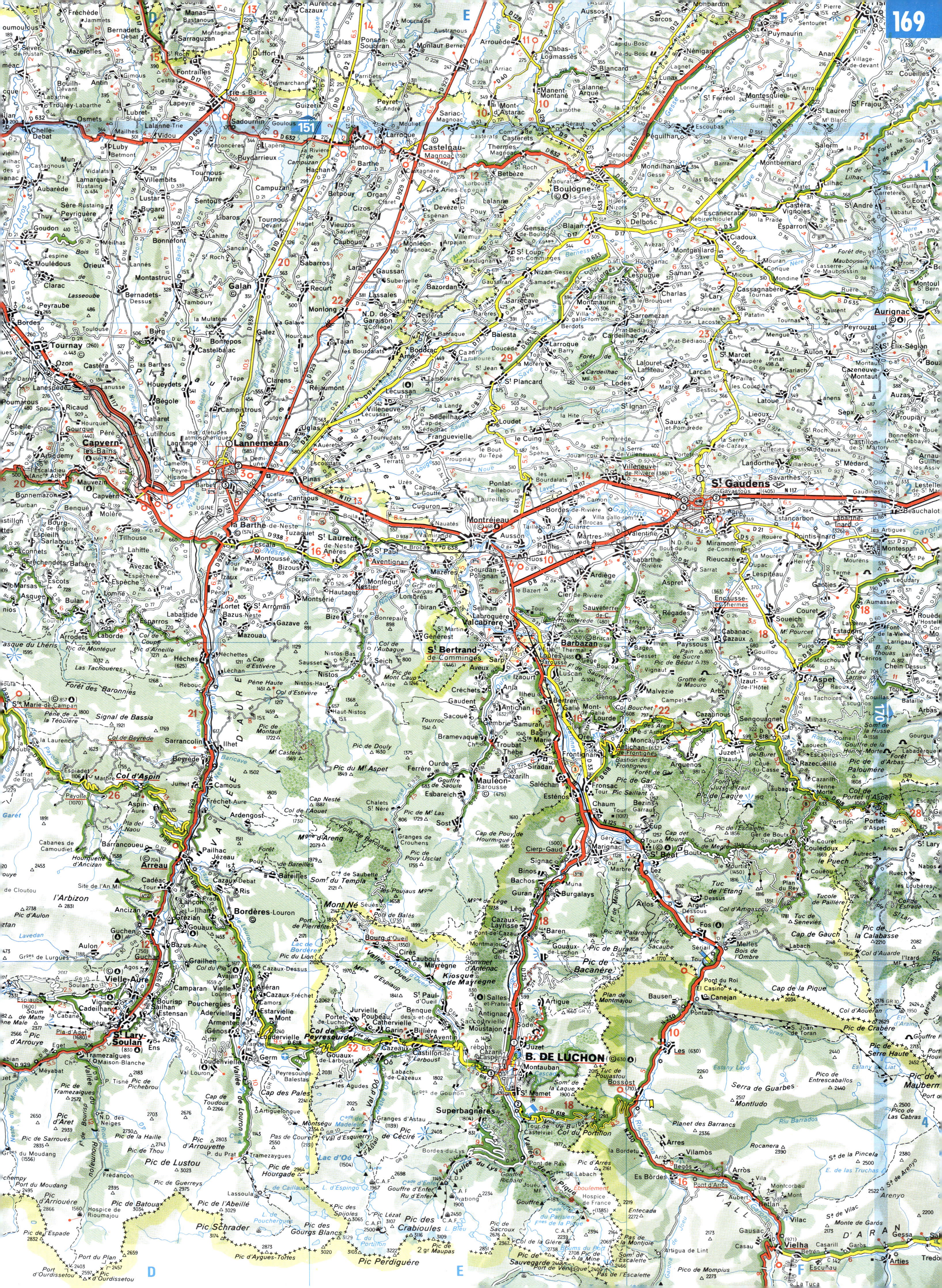

CARCASSONNE
la Cité
Limoux
Quillan
Couiza
Lézignan-Corbières
Capendu
Trèbes
Olonzac
Minerve
Peyriac-Minervois
Rieux-Minervois
Conques-s-Orbiel
Mas-Cabardès
Montolieu
Alzonne
Lagrasse
Montagne d'Alaric
Plateau de Lacamp
Mouthoumet
Tuchan
Durban-Corbières
St Hilaire
Arques
Chau de Peyrepertuse
Cucugnan
Chau de Quéribus
Grau de Maury
Maury
St Paul-de-Fenouillet
Axat
Pic de Bugarach
Bugarach
Sournia
Latour-de-France
Estagel
Millas
Força Réal
Fontjoncouse
Villerouge-Termenès
Félines-Termenès
Albas
Cascastel-des-Corbières
Embres-et-Castelmaure
Villeneuve-les-Corbières
St Laurent-de-la-Cabrerisse
Ribaute
Ferrals-les-Corbières
Fabrezan
Boutenac
Montséret
Homps
Azille
Laure-Minervois
Villeneuve-Minervois
Caunes-Minervois
Salsigne
Aragon
Pennautier
Pezens
Leuc
Couffoulens
Montclar
Pomas
Pieusse
Roquefeuil
Campagne-les-Bains
Rennes-les-Bains
Sougraigne
Camps-s-l'Agly
Cubières-s-Cinoble
Soulatge
Padern
Paziols
Vingrau
Tautavel
Cases-de-Pène
Baixas
St Estève
Rivesaltes
A 61
N 113
D 118
D 117
154
155
176
177

Foix
Montgaillard
Lavelanet
Bélesta
Chalabre
Tarascon-s-Ariège
Les Cabannes
Ax-les-Thermes
Vicdessos
Belcaire
Mérens-les-Vals
Pic Carlit
Col de Puymorens
Porté-Puymorens
Font-Romeu
Andorra la Vella
Les Escaldes
Sant Julià de Lòria
Encamp
Canillo
Soldeu
Pas de la Casa
Port d'Envalira
Puigcerdà
Bourg-Madame
Llívia
La Seu d'Urgell
Bellver de Cerdanya
La Molina
Pic d'Estats
Pic de Montcalm
Pic des 3 Seigneurs
Pic de Tarbézou
Pic de Serembarre
Pic Pédrous
Pic Peric
Puig Pedros
Pic Rouge de Bassiès
Montségur
Laroque-d'Olmes
Pic de Saint-Barthélemy
Montagne de Tabe
Plateau de Sault
Lleida
Ripoll Barcelona
Túnel del Cadí Barcelona
170
171

A
B
C

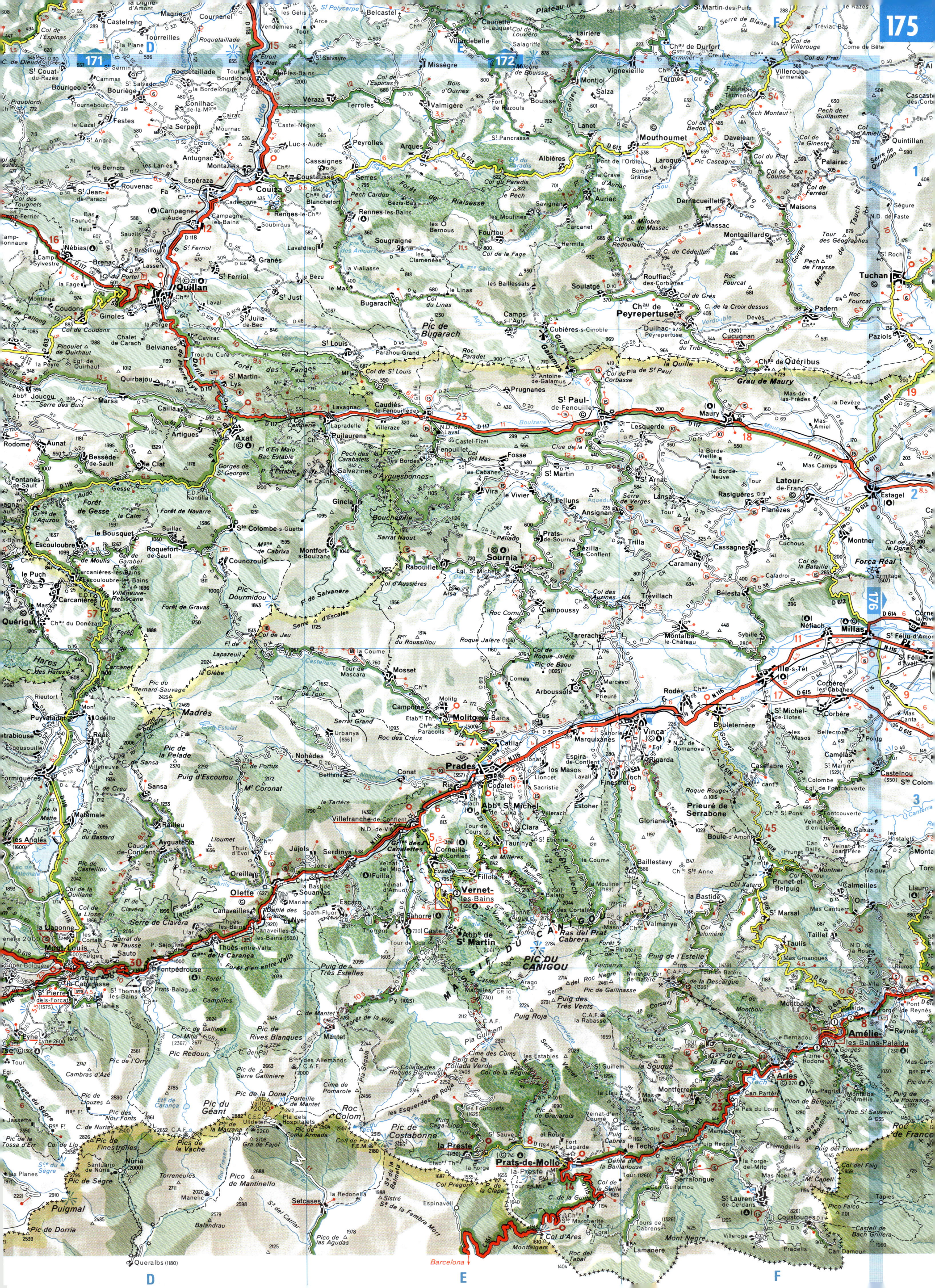

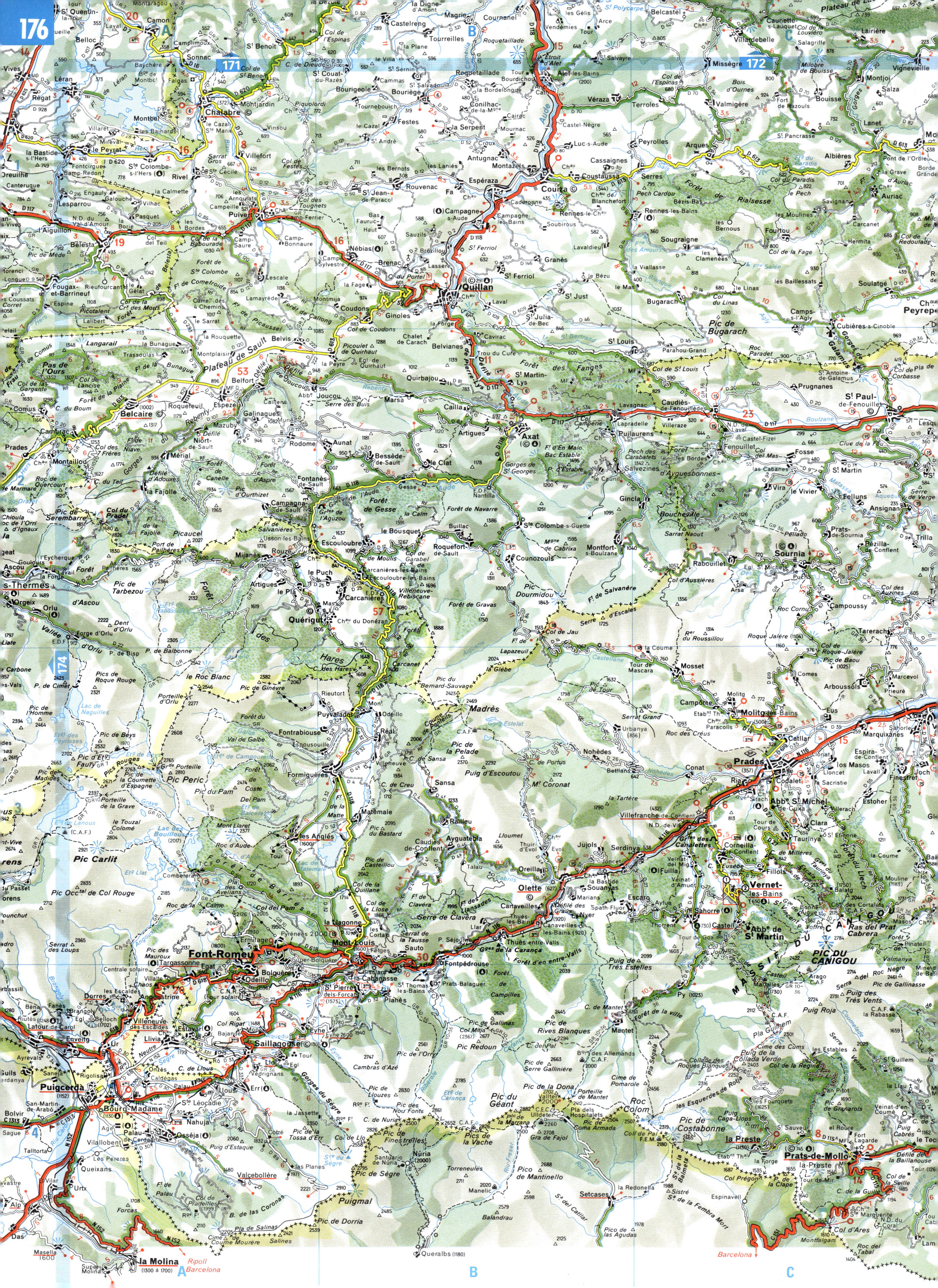

172
173
Sigean
Port-la-Nouvelle
Durban-Corbières
Albas
Villeneuve-les-Corbières
Cascastel-des-Corbières
Roquefort-des-Corbières
Lapalme
St Jean-de-Barrou
Fraissé-des-Corbières
Embres-et-Castelmaure
Feuilla
Caves
Treilles
Grau de la Franqui
la Franqui
Leucate
Cap Leucate
Leucate-Plage
Fitou
Montgaillard
Maisons
Tuchan
Padern
Paziols
Cucugnan
Quéribus
Grau de Maury
Maury
Vingrau
Opoul-Périllos
Fort de Salses
Salses-le-Château
Étang de Leucate ou de Salses
Port-Leucate
Port-Barcarès
le Barcarès
Tautavel
Estagel
Cases-de-Pène
Espira-de-l'Agly
Rivesaltes
St Hippolyte
St Laurent-de-la-Salanque
Torreilles
Latour-de-France
Planèzes
Cassagnes
Força Réal
Caramany
Bélesta
Montner
Calce
Baixas
Peyrestortes
Pia
Bompas
Claira
Villelongue-de-la-Salanque
Ste Marie
Ste Marie-Plage
Canet-en-Roussillon
Canet-Plage
Millas
St Féliu-d'Amont
Corneilla-la-Rivière
Pézilla-la-Rivière
le Soler
Villeneuve-la-Rivière
St Estève
Baho
PERPIGNAN
Cabestany
St Nazaire
Ille-s-Têt
Néfiach
Corbère
Toulouges
Canohès
Pollestres
Saleilles
Alénya
Théza
Corneilla-del-Vercol
St Cyprien
St Cyprien-Plage
Thuir
Ponteilla
Villeneuve-de-la-Raho
Llupia
Trouillas
Bages
Montescot
Elne
Latour-Bas-Elne
Castelnou
Ste Colombe
Prieuré de Serrabone
Boule-d'Amont
Fourques
Passa
Tresserre
St Jean-Lasseille
Banyuls-dels-Aspres
Brouilla
Ortaffa
Palau-del-Vidre
St André
Argelès-Plage
Argelès-s-Mer
Collioure
Port-Vendres
Cap Béar
Banyuls-s-Mer
Cap l'Abeille
Cap Rederis
Cap Peyrefite
Cap Canadell
Cerbère
Cap Cerbère
CÔTE VERMEILLE
Le Boulou
Montesquieu
Laroque-des-Albères
Sorède
St Génis
Villelongue-dels-Monts
Céret
Maureillas-las-Illas
St Martin-de-Fenollar
le Perthus
Amélie-les-Bains-Palalda
Arles
Reynès
Tour Madeloc
La Jonquera
Cantallops
Portbou
Colera
Llançà
Espolla
Rabós
Vilamaniscle
Agullana
Darnius
Capmany
Sant Climent Sescebes
Masarac
Mollet
Delfià
St Laurent-de-Cerdans
Coustouges
Serralongue
Roc de France
Barcelona
A9
N9
D
E
F
1
2
3
4

Index Register

Comment se servir de cet index
How to use this index
Toelichting bij het register
Zum Gebrauch des Registers

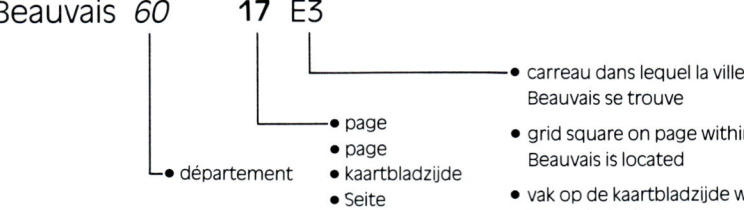

- carreau dans lequel la ville de Beauvais se trouve
- grid square on page within which Beauvais is located
- vak op de kaartbladzijde waarin Beauvais te vinden is
- Planquadrat in dem Beauvais liegt

- page
- page
- kaartbladzijde
- Seite

- département

Les localités de cet index ont un bureau de poste distributeur.

Les sorties de ville indiquées par un numéro cerné de noir sont identiques sur les plans et les cartes au 1/200 000.

This index lists all prefectures, sub-prefectures and postal centres in France.

The prominent black numbers in circles at the sides of the city maps correspond with the numbers given for main routes on the 1:200 000 maps.

Dit register bevat de namen van de belangrijkste plaatsen, namelijk de vestigingsplaatsen van de Franse overheden (préfecturen en onderprefecturen) alsmede alle plaatsen met een belangrijk postkantoor.

De overzichtskaartjes van de grote steden geven de verbindingen aan voor het doorgaande verkeer. De omcirkelde zwarte cijfers aan de rand van deze kaartjes verwijzen naar de cijfers van de uitvalswegen op de kaartbladzijden in deze atlas.

Die im Register enthaltenen Orte sind entweder Präfekturen, Unterpräfekturen oder Postleitzentren in Frankreich.

Die in schwarz gedruckten und durch Kreise hervorgehobenen Zahlen an den Seitenleisten der Übersichtspläne der wichtigsten Städte entsprechen in den Karten 1:200.000 der für Durchgangsstraßen verwendeten Numerierung.

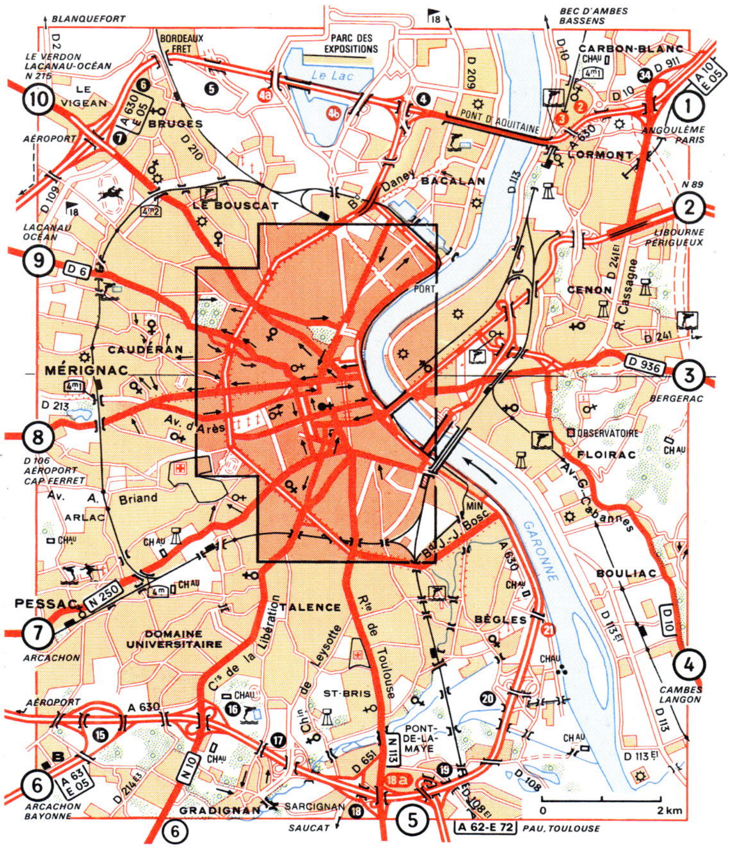

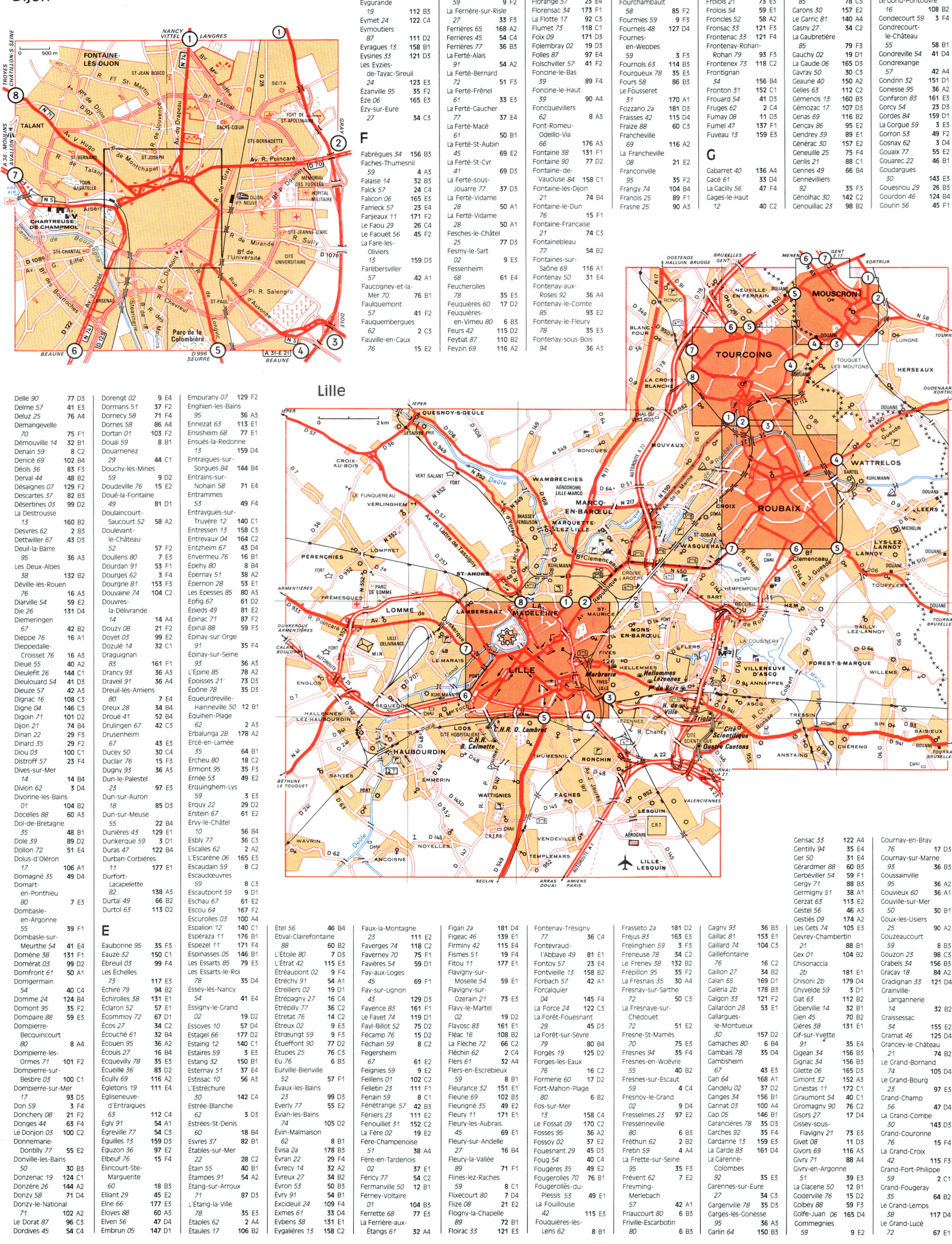

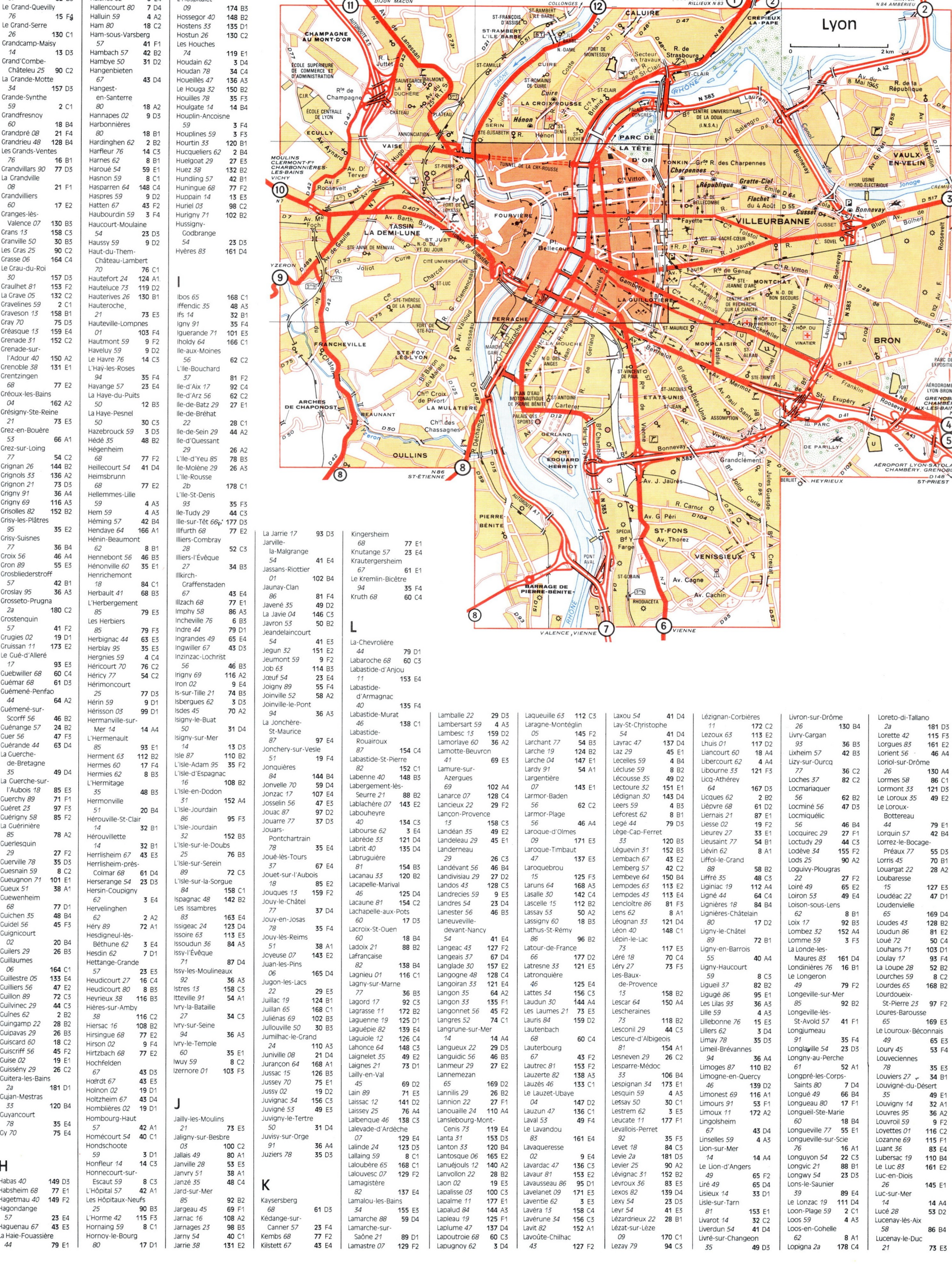

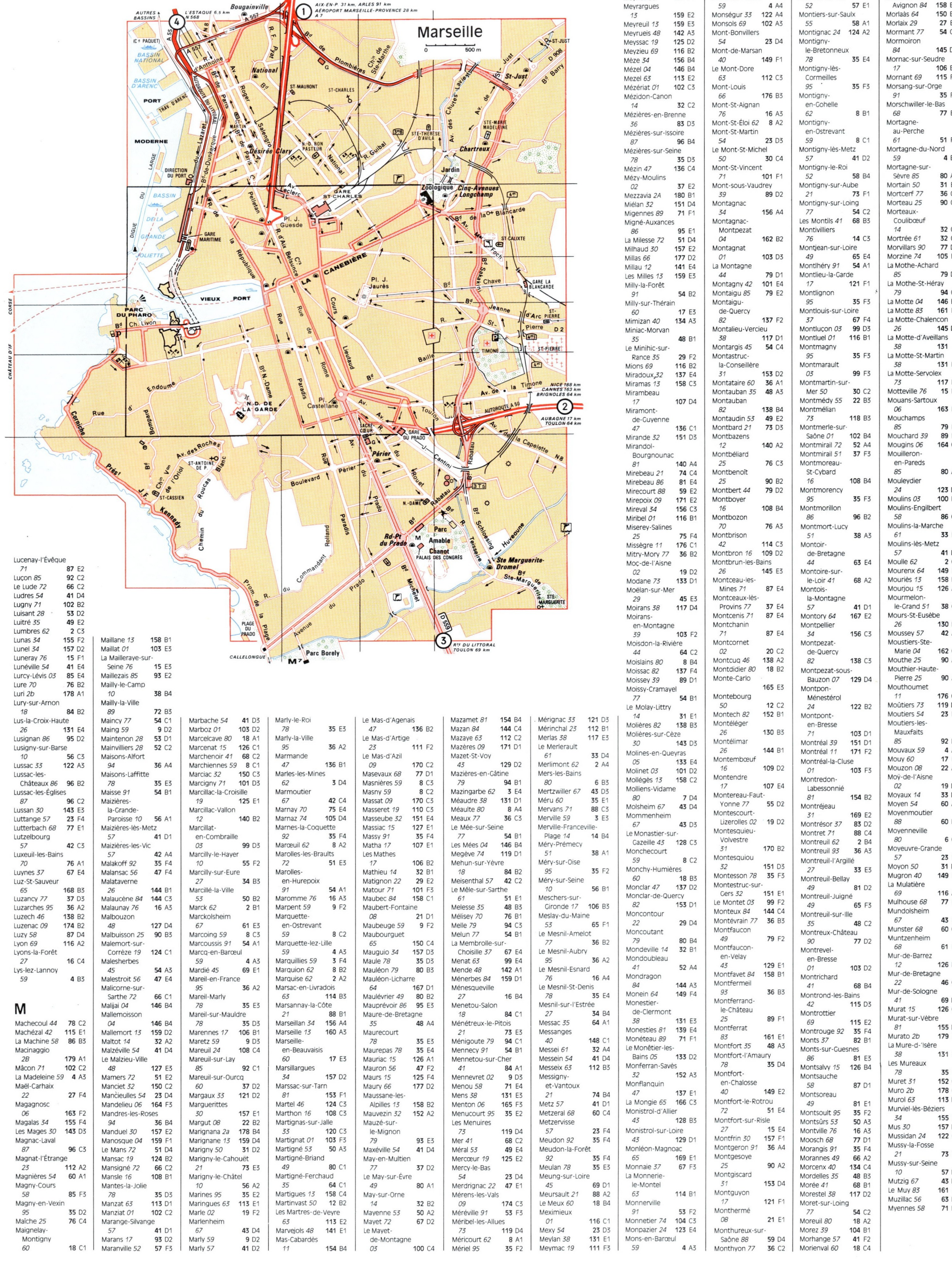

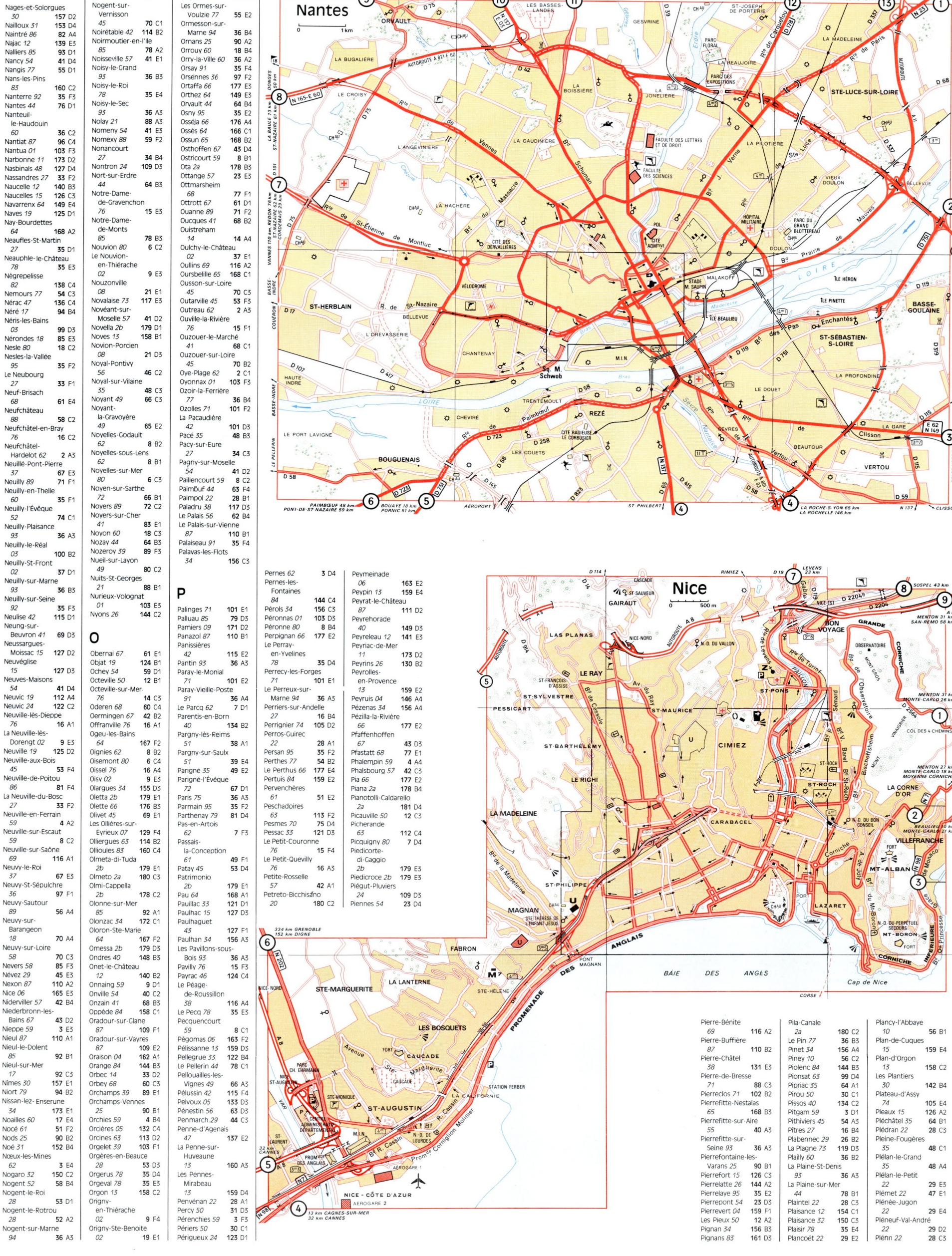

Rouen

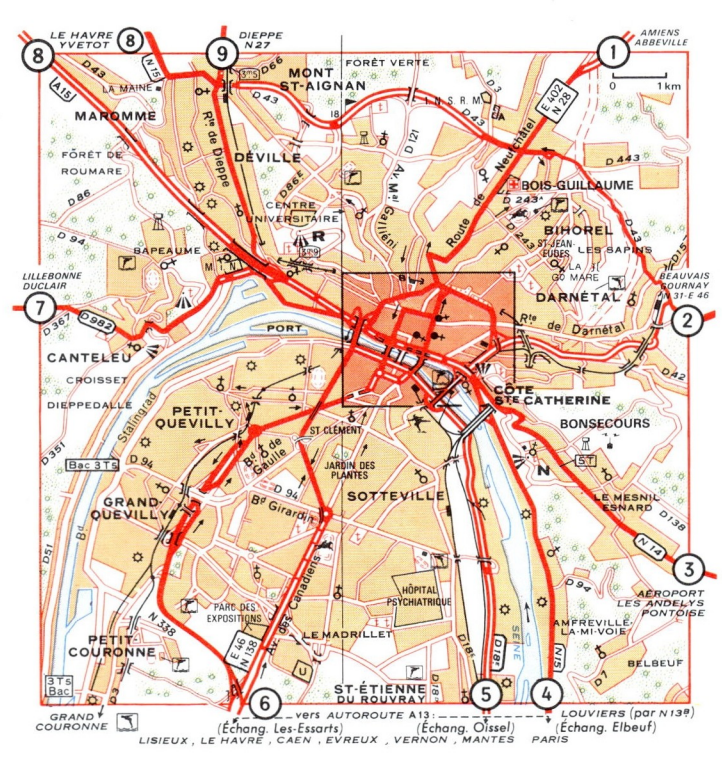

190

189

Strasbourg

Map of Strasbourg and surrounding areas including Lampertheim, Mundolsheim, Niederhausbergen, Hoenheim, Bischheim, Mittelhausbergen, Schiltigheim, Oberhausbergen, Eckbolsheim, Kehl, Lingolsheim, Ostwald, Illkirch-Graffenstaden, Neuhof, Stockfeld.

Index (S continued – T)

Name	Dept	Ref
St-Jean-de-la-Ruelle 45	69	E1
St-Jean-de-Sauves 86	81	E3
St-Jean-de-Védas 34	156	C3
St-Jean-des-Baisants 50	31	E2
St-Jean-du-Gard 30	142	C4
St-Jeoire 74	105	D3
St-Joachim 44	63	E4
St-Jorioz 74	118	B1
St-Jory 31	152	C2
St-Joseph-de-Rivière 38	117	E4
St-Juéry 81	154	A1
St-Julien 39	103	E2
St-Julien-l'Ars 86	95	E1
St-Julien-Chapteuil 43	129	D2
St-Julien-en-Born 40	134	A4
St-Julien-en-Genevois 74	104	B3
St-Julien-Mont-Denis 73	152	C1
St-Julien-les-Villas 10	56	C3
St-Julien-de-Civry 71	101	E4
St-Julien-de-Concelles 44	64	C4
St-Julien-de-Peyrolas 30	143	F3
St-Julien-de-Vouvantes 44	65	D2
St-Julien-du-Sault 89	55	E4
St-Junien 87	109	E1
St-Just-en-Bas 42	114	C2
St-Just-en-Chaussée 60	17	F3
St-Just-en-Chevalet 42	114	A1
St-Just-Malmont 43	115	E4
St-Just-le-Martel 87	110	B1
St-Just-la-Pendue 42	115	D1
St-Just-Luzac 17	106	C2
St-Just-Saint-Rambert 42	115	D2
St-Lary-Soulan 65	169	D4
St-Lattier 38	130	C2
St-Laurent-Blangy 62	8	A2
St-Laurent-de-Cerdans 66	177	D4
St-Laurent-de-Chamousset 69	115	E2
St-Laurent-de-Mure 69	116	B2
St-Laurent-de-Neste 65	169	E2
St-Laurent-de-la-Salanque 66	177	F4
St-Laurent-des-Autels 49	65	D4
St-Laurent-du-Pont 38	117	E4
St-Laurent-du-Var 06	165	D4
St-Laurent-en-Grandvaux 39	104	B1
St-Laurent-et-Benon 33	120	C1
St-Laurent-sur-Gorre 87	109	F2
St-Laurent-sur-Saône 01	102	C3
St-Léger-lès-Domart 80	7	D3
St-Léger-sous-Beuvray 71	87	D3
St-Léger-sur-Dheune 71	88	A3
St-Léger-Vauban 89	72	C4
St-Léonard-de-Noblat 87	110	C1
St-Léons 12	141	D1
St-Leu-d'Esserent 60	36	A1
St-Leu-la-Forêt 95	35	F3
St-Lizier 09	170	B4
St-Lô 50	31	D1
St-Loubès 33	121	E3
St-Louis 68	77	F2
St-Loup-de-la-Salle 71	88	B3
St-Loup-du-Dorat 53	66	A1
St-Loup-sur-Semouse 70	76	A1
St-Lubin-de-la-Haye 28	34	C3
St-Lubin-des-Joncherets 28	34	B4
St-Lupicin 39	104	A2
St-Lys 31	152	B3
St-Macaire 33	135	F1
St-Macaire-en-Mauges 49	80	A2
St-Maixent-l'École 79	94	C1
St-Malo 35	29	F2
St-Malo-de-Guersac 44	63	E4
St-Mamert-du-Gard 30	157	D1
St-Mamet-la-Salvetat 15	126	A3
St-Mammès 77	54	C2
St-Mandé 94	36	A3
St-Mandrier-sur-Mer 83	160	C4
St-Marcel 27	34	C2
St-Marcel 71	88	B4
St-Marcel-de-Félines 42	115	D1
St-Marcel-lès-Valence 26	130	B3
St-Marcellin 38	130	C1
St-Marcellin-en-Forez 42	115	D3
St-Mars-la-Brière 72	51	E4
St-Mars-d'Outillé 72	67	D3
St-Mars-la-Jaille 44	65	D3
St-Martial-le-Vieux 23	112	A2
St-Martin-Belle-Roche 71	102	B3
St-Martin-en-Bresse 71	88	B3
St-Martin-en-Haut 69	115	E2
St-Martin-Valmeroux 15	112	A2
St-Martin-le-Vinoux 38	131	E1
St-Martin-d'Auxigny 18	84	C1
St-Martin-de-Belleville 73	119	D4
St-Martin-de-Boscherville 76	15	F3
St-Martin-de-la-Brasque 84	159	E2
St-Martin-de-Castillon 84	159	E2
St-Martin-de-Crau 13	158	A3
St-Martin-de-Landelles 50	49	E1
St-Martin-de-Londres 34	156	B2
St-Martin-de-Ré 17	92	C3
St-Martin-de-Seignanx 40	148	B3
St-Martin-de-Valamas 07	129	E3
St-Martin-de-Valgalgues 30	143	D3
St-Martin-d'Estréaux 42	100	C3
St-Martin-d'Hères 38	131	E1
St-Martin-du-Bois 49	65	F2
St-Martin-du-Var 06	165	D3
St-Martory 31	170	A2
St-Mathieu 87	109	E2
St-Mathieu-de-Tréviers 34	156	C3
St-Mathieu (Pointe de) 29	26	A3
St-Maur 36	83	F4
St-Maur-des-Fossés 94	36	A4
St-Maurice 94	36	A3
St-Maurice-sur-Moselle 88	76	C1
St-Max 54	41	D4
St-Maximin 60	36	A1
St-Maximin-la-Ste-Baume 83	160	C2
St-Médard-en-Jalles 33	121	D3
St-Méen-le-Grand 35	47	F1
St-Méloir-des-Ondes 35	30	A4
St-Même-les-Carrières 16	108	B3
St-Michel 16	108	B3
St-Michel 02	10	B4
St-Michel-Chef-Chef 44	78	B1
St-Michel-de-Fronsac 33	121	E3
St-Michel-de-Maurienne 73	132	C1
St-Michel-en-l'Herm 85	92	B2
St-Michel-l'Observatoire 04	159	F1
St-Michel-Mont-Mercure 85	80	B3
St-Michel-sur-Orge 91	36	A4
St-Mihiel 55	40	B3
St-Mitre-les-Remparts 13	158	A4
St-Nazaire 44	63	E4
St-Nectaire 63	113	D1
St-Nicolas-d'Aliermont 76	16	B1
St-Nicolas-de-la-Grave 82	137	D2
St-Nicolas-de-Port 54	41	E4
St-Nicolas-de-Redon 44	63	F2
St-Nicolas-du-Pélem 22	28	B4
St-Nom-la-Bretèche 78	35	E3
St-Omer 62	2	C2
St-Omer-en-Chaussée 60	17	D3
St-Oradoux-de-Chirouze 23	112	A2
St-Orens-de-Gameville 31	153	D3
St-Ouen 93	36	A3
St-Ouen 80	7	E3
St-Ouen-l'Aumône 95	35	E2
St-Pair-sur-Mer 50	30	B3
St-Palais 64	149	D4
St-Palais-sur-Mer 17	106	B2
St-Pardoux 63	99	F4
St-Pardoux-la-Rivière 24	109	E3
St-Parize-le-Châtel 58	86	B4
St-Parres-lès-Vaudes 10	56	C3
St-Paterne 72	51	D2
St-Pathus 77	36	C2
St-Paul 04	147	E1
St-Paul 06	165	D3
St-Paul-Cap-de-Joux 81	154	A1
St-Paul-la-Coste 30	142	C3
St-Paul-lès-Dax 40	148	C3
St-Paul-de-Fenouillet 66	176	C2
St-Paul-de-Varax 01	103	D4
St-Paul-de-Vence 06	165	D3
St-Paul-Saint-Saturnin 63	113	E2
St-Paul-Trois-Châteaux 26	144	B2
St-Paulien 43	128	C2
St-Pé-de-Bigorre 65	168	B2
St-Péray 07	130	A3
St-Père-en-Retz 44	78	B1
St-Philbert-de-Bouaine 85	79	D2
St-Philbert-de-Grand-Lieu 44	79	D2
St-Pierre-d'Albigny 73	118	B3
St-Pierre-d'Allevard 38	118	B4
St-Pierre-de-Bailleul 27	34	B2
St-Pierre-de-Chignac 24	123	E1
St-Pierre-de-Maillé 86	82	B4
St-Pierre-de-Plesguen 35	48	B1
St-Pierre-des-Corps 37	67	F4
St-Pierre-des-Nids 53	51	D2
St-Pierre-d'Irube 64	148	B3
St-Pierre-d'Oléron 17	106	B2
St-Pierre-du-Vauvray 27	34	B2
St-Pierre-Église 50	12	C1
St-Pierre-Montlimart 49	65	D4
St-Pierre-le-Moûtier 58	85	E4
St-Pierre-Quiberon 56	62	B3
St-Pierre-sur-Dives 14	32	C2
St-Pois 50	31	D4
St-Pol-de-Léon 29	27	D1
St-Pol-sur-Mer 59	3	D1
St-Pol-sur-Ternoise 62	7	E1
St-Pons-de-Thomières 34	155	D4
St-Porchaire 17	106	C1
St-Pourçain-sur-Sioule 03	100	A3
St-Priest 69	116	B2
St-Priest-des-Champs 63	112	C1
St-Priest-en-Jarez 42	115	E3
St-Priest-la-Prugne 42	101	C2
St-Priest-la-Roche 42	115	D1
St-Priest-Taurion 87	110	B1
St-Privat 19	125	E2
St-Privat-d'Allier 43	128	B2
St-Privat-de-Vallongue 48	142	C3
St-Privat-la-Montagne 57	41	D1
St-Prix 95	35	E3
St-Pryvé-St-Mesmin 45	69	E1
St-Quay-Portrieux 22	28	C3
St-Quentin 02	19	D1
St-Rambert-d'Albon 26	130	A1
St-Rambert-en-Bugey 01	117	D1
St-Raphaël 83	163	E3
St-Rémy-de-Maurienne 73	118	C4
St-Rémy-de-Provence 13	158	B2
St-Rémy-des-Monts 72	51	E2
St-Rémy-en-Bouzemont 51	57	E1
St-Rémy-sur-Avre 28	34	B4
St-Rémy-sur-Durolle 63	114	A1
St-Renan 29	26	A3
St-Révérien 58	86	B1
St-Riquier 80	7	D3
St-Romain-le-Puy 42	115	D3
St-Romain-de-Colbosc 76	15	D3
St-Rome-de-Cernon 12	141	D1
St-Saëns 76	16	B2
St-Saturnin-lès-Avignon 84	158	C1
St-Saturnin-d'Apt 84	159	E2
St-Saulge 58	86	B2
St-Sauveur 59	9	D1
St-Sauveur-d'Auvergne 63	112	C2
St-Sauveur-d'Aunis 17	93	E3
St-Sauveur-de-Montagut 07	129	F3
St-Sauveur-en-Puisaye 89	71	E3
St-Sauveur-Lendelin 50	30	C2
St-Sauveur-le-Vicomte 50	12	B3
St-Savin 86	96	B2
St-Savin 33	121	E2
St-Savinien 17	107	D1
St-Savournin 13	159	E4
St-Sébastien 23	97	E2
St-Sébastien-sur-Loire 44	79	E1
St-Séglin 35	48	B3
St-Seine-l'Abbaye 21	73	F4
St-Sernin-sur-Rance 12	154	A1
St-Seurin-sur-l'Isle 33	122	A2
St-Sever 40	149	F2
St-Sever-Calvados 14	31	E3
St-Siméon 77	37	D4
St-Siméon-de-Bressieux 38	116	A4
St-Simon 02	19	D2
St-Sorlin-en-Vallorie 26	130	B1
St-Soupplets 77	36	C2
St-Sulpice 81	153	D2
St-Sulpice-des-Champs 23	98	B4
St-Sulpice-de-Favières 91	54	A1
St-Sulpice-les-Feuilles 87	97	D4
St-Sulpice-Laurière 87	97	D4
St-Sylvain 19	125	D1
St-Sylvain-d'Anjou 49	65	A3
St-Symphorien 35	135	D2
St-Symphorien-de-Lay 42	115	D1
Stes-Maries-de-la-Mer 13	157	E4
Les Saisies 73	119	D2
Saissac 11	171	F1
Salbris 41	69	F4
Salernes 83	161	D1
Salers 15	126	B2
Saleux 80	17	F1
Salies-de-Béarn 64	149	E3
Salies-du-Salat 31	168	A2
Salignac-Eyvignes 24	124	C3
Saligny-sur-Roudon 03	100	C2

Name	Dept	Ref
St-Tropez 83	161	F3
St-Vaast-la-Hougue 50	12	C2
St-Valérien 89	55	D3
St-Valery-en-Caux 76	15	E1
St-Valery-sur-Somme 80	6	C2
St-Vallier 71	101	F1
St-Vallier 26	130	A1
St-Vallier-de-Thiey 06	164	C3
St-Varent 79	81	D3
St-Vaury 23	97	F3
St-Venant 62	3	D2
St-Véran 05	133	E4
St-Victoret 13	159	D4
St-Victurnien 87	109	F1
St-Vincent-de-Tyrosse 40	148	C3
St-Vincent-les-Forts 04	146	C1
St-Vit 25	89	E1
St-Vivien-de-Médoc 33	106	B4
St-Vrain 91	54	A1
St-Yorre 03	100	B4
St-Yrieix-la-Perche 87	110	B3
St-Yrieix-sur-Charente 16	108	B2
St-Zacharie 83	160	C2
Ste-Adresse 76	14	C3
Ste-Alvère 24	123	E2
Ste-Cécile 71	101	F3
Ste-Cécile-les-Vignes 84	144	B3
Ste-Colombe 69	116	A3
Ste-Colombe-la-Commanderie 27	34	A1
Ste-Croix-Vallée-Française 48	142	C3
Ste-Croix-Volvestre 09	170	A2
Ste-Enimie 48	141	E2
Ste-Eusoye 60	17	F3
Ste-Florine 43	113	E4
Ste-Fortunade 19	125	D1
Ste-Foy-l'Argentière 69	115	E2
Ste-Foy-la-Grande 33	122	B3
Ste-Foy-lès-Lyon 69	116	A2
Ste-Foy-Tarentaise 73	119	E2
Ste-Gauburge-Ste-Colombe 61	33	E4
Ste-Geneviève 60	35	F1
Ste-Geneviève-des-Bois 91	54	A1
Ste-Geneviève-sur-Argence 12	126	C2
Ste-Hermine 85	92	C1
Ste-Jamme-sur-Sarthe 72	9	F3
Ste-Livrade-sur-Lot 47	137	D2
Ste-Lucie-de-Porto-Vecchio 2A	181	E3
Ste-Lucie-de-Tallano 2a	181	D1
Ste-Marie 25	76	C3
Ste-Marie-aux-Chênes 57	41	D1
Ste-Marie-aux-Mines 68	60	C2
Ste-Marie-de-Ré 17	92	C3
Ste-Marie-du-Mont 50	12	C3
Ste-Marie-Kerque 62	2	C2
Ste-Marie-la-Mer 66	177	F4
Ste-Maure-de-Touraine 37	82	B2
Ste-Maxime 83	161	F3
Ste-Menehould 51	39	E2
Ste-Mère-Église 50	12	C2
Ste-Pazanne 44	78	C1
Ste-Pience 50	30	C3
Ste-Savine 10	56	B3
Ste-Sévère-sur-Indre 36	98	B2
Ste-Sigolène 43	129	D1
Ste-Suzanne 53	50	B4
Ste-Tulle 04	159	F2
Saintes 17	107	D1
Saissac 11	171	F1
Salbris 41	69	F4
Salernes 83	161	D1
Salers 15	126	B2
Saleux 80	17	F1
Salies-de-Béarn 64	149	E3
Salies-du-Salat 31	168	A2
Salignac-Eyvignes 24	124	C3
Saligny-sur-Roudon 03	100	C2
Salindres 30	143	D3
Salin-de-Giraud 13	158	B4
Salins 77	55	D2
Salins-les-Bains 39	103	F1
Sallanches 74	105	E4
Sallaumines 62	8	B1
La Salle 05	133	D2
Sallenelles 14	32	B1
Salles 33	134	C1
Salles-Curan 12	140	C2
Salles-sur-l'Hers 11	171	E1
Salon-de-Provence 13	159	D4
Salornay-sur-Guye 71	102	A1
La Salvetat-Peyralès 12	140	B1
La Salvetat-sur-Agout 34	155	B3
Salviac 46	124	B3
Samatan 32	152	A3
Samer 62	2	A3
Samoëns 74	105	E3
Samois-sur-Seine 77	54	C2
San-Lorenzo 2b	179	E3
San-Nicolao 2b	179	E3
Sanary-sur-Mer 83	160	C4
Sancergues 18	85	E3
Sancerre 18	70	C4
Sancey-le-Grand 25	76	B4
Sancoins 18	85	E3
Sandarville 28	52	C2
Sandillon 45	69	E1
Sanguinet 40	134	B1
Sannerville 14	32	B1
Sannois 95	35	F3
Santa-Lucia-di-Tallano 2A	181	D1
Santa-Maria-Siché 2a	180	C2
Santenay 21	88	B3
Santes 59	3	E1
Santo-Pietro-di-Tenda 2b	179	D1
Sanvignes-les-Mines 71	87	E4
Le Sap 61	33	E2
Saramon 32	151	F3
Sarcelles 95	36	A2
Sari-di-Porto-Vecchio 2A	181	E2
Sari-d'Orcino 2a	180	B1
Sarlat-la-Canéda 24	124	B3
Sarralbe 57	42	B2
Sarrancolin 65	169	D2
Sarras 07	130	A1
Sarre-Union 67	42	C1
Sarrebourg 57	42	B1
Sarreguemines 57	42	B1
Sarreinsming 57	42	B1
Sarrians 84	144	B4
Sars-Poteries 59	9	F3
Sartène 2a	180	C3
Sartilly 50	30	B3
Sartrouville 78	35	F3
Sarzeau 56	62	C2
Sassenage 38	131	E1
Sathonay-Camp 69	116	A2
Satillieu 07	129	F2
Saugues 43	127	F3
Saujon 17	106	C2
Saulce-sur-Rhône 26	146	B2
Saulcy-sur-Meurthe 88	60	C2
Saulieu 21	87	F1
Saulnes 54	23	D1
Saulon-la-Chapelle 21	88	B1
Sault 84	145	D2
Sault-Brénaz 01	117	D1
Saulx 70	76	A2
Saulxures-lès-Nancy 54	41	E4
Saulxures-sur-Moselotte 88	60	B4
Saulzais-le-Potier 18	99	D1
Saulzoir 59	9	D2
Saumane 30	142	C4
Saumur 49	81	D1
Sausheim 68	77	E1
Sausset-les-Pins 13	158	C4
Sautron 44	64	B4
Sauve 30	156	C1
Sauveterre-de-Béarn 64	149	D3
Sauveterre-de-Guyenne 33	122	A4
Sauxillanges 63	113	E3
Sauzé-Vaussais 79	95	D3
Sauzet 26	144	B1
Savenay 44	63	F4
Saverdun 09	171	D1
Saverne 67	42	C2
Saviers 80	9	F5
Savignac-les-Églises 24	123	E1
Savigné-l'Évêque 72	51	E4
Savigné-sur-Lathan 37	67	D4
Savigny-lès-Beaune 21	88	A2

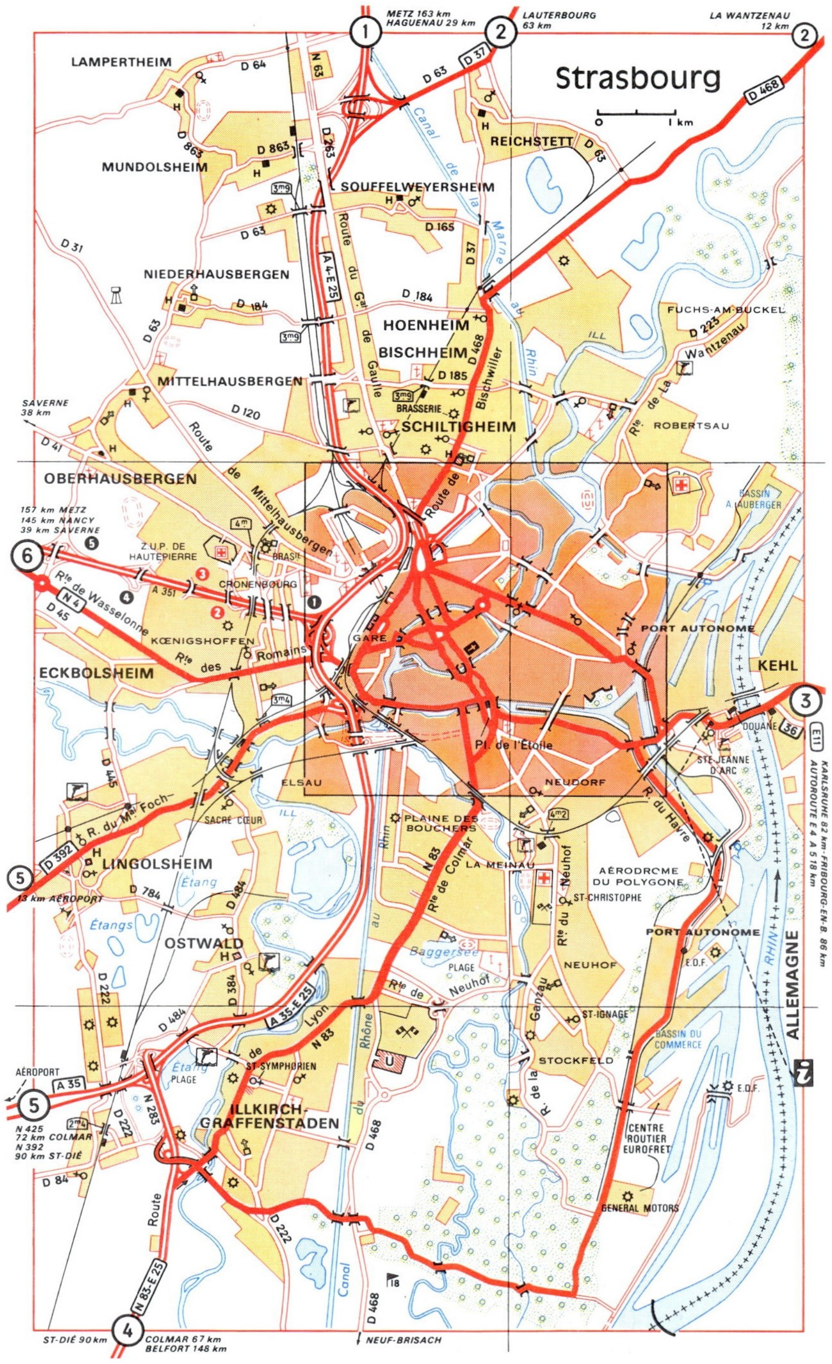

Name	Dept	Ref
Savigny-sur-Braye 41	67	F1
Savigny-sur-Orge 91	35	F4
Savigny-le-Temple 77	36	B4
Savines-le-Lac 05	146	C1
Scaër 29	45	E2
Sceaux 92	35	F4
Scey-sur-Saône-et-St-Albin 70	75	D2
Scherwiller 67	61	D2
Schiltigheim 67	43	E4
Schirmeck 67	60	C1
Schweighouse-sur-Moder 67	43	E3
La Scheinie 43	129	D3
Seclin 59	3	E2
Secondigny 79	93	F1
Sedan 08	21	F2
Séderon 26	145	E3
Sées 61	51	D1
Segonzac 16	108	A3
Segré 49	65	E2
Seichamps 54	41	E4
Seiches-sur-le-Loir 49	66	A3
Seignelay 89	71	F1
Seignosse 40	148	C2
Seigny 21	73	E3
Seilhac 19	111	A4
Seine-Port 77	36	B4
Seissan 32	151	E3
Seix 09	170	B3
Le Sel-de-Bretagne 35	49	D4
Sélestat 67	61	D2
Selles-sur-Cher 41	83	C1
Sellières 39	12	F1
Selongey 21	74	C3
Selonnet 04	146	C2
Sémeac 65	168	C1
Séméac 59	9	F5
Semur-en-Auxois 21	73	D3
Senan 87	71	F1
Sénas 13	158	C2
Séné 56	62	C2
Senlis 60	36	B1
Sennecey-le-Grand 71	102	B1
Senonches 28	52	B1
Senones 88	60	B2
Sens 89	55	E3
Sens-de-Bretagne 35	48	C2
Sentheim 68	77	D1
La Sentinelle 59	9	E2
Seppois-le-Bas 68	77	E2
Septeuil 78	35	D3
Septfonds 82	138	C3
Septmoncel 39	104	B2
Seraucourt-le-Grand 02	19	D2
Séreilhac 87	110	A2
Sérent 56	47	E3
Sérifontaine 60	17	E4
Sérignan 34	173	E1
Sérignan-du-Comtat 84	144	B3
Sermaize-les-Bains 51	39	F3
Serques 62	2	C2
Serquigny 27	33	F2
Serra-di-Scopamène 2a	181	D2
Serres 05	145	F3
Serres-Castet 64	168	A1
Serrières 07	116	A4
Serrières-de-Briord 01	117	D2
Servance 70	76	C1
Servian 34	155	F4
Sessenheim 67	43	F3
Sète 34	156	C4
Seurre 21	88	C2
Sévérac-le-Château 12	141	E2
Sevran 93	36	B3
Sèvres 92	35	F3
Sévrier 74	118	A2
Seyches 47	122	C4
Seyne 04	146	C2
La Seyne-sur-Mer 83	160	C4
Seyssel 74	117	E2
Seyssel 01	104	A4
Seysses 31	152	C3
Seyssinet-Pariset 38	131	E1
Sézanne 51	37	F4
Sierck-les-Bains 57	23	F1
Senonches 28	52	B1

Name	Dept	Ref
Sierentz 68	77	F2
Sigean 11	173	D3
Signes 83	160	C3
Signy-l'Abbaye 08	21	D2
Signy-le-Petit 08	20	C1
Sigoulès 24	122	C3
Sille-le-Guillaume 72	50	C4
Simiane-Collongue 13	159	D4
Simorre 32	151	F4
Sin-le-Noble 59	8	C2
Sisco 2b	178	E2
Sissonne 02	20	B3
Sisteron 04	146	A3
Sivry-Courtry 77	54	C1
Six-Fours-les-Plages 83	160	C4
Sixt-Fer-à-Cheval 74	105	E4
Sizun 29	27	D3
Soccia 2a	178	C4
Sochaux 25	76	C2
Soignolles-en-Brie 77	54	C2
Soissons 02	19	D4
Soisy-sous-Montmorency 95	36	A2
Soisy-sur-École 91	54	B1
Soisy-sur-Seine 91	36	A4
Solenzara 2A	181	E2
Le Soler 66	177	E4
Solesmes 59	9	D3
Solignac 87	110	B2
Solignac-sur-Loire 43	128	C3
Solliès-Pont 83	161	D4
Solre-le-Château 59	9	F2
Somain 59	8	C2
Somberon 21	73	F4
Sommières 30	157	D1
Sompuis 51	39	D2
Songeons 60	17	D3
Soorts-Hossegor 40	148	B3
Sorbiers 42	115	D2
Sorbollano 2a	181	D2
Sore 40	135	D1
Sorel-Moussel 28	34	C3
Sorèze 81	153	F4
Sorgues 84	144	B4
Sormery 89	56	A4
Sornac 19	112	A2
Sospel 06	165	F2
Sotta 2a	181	E3
Sotteville-lès-Rouen 76	16	A4
Soubise 17	106	B1
Souchez 62	8	A1
Soues 65	168	C1
Soufflenheim 67	43	F3
Souffelweyersheim 67	43	E4
Souillac 46	124	C3
Souilly 55	40	B2
Soulac-sur-Mer 33	106	B4
Soultz-Haut-Rhin 68	77	E1
Soultz-sous-Forêts 67	43	F2
Soultzmatt 68	61	D4
Soumoulou 64	168	B1
Souppes-sur-Loing 77	54	C2
Sourdeval 50	31	E3
Sourdun 77	55	F1
Sournia 66	176	C2
Souscyrac 46	125	D3
Soustons 40	148	C2
La Souterraine 23	97	E3
Souvigny 03	100	A1
Soyaux 16	108	B3
Spézet 29	45	E1
Spincourt 55	22	C4
Staffelden 68	77	E1
Stains 93	36	A3
Steenbecque 59	3	D3
Steenvoorde 59	3	E1
Steenwerck 59	3	E1
Steinbourg 67	42	C2
Stenay 55	21	F3
Strasbourg 67	43	E4
Sucy-en-Brie 94	36	B4
Suippes 51	39	D2
Sully-sur-Loire 45	70	A2
Sumène 30	156	B1
Sundhouse 67	61	E3
Suresnes 92	35	F3
Surgères 17	93	E3
Sury-le-Comtal 42	115	D3

T

Name	Dept	Ref
Tain-l'Hermitage 26	130	A2
Taingy 89	71	E3
Talant 21	74	B4
La Talaudière 42	115	E4
Talence 33	121	D3
Tallard 05	146	B1
Talloires 74	118	A3
Talmont-St-Hilaire 85	92	A1
Taninges 74	105	D3
Tanlay 89	72	C1
Tannay 58	71	F4
Tantonville 54	60	A1
Tarare 69	115	E1
Tarascon 13	158	A2
Tarascon-sur-Ariège 09	171	D2
Tarbes 65	168	C1
Tardets-Sorholus 64	167	E2
Tardinghen 62	2	A2
Targon 33	121	F4
Tarnos 40	148	B3
Tartas 40	149	E2
Tassin-la-Demi-Lune 69	116	A2
Taulé 29	27	D2
Tauriac 46	125	D3
Taussat 33	120	A4
Tauves 63	112	B2
Tavaux 39	89	D2
Tavel 30	144	B4
Tavera 2a	178	C4
Taverny 95	35	F3
Le Teil 07	144	A1
Le Teilleul 50	49	F1
Teloché 72	67	D1
Templemars 59	4	A4
Templeuve 59	4	A4
Tenay 01	117	D2
Tence 43	129	E2
Tende 06	165	F1
Tergnier 02	19	D2
Ternay-Melay-et-St-Hilaire 70	76	A1
Terrasson-la-Villedieu 24	124	B2

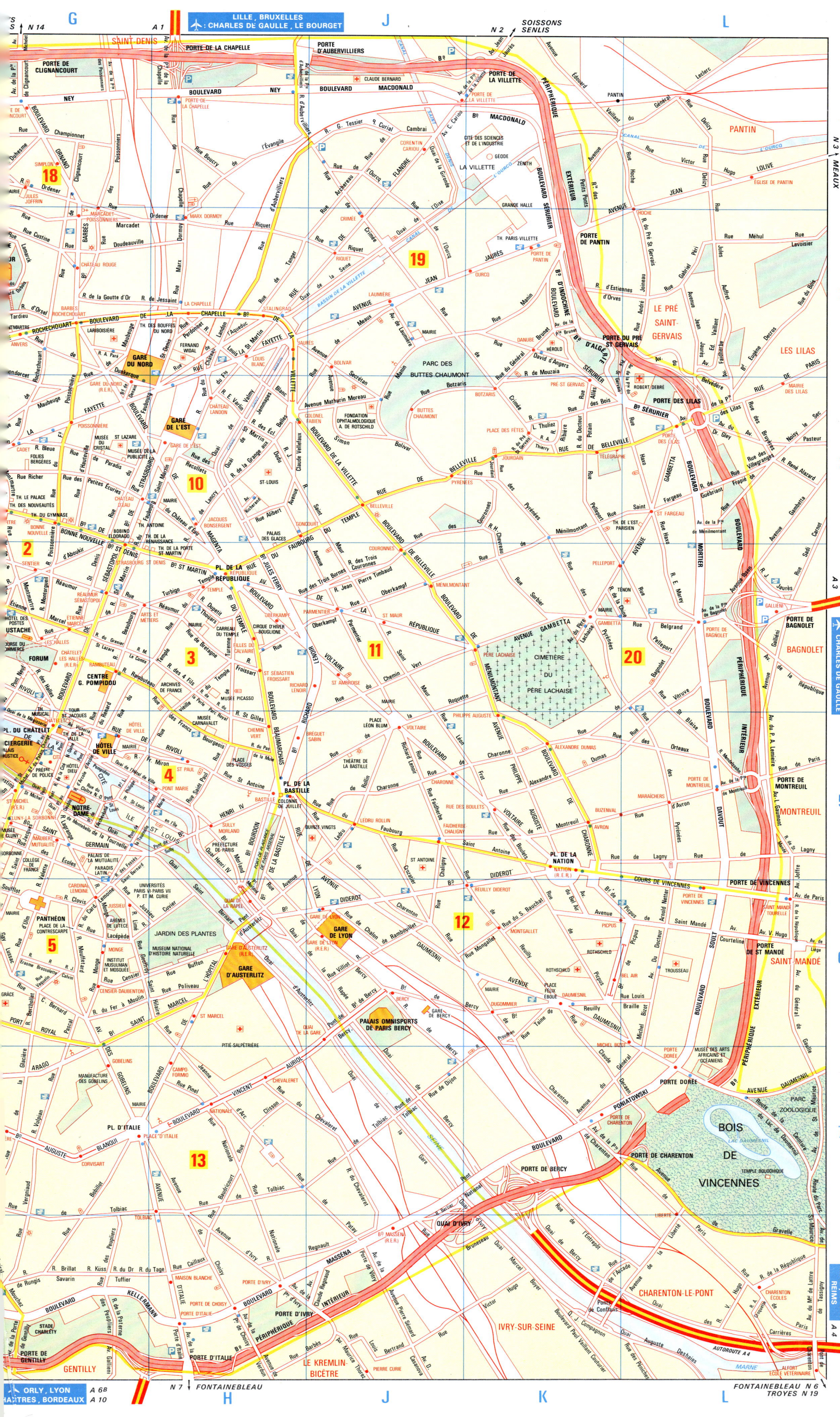

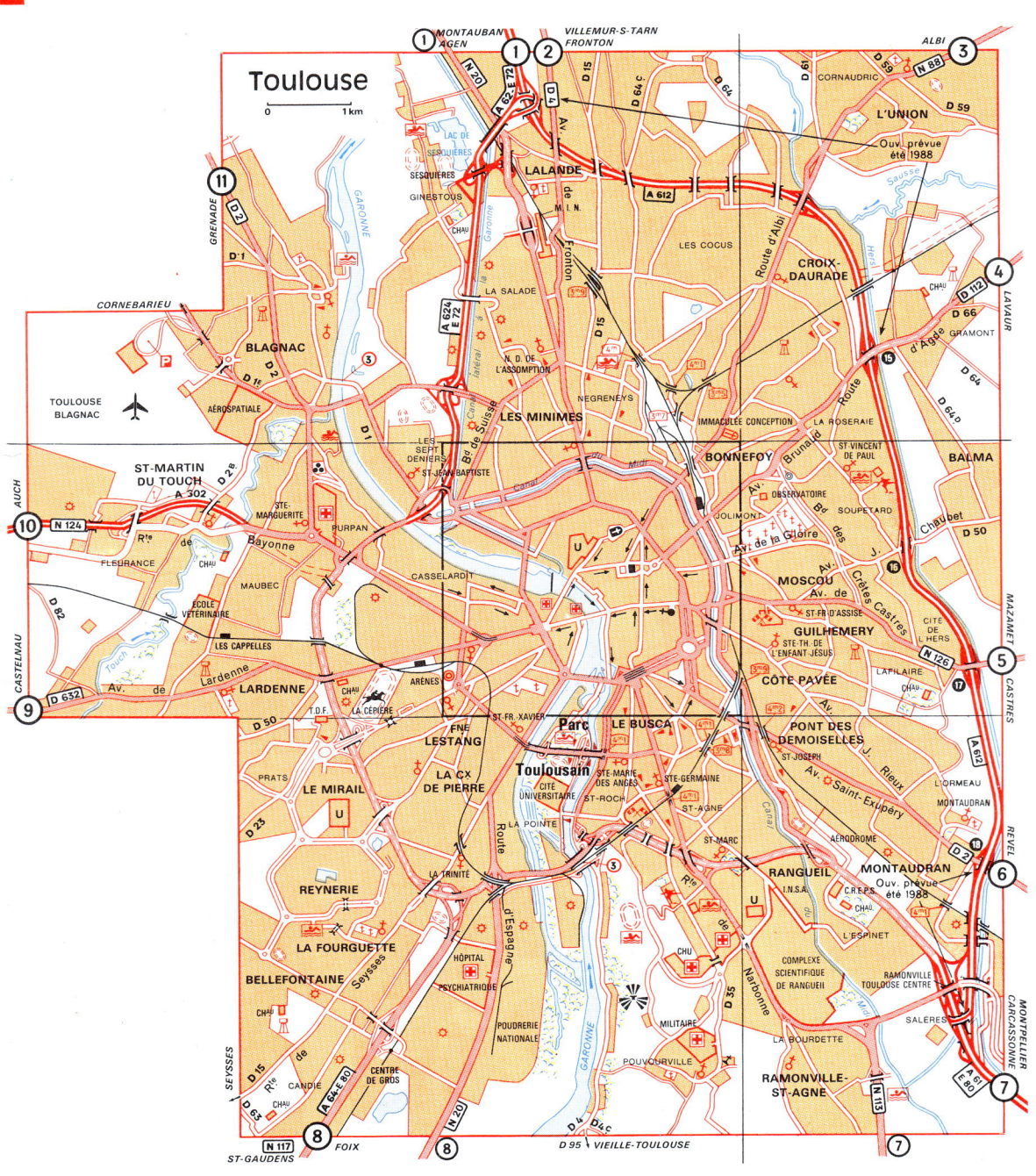